THE WILL TO LIVE

THE WILL TO LIVE

ARNOLD A. HUTSCHNECKER, M.D.

NEW YORK: THOMAS Y. CROWELL COMPANY

Distributed by
DeVorss & Co.
520 W. Ninth
Los Angeles 15

To
the memory of
MY MOTHER

ACKNOWLEDGMENTS

THIS BOOK has grown out of the following beliefs: Mind and body are one. Their dynamic interaction can be understood only if we are willing to accept psychological principles with the same objectivity as we have learned to scrutinize physiological processes.

Psychosomatic medicine deals with that interrelationship in accordance with scientific standards.

The literature on that subject opens immense new vistas vital for both the understanding and the treatment of illness. These gains must not remain merely another specialty but must become an integrated part of all medicine, for the benefit of the individual and of mankind as a whole.

I acknowledge gratefully the works of all men and women who have contributed to the new medical concept.

Dr. Franz Alexander's book, *Psychosomatic Medicine, Its Principles and Applications* (W. W. Norton & Company), has been an inspiring source of concise information. I wish to thank Dr. Alexander for his willingness to read my galley proof and I am indebted to his publisher for permission to reprint some passages.

Dr. Carl Binger was the first authority to read my manuscript. I wish to thank him for his encouragement and criticism. I acknowledge the permission of W. W. Norton & Company to use some quotations from Dr. Binger's book, *The Doctor's Job*.

I wish to thank Dr. George Draper, one of the medical pioneers of the psychosomatic concept, for reading the galley proof and for his heartening, commending letter.

Dr. Flanders Dunbar's book, *Emotions and Bodily Changes*, was an incessant spring of case and reference material. I wish to thank her publisher, Columbia University Press, for allowing me to reprint some passages.

Psychosomatic Medicine by Drs. E. Weiss and S. O. English, published by W. B. Saunders Company, was another source of valuable information. I am indebted to this publisher for permitting me to use quotations from the book.

Dr. Karl Menninger's book, *Man Against Himself* (Harcourt, Brace & Company), was inspirational and reassuring in its enlightening, forward ideas.

The limited space does not permit me to state the various other sources of facts. Because of their importance I feel obliged to name Freud's *Collected First Papers* (Hogarth Press, London, and the Institute of Psycho-Analysis), as well as *The Outline of Psychoanalysis, The Problem of Anxiety, The Question of Lay Analysis,* published by W. W. Norton & Company.

I wish to give credit to the *Journal of the American Medical Association,* to Dr. Hans Selye's book *Stress,* and to *Principles of Internal Medicine* edited by Dr. T. R. Harrison.

I am indebted to various specialists—Drs. Franz Groedel, Francis P. Corrigan, Ernest Grafenberg, Ralph Jacoby—for reading my manuscript and for their reassuring comments.

To Ruth Goode I am greatly indebted for her assistance, her enthusiasm and her steadfastness with which she helped me in preparing and organizing this book.

Others who deserve credit are Charlotte Seitlin, Harry Logan, Jean Dalrymple, Harold H. Corbin, Freda Kirchwey, Lillie Schultz, and last but not least my wife, who was my first reader and critic.

Schopenhauer's "Characteristic of the Will to Live" was an incentive in my deciding on the title of the book.

Yet my greatest debt I owe to my patients. Their physical and emotional suffering made every single one a teacher. No better words were spoken to describe their contribution than those by Sir William Osler: "To study the phenomena of disease without books is to sail an uncharted sea, while to study books without patients is not to go to sea at all."

CONTENTS

INTRODUCTION

THE WORLD is sick. We have said it, and heard it said. We say it dismissively, as an excuse for the world's confusion and man's foolish behavior. But it is literally true.

A new study of world health reveals that half the human race is physically ill: one and three-quarter *billions* of people. The psychiatrist Flanders Dunbar, summing up industrial and army records, tells us that eighty per cent of the population of the United States needs the services of a psychiatrist.

These statements are more than disconcerting. They are actually incredible, standing as they do side by side in the newspaper columns with accounts of the continuous progress of medical science.

Almost every day new and miraculous drugs are discovered, more infectious diseases conquered, new marvels of surgical technique developed. Physicians and scientific researchers have paid even with their lives for progress; modern medicine has stopped at no sacrifice, and truly it has made giant strides.

Yet uncounted millions of people still live in pain and anguish. For all its heroic striving, the science of medicine seems never to catch up in the race against disease and death. As bacteria are overcome, viruses arise. As tuberculosis and pneumonia decline, heart disease and cancer become the new killers. Each time a new defense is discovered against some old enemy of man, a new enemy springs up. The number of physically ill does not diminish. Nervous breakdowns increase at an ever-faster rate, and the sick in mind fill our mental hospitals to overflowing.

More sinister still—and more bewildering—is another estimate, a conservative one, that thirty to fifty per cent of all patients passing through doctor's offices complain of symptoms for which little or no physical causes can be found. For all his streamlined machinery, his miracle drugs, his surgical skills, the doctor can find no help for approximately half the sufferers who come to him for help. He cannot even discover what is wrong with them.

Why is this so? What are these mysterious illnesses?

Moreover, why do some people become ill while others stay well? Why does one man's heart give out at fifty and another's beat strongly long past the allotted three score and ten? Why, when many suffer the same exposure, do some catch cold while others do not?

Medical science has its ready answers: susceptibility, inherited tendency, constitutional weakness, environmental factors. These and many others are offered to explain the point of lowest resistance. All are merely different ways of saying the same thing: that we don't know. For none holds up under persistent examination. They are explanations which do not explain, answers which lead only to more questions.

Medical science long ago drew a line between the mental and the physical. It mapped the body of man as the physician's only proper concern. A professor in the university where I earned my degree warned his students against crossing the boundary.

"I have sliced the human brain into thousands of slides. I have stained them. I have microscoped them," he would say, and add thunderously, "and never have I found any trace of a soul!"

Scientifically, methodically, as medical knowledge grew too vast for one mind to encompass, modern medicine divided man into segments, with each segment presided over by a specialist. I remember a case reported at a medical meeting. A battery of physicians had been assigned to examine a man who had applied for an extraordinarily large life insurance policy.

Everything was normal, including the electrocardiogram. A few days after the policy was issued the man dropped dead.

It is like the story told of Forain, the French painter, who became ill and was examined by half a dozen specialists. The heart specialist pronounced his heart in good shape, the lung specialist declared his lungs to be fine, the kidney specialist reported that his kidneys were functioning properly, and so on until Forain broke in: "Then, gentlemen, it seems that I am dying in perfect health!"

Not often do physicians suffer so dramatic an affront as the death of a man whom they have just pronounced perfectly well. But what of the fifty per cent of patients, those in whom the doctor can find no organic cause of illness, neither by examination, X-ray, laboratory tests, or exploratory surgery? These are a daily reproach to the physician, a plague and a cross to the profession.

Doctors simply shrug their shoulders. Some, standing on their ethical pride, mindful of the many "really sick" who need them, decline to waste time with these "imaginary ill." The doctor says, pleased with his own blunt honesty, "Forget it—pull yourself together—there's nothing wrong with you."

What a slap in the face of a confused, suffering human being! What arrogance, to stand in judgment, only because no "objective" symptom can be found!

And the patient? The doctor has told him there is nothing wrong. Why, then, does he not rejoice? Why, instead, does he go from doctor to doctor, seeking recognition for his suffering, begging for understanding, sinking ever deeper into defeat and despair? Why, when at last the tortured body produces an ulcer or gallstone which the X-ray finally reveals, does he greet the dire news with relief, and gratefully sacrifice one organ after another to the surgeon's knife?

Some patients can exhibit at least a spastic colon, a rapid pulse, a twitch here and a pain there. Doctors call these disorders functional, as opposed to organic illness. Asked what "functional" means, the doctor explains: the organ is not diseased; it is only a nervous condition. He prescribes vita-

mins, antibiotics, diathermy, sleeping pills, a vacation in
Florida. But he knows—and in time the patient knows, to his
sorrow—that relief is temporary, and that sooner or later the
same patient will sit in the same or another office with the
same or a new set of symptoms.

We used to call these patients hypochondriacs, hysterics,
neurotics and psychoneurotics. Now a new word has come
into the layman's vocabulary. A patient will say, "Sometimes
I think I'm going psychosomatic," much as he used to say,
"Sometimes I think I'm going crazy." Or he will say of his
headache, for example, "It's purely psychosomatic," as until
recently he said, "It's just nerves." Mistakenly he identifies
"psychosomatic" with "mental" and "mental" with "imaginary." With many laymen, to call an illness psychosomatic is
to regard it with moral disapproval as a morbid fancy, a sign
of weakness. Tell a man his symptoms are psychosomatic, and
unless he really understands the term, he will shamefacedly
try to ignore his illness—a dangerous attitude, since whatever
its origin, illness is a medical matter and should be so treated.

Suffering man is tossed between Scylla and Charybdis. On
the one side, medicine either rejects his illness altogether or
sends him from specialist to specialist. On the other side are
the psychiatrists. The ordinary man hugs his physical symptoms closer, frightened at the implication that he may be
mentally ill.

What is illness?

For more than a generation now, great physicians have been
preaching that man is not a machine put together on an assembly line, but one complex and mysterious whole. Slowly
we are relearning the ancient truth that if a part is ill, the
whole is ill.

Illness of the body is more than merely physical distress. Illness is not only a malfunctioning organ or a diseased one.
Illness is an outer expression of a deep and dangerous destructive force at work. Illness is an S.O.S. from a ship at sea with
a fire raging in the hold.

The new understanding points toward a time when we

will recognize that in physical illness of any kind, from the common cold to cancer, *emotional disturbance* has contributed to the disposition to disease. The physical agent that we name as the cause of illness—the cold germ or the malignant cell—is like the shot at Sarajevo as the cause of World War I. We must come to recognize illness not only as a picture of a group of morbid physical symptoms, but also as evidence of a life-and-death struggle between two basic, all-powerful drives, the creative instinct and the destructive instinct. When the destructive instinct gains over the creative instinct, illness is a result.

Sigmund Freud's last and perhaps greatest work was his theory of these two basic instincts, their action and interaction, in man. Many of Freud's own disciples still reject this concept. To me, however, it seems that without it we see a two-dimensional picture only. With it we gain vision in depth. It is like looking into a stereoscope which blends into one image pictures from different points of view. To recognize it is to find a master key to man's most baffling and mysterious behavior.

The "will to live" is a familiar enough phrase. It is ordinary man's intuitive recognition of the powerful drive within him to stay alive, and more than this, to create, discover, accomplish. It is the motor for man's biological impulse toward self-preservation and preservation of the species, and for his need for achievement without which life becomes meaningless. Doctors make obeisance to it when, in a crisis of illness, they say, "We have done all we can—now it is up to the patient," and summon a child or wife or mother to the dying man's bedside to rekindle the will to live.

The destructive instinct is less readily observed. We see it in nature as storm, flood, erupting volcano, and the gradual disintegration which we call death. We see it in man's world as hatred and intolerance. We see it in international intrigue, in the drive to war. We stand aghast at the realization that despite religious and moral teachings, the destructive force seems the more passionate of the two.

It is easy to understand that a man who puts a bullet into his own heart does so to destroy himself. It is more difficult to see that another man is killing himself on the installment plan, by means of illness.

Shall we believe, then, that this poor sufferer, dragging himself from doctor to doctor, exhausting his small store of energy in the effort to get well, is really trying to kill himself?

So far only the psychiatrists have dared to approach illness of the body as an evidence and a consequence—desperately, physically real—of psychic disturbance. Medical men, so far as the public is concerned, have remained virtually silent.

Yet the miracles like those of Lourdes, the extraordinary cures in every doctor's experience no less than many of the failures, are inexplicable by the logic of purely biological science. Almost everyone knows of some recovery in which medicine has played a minor role. The principal actor has been the patient himself. At the edge of the abyss some sudden light, some new hope has made him turn. Freud has given us the psychological interpretation of Goethe's two souls battling tragically within the human breast.

In this book I have attempted to bring hope and understanding to the sick, to those who try to avoid sickness, and to those dismayed by the sickness of others near to them. I have drawn from my own and others' observations of men and women in these deep waters, some who swam to safety and some who did not. My purpose is to make people understand the enigma of health. My wish is to present a method by which modern medicine can give them strength to discover and engage the hidden ravaging power within themselves. For it is only ourselves who permit the destructive force to avalanche into a wish to die, thus wilfully though unconsciously overwhelming that positive force within us which is called the will to live.

PART I THE BATTLE OF THE INSTINCTS

> Two souls, alas! are lodg'd
> within my breast,
> which struggle there for
> undivided reign.
>
> GOETHE

1. THE LEGION OF THE TIRED

THE PATIENT sat on the edge of her chair, ready to run away. "Probably I shouldn't have come at all," she said. "I've been to so many doctors. Maybe there's no help for me."

After a hesitant pause, she went on. "First I was treated by our family physician. After two years of trying, he gave up. He said he had given me 'everything in the book.' He sent me to a specialist."

Then the patient named specialist after specialist: gynecologists, cardiologists, internists, surgeons, and even a chiropractor. She had had two years of psychiatric treatment. She had undergone two operations.

Each doctor made a different diagnosis. She was told she had low blood sugar, an asthenic heart, an anemic condition. One doctor suspected cancer of the pancreas and operated on her; there was no cancer. Each time a doctor succeeded in relieving one symptom, another sprang up. She had dizzy spells, palpitations, headaches, stomach pains.

I asked her what troubled her now. "I feel terribly tired," she said. "My legs are heavy. I can barely get through the day. I can't stand noise. I can't stand crowds. I have indigestion no matter what I eat. I have no energy . . ."

As she talked, I saw in my mind's eye the multitudes who

7

pass through doctors' offices, mine and others': men and women suffering from many and varied symptoms. Some have feelings of weakness, of inner shakiness. Some feel bloated. Some cannot sleep. Some have pains in the legs, shoulders, back. They express their trouble in many ways. They say that they are nervous, that they are depressed, that they have lost their zest for living. A few admit that they are confused.

But with them all the principal theme remains the same. All are inexpressibly, unrelievedly *tired*.

This is not merely one doctor's observation. Dr. Dwight L. Wilbur of Stanford University reported in the *Journal of the American Medical Association* recently that up to two-thirds of all patients seen by doctors suffer from a "tired feeling."

These tired people often speak with envy of someone they know who seems never to be tired, who moves and talks with inexhaustible vigor. They wonder at such an abundance of energy. They are jealous of anyone who can eat and digest, who can fall asleep and arise refreshed.

"With me," they say ruefully, "I wake up more tired than when I went to bed!"

Resignedly they console themselves with the thought that fate has favored the envied one with more energy, as it grants some an elegant figure, a handsome face, or an outstanding talent. They are dashed to learn that the vigorous man does not necessarily produce more energy, but only uses it more effectively, that his energy is not dissipated but channeled.

With these weary men and women, energy seems to ooze away. It disappears like a river which vanishes underground, leaving barely a trickle on the surface. But energy does not simply disappear. It is a law of physics that no energy is lost. Where does it go then?

In a state of bewilderment, these people fill doctors' offices, seeking an explanation. The doctors probe and examine. They search the patient with X-ray. They measure his breathing and trace the pumping of his heart. They study the evidence of their many perfected machines and their sensitive chemical tests, and finally they arrive at an opinion. But there are almost as many opinions as there are symptoms.

Hyperacidity, says one doctor. Sinus condition, says another. Allergy, declares a third. Herniated vertebral disc, states a fourth.

If the cause of illness has been found and treated, then the patient should be cured. Yet all too often he returns with a relapse. Or he produces a new illness. Again the tests and the investigations begin, and somehow they can always reveal still another disorder to treat, still another organ on which to operate.

Or the doctors can find nothing wrong—nothing, that is, which shows on the X-ray film or in the test tube. Still these people are sick. They say so and they look it. It is obvious that their strength is being depleted in some way that the doctors seem unable to fathom.

What is wrong with all these people? What is this strange malady that produces such numerous and varied symptoms, or else no objective symptoms at all? Why does its cause remain undetected by all of modern medicine's brilliant techniques of diagnosis? Why do its symptoms stubbornly refuse to yield to the specialist and all his wonder drugs? Can it be that some secret enemy is destroying these people? Can it be that their bodies have become a battleground, that their energies are being devoured in some inner struggle?

A man in conflict is like a country in a state of civil war. He is battling desperately against rebellious forces within himself.

A man who commits suicide is one who has surrendered to this inner enemy, and by his own hand completes his destruction.

A mental patient has surrendered not his body but his mind to the enemy. Dr. Karl Menninger has reported startling evidence of this from his Topeka, Kansas, clinic. He finds that psychotics as a rule enjoy the most robust health, and that they do not begin to suffer physical illness until they are on the way to regaining their mental health. As they return to reality and engage once more in the struggle of living, they become once more vulnerable to illness of the body.

The man whose illness is of the body has not given up. He may surrender organ after organ to disease, as a retreating army surrenders town after town. He may give up, step by step, his capacity for active living. He is fighting, but it is a losing battle. He turns to the physician for help, only to find too often that the physician is as helpless as himself.

Until the sick man and his physician confront the cause of the war as well as its damage, his sickness will not be healed.

For each man has within himself the power of self-destruction, as well as the power of self-preservation.

The Destructive Instinct

To understand the woman whom we have left sitting on the edge of her chair in my office, as well as the millions of sufferers like her, let us investigate this potential enemy within each one of us.

Einstein once declared that "the grand aim of all science is to cover the greatest number of empirical facts by logical deductions from the smallest number of hypotheses or axioms."

Applying this definition to medicine, we find just such a grand aim accomplished. One man, almost at the end of a long life of study, arrived at a single formula which seems to explain the great and infinitely varied array of man's symptoms of illness.

The man was Sigmund Freud; the formula, his theory of the instincts. The thesis stated in his last papers is still a subject of argument. Yet it has the potency of an all-embracing, master-key conception. It seems to give the only single logical explanation for man's otherwise incomprehensible involvements and dilemmas.

Long before Freud, it was known that man's strongest drives are instinctual; that is, they are born within him and constitute an essential part of his nature. It is important to remember that the instincts are not conscious or reasoned, although they are guided or controlled to a degree by the conscious mind.

Scientists engaged in the study of man have named a large number of instincts. They have debated whether this or that one is actually an instinct, a product of man's environment or experience, or an instinct modified by experience.

Freud came to the conclusion that although there are an indeterminate number of instincts, we may trace all of them to a few fundamental ones.

And so he wrote: "After long doubts and vacillations we have decided to assume the existence of only *two basic instincts,* Eros and the destructive instinct."

Eros, named for the god of love, is the creative instinct. We think of love as principally bringing together man and woman for the purpose of procreation. But the instinct for the preservation of man and his species is only one aspect of the fundamental instinct of creation. Love in its all-embracing sense, as the Bible speaks of love, is the creative instinct.

This instinct is the father of all man's creative works. His devotion to his crafts and his arts, his intellectual and scientific achievements, his ceaseless struggle to advance himself and to improve his world—all these untiring efforts are further expressions of this one compelling force, the creative instinct. It is the will to live and to nurture life in all its varied flowering.

The destructive instinct is to most of us a new and difficult concept. It is also called the death instinct, and sometimes Thanatos, after the Greek god of death. It is that smoldering, belligerent force within us which aims directly and wishfully to destroy us so that we may be decomposed into an inorganic state, so that man may be returned to the dust whence he came. It is nature's instrument to end life. The ending of life, as the physiologist Rubner observes, must be a necessity since it appears everywhere in the kingdom of the living.

If we would understand the dynamics of the destructive instinct, we must regard it as an active principle, checked only by the stronger force of the creative instinct. We can observe how in nature these two instincts balance each other. We can also observe how, in nature as in man, the destructive instinct gains momentum as the creative powers in an individual are exhausted. This is the natural progress of all living things toward dissolution or death.

The awareness of these two forces in the world is probably as old as man's first thought. The Greek philosopher and physician Empedocles, more than two thousand years ago, taught that two dynamic principles determine the phenomena of the visible world. He called them Friendship and Strife.

Freud himself stated the parallel: "The analogy of our two basic instincts extends from the region of animate things to the pair of opposing forces—Attraction and Repulsion—which rule the inorganic world."

Whether we call them attraction and repulsion, fusion and fission, friendship and strife, love and hate, peace and war, good and evil, the concept is the same: two forces are pitted against each other, in the vasts of the universe, in the miniature cosmos of the atom, and in the inner world of every man.

Freud did not formulate his theory of the instincts until he had delved deeply into man's inner world. First he had made his tremendous revelation that all of us live another life beyond our conscious life, beyond our reason and our conscious control. He had traced how the unconscious impulses, the fears and desires hidden in that dark continent of man's mind, actually influence and guide the conscious acts. He had shown how reason often follows meekly after, hurrying up with explanations and justifications—rationalizations, we have come to call them—of acts and opinions determined upon in the unconscious sphere.

Thus it was in his later years, when genius had been mellowed by wisdom and experience, that Freud came to the culmination of his researches with his theory that two dynamic principles, the creative and the destructive instincts, are the basic forces from which all other instincts emanate.

These two opposing forces are common to all of us. How

they function in each individual, in harmony or disharmony, for health or sickness, for long life or early death, for the fullness of living or the poverty of it, depends upon the individual himself.

There are those who believe that we determine not only our end but also the means by which we die. As Menninger stated it: "In the end each man kills himself in his own selected way, fast or slow, soon or late."

The Enigma of Health and Illness

How does this excursion into theory help us to understand health and illness? How does it explain the weary sufferers who drag their pain of body and anguish of mind in vain from doctor to doctor?

What Freud pointed out to us, and what we are only beginning to understand, is that man turns his creative and destructive instincts not only upon the world around him *but also upon himself.*

Let us examine this idea further. We understand how the creative impulse is exerted upon the world around us. We see it everywhere. From a Michelangelo painting his frescoes to a housewife baking a good pie for her family, in whatever work we do, if we do it with a loving purpose, we are following the drive of the creative instinct.

The destructive instinct is not always an opposing force. It also moves hand in hand with the creative instinct. Hercules in his cradle killed the serpent which would otherwise have killed him. We cut down a living tree to build a house. When we eat we destroy; that is, we convert matter from its original form to another form, for the sake of our own survival. The act of sexual love, the universal symbol of creativity, usually has in it some element of the destructive impulse, as for example the conquest of the loved one.

We have still to answer the crucial question: how do we turn the destructive instinct against ourselves? And the further question, why does an individual seek to destroy himself?

Look in any newspaper for the account of a suicide. The deceased, it says tersely, had suffered a reversal in business, a rejection in love, a frustration in his career.

We readily understand a man or woman who seeks, at the end of a rope or through an open window, with a drug or by turning on the gas, *escape from a situation which cannot be changed or endured.*

Let us restate this in terms of the two instincts. The creative instinct might have saved the suicide's life by seeking a way to solve his dilemma. But for some reason the creative instinct failed him. He had given himself over to the destructive instinct.

Cannot the same be true in illness, the slow suicide?

In suicide the creative instinct has resigned entirely. In illness perhaps the creative instinct, though not strong enough to maintain health, is yet strong enough to hold back the final fatal resolution of a dilemma. It is yet strong enough to turn us again and again toward life, toward our friends for understanding, toward the doctor for help.

If we could find and remove what is crippling the creative instinct, if we could restore it to its normal power, then we should be able to halt the slow suicidal trend and turn the patient back toward health.

If this is true, then we may hope to solve at last the enigma of health and illness.

The Inner Battle

Let us return now to the anxious patient in my office. We need not go deeper into the physical particulars of her suffering. If we are right, and her illness is an evidence of an inner battle between her instinct to live and a drive to self-destruction, then we should find her in a situation which she can neither accept nor resolve. We should discover reasons why she has turned her destructive instinct against herself, in an unconscious effort to escape from an unendurable dilemma.

She had suffered no serious illness except appendicitis, and no nervous disturbance, until her marriage at the age of twenty-two. She had continued her job after marriage.

With her marriage a sequence of troubles began. Every evening before she left her work she fell into a fit of weeping It was only after this release that she was able to travel home. She had been married barely six months when she developed an ovarian cyst which required an operation.

Could there be a connection? She was so depressed each evening at the moment of going home that she broke down and wept. In six months she had a growth which demanded surgery.

Surgeons maintain that "medicine does not know the cause of growth." But medical literature challenges this. Kehrer, a noted German gynecologist, wrote in the mid-twenties:

"Every patient with a fibroid tumor has a history of chronic psycho-sexual disturbance. Women leading satisfactory sexual lives remain free from fibromata. . . . Furthermore, from the size of a myoma and the degree of certain other accompanying manifestations of chronic sexual hyperemia [congestion of blood] even the duration of the psycho-sexual disturbance can be judged with striking accuracy."

This was the statement of a physician who had elsewhere declared himself "free from such teachings of Freud and his school as rest on exaggerated emphasis of the sexual life." By an entirely different path, that of gynecological examination and observation, he had arrived at virtually the same conclusion.

In our patient's story, not only the growth which required surgery but the entire medical picture suggested an emotional difficulty in her marriage. Her illness had begun with marriage; until then she had been well. Obviously we needed to know more about her home life and her husband.

Her husband was a fine man, she said, a man of good character. He was a lawyer, conscientious and punctual in the pur-

suit of his profession. He left home for his office at the same
time each morning and returned home with the same regular-
ity at night. Four nights a week he went out, to a club meeting
or an evening at cards. Once a week they went together to a
neighborhood motion picture. He was a shy man, she added.

Twice during her marriage she had become pregnant, once
on the advice of a doctor, the second time by her own decision
in an effort to regain her health. Those were the only periods
during the fourteen years of her marriage when she had felt
well. Why? Because of biological changes? Even so, are not
those very biological changes the consequence of creative activity in the body, expressions of the creative instinct? Indeed,
her well-being lasted only until the end of each pregnancy,
when she had given life each time to a healthy child.

We talked of her sexual relationship with her husband. She
was not quite sure what sexual satisfaction meant. She might
have experienced it occasionally at the beginning of her pregnancies. She was certain she had not, in the years since.

One of my medical teachers used to say that the shortest
definition of frigidity was "wrong partner." This is correct
but superficial. Frigidity or impotence reveals something more
fundamental about the individual. Both are expressions of
the destructive instinct turned against the self.

Freud explained how the two basic instincts function har-
moniously in the sexual act. A surplus of sexual aggressive-
ness will change the lover, he says, into a sexual murderer.
An inhibition of the aggressive factor—through conscience or
fear—will lead to shyness or impotence. When the aggressive
factor is prevented from expressing itself outwardly, it turns
against the self, in an unconscious effort to curb the guilty impulse. Thus sexual shyness, frigidity, and impotence are seen
to be expressions of the destructive instinct, in the sense that
they seek to destroy or to deny a part of the self.

As our patient's personality emerged it became clear that
she was denying herself not only sexual expression but also
expression in other creative directions. Although she had had
a job before her marriage and for a while afterward, she had

never had an interest in business as a career. She had no interest in artistic or intellectual pursuits. She did not join her husband in his social life because she had never cared for cards and she found groups of people exhausting.

As she talked about her marriage, she herself realized how barren and unsatisfactory it was. She was a Catholic and had not thought of divorce.

Apart from religious or moral scruples, a physician would be oversimplifying a situation if he advised a patient to dissolve a marriage in order to cure her ills. Divorce is not always a solution. The situation leading to divorce is often brought on, not by incompatibility with a given partner, but by dissatisfaction with oneself during a phase of inner strife. Or there may be a permanent maladjustment in one or the other partner.

We had begun medical treatment for the patient's symptoms. As her visits continued over the weeks and our talks proceeded, her negative response toward her marriage became ever clearer. She was a dutiful wife and mother, but the active, loving, creative impulse was lacking. Though outwardly submissive to her marriage, she was in unconscious rebellion against it, unconscious because her religious scruples would not permit open protest. This was her conflict: she rebelled against her marriage while at the same time accepting the commandment that marriage is indissoluble except by death.

She thus had only one alternative left. She must accept her marriage. There was no other solution except to make a positive adjustment.

She had never faced this decision. She had never realized that she had a decision to make, until she saw her situation clear in the light of our discussions. She thought she had accepted her marriage, since she had no thought of ending it. But in her heart she had rejected it. In all the creative aspects of marriage, from sexual union to social companionship, she had remained withdrawn and negative.

This troubled soul reminded me of an experience I once had during a hurricane in the Indian Ocean, when our ship was slowly sucked into the low barometric center of the storm. Though this woman's progress was less obvious and less dramatic, she was just as surely being drawn toward the whirlpool of final destruction. By refusing to face the issue, she had set loose within herself a force which was destroying her happiness, her health, and might end by destroying her life. By choosing to live in indecision, by negating the creative impulse which she might have exerted in her marriage, she had unconsciously chosen to go down the path of slow suicide.

It mattered little how her situation had originally come about. She recalled that she had stumbled into her marriage in a state of confusion. She and her husband had had to live with her parents for the first year. Whether her original decision to marry had been ill considered or immature, whether she had married out of infatuation or on the rebound or for whatever irrelevant reason, whether the crucial first year spent in the inhibiting atmosphere of her parents' home had set or developed the pattern, the result was an unhappy marriage.

The fact that her husband spent so much of his leisure time away from her could be understood as his unconscious answer to her inability to love him. The effect on her was still further discouragement, still further withdrawal. She could not share a normal social life with him. Crowds upset her; parties exhausted her. She was too sick—or too preoccupied with herself—for any enjoyment. Her illness, which began as a retreat from a life which she could not accept, now was its own reason for her further retreat from life. This is the vicious circle of illness.

Behind the Veil of Time

It is always painful to awaken from self-deception to reality. If the reality turns out to be a trap with no hope of escape, it is frightening. Fear becomes panic when the original problem has been driven into the unconscious where we bury the things we cannot face.

A decision we cannot make, an obstacle we cannot surmount is pushed down below the level of consciousness where we no longer feel its pain. Time lays veil after veil over hurtful events, so that when we later come to a crisis or a point of decision the source of our difficulty is obscured from understanding and beyond the reach of conscious reason.

If a man does not even know what troubles him, how can he know that this trouble is making him sick? Confused, he exhausts himself in futile search for a way out. The harder he tries, the weaker he becomes, the wearier and the more haunted. A new depth of depression acknowledges each new attempt to break out and each consequent realization of defeat.

Each defeat has its effect both consciously and unconsciously. As his physical energy is depleted, his problem grows to monstrous proportions. Sleepless nights or nights spent tossing in fitful sleep end in still greater fatigue, deeper depression, darker hopelessness.

Though the struggle may seem to end in resignation—as with our patient who seemed to resign herself to her marriage —in the unconscious mind it continues, exerting its subtle pressures on the body. Eventually the tortured man or woman joins the throng of fellow-sufferers who crowd the waiting rooms of the famous specialists, to be treated for their asthma, their heart trouble, their colitis, gastritis, bursitis, neuritis, arthritis, and the many other varieties of *itis*.

One who is physically depleted by this inner struggle moves like a spiritless, beaten army. Like the beaten army, he does not dare to counterattack. If his adversary—the situation he must resolve or the decision he must make—has grown to the strength of, let us say, ten army divisions, while all he can oppose to it in his own estimation may equal not even five divisions, he is not likely to attack. He will avoid facing the issue as a weakened army will avoid engaging the enemy. He will resign himself to defeat. He will pay tribute to the enemy in the form of loss of zest for living, loss of health, perhaps loss of life itself.

But if we can raise his strength to equal that of his adversary, and give him the reassurance besides of perhaps five fresh divisions in reserve, would he not be nerved to face his enemy? And if we can show him the nature of the enemy and where it hides, would he not seek out the destroying force and deal with it once and for all?

So it was with our patient. Clinical medicine had the answer to her physical and nervous symptoms. But now she knew that her treatments were double-pronged, that they were aimed not only at the symptoms but at the cause itself. The physical part of her new regimen was directed at repairing the disturbance of her bodily functions. But the main strategy was to build up her strength to deal with her inner enemy, the conflict within her marriage. (For the full story of how modern medicine can rebuild strength in both body and mind to meet the real enemy, the emotional cause of illness, we must wait for a later chapter.)

The day when this patient discovered that her marriage was the source of her trouble was the day on which she began her upward climb. Such a revelation is, of course, not fully absorbed at once. She needed time to examine her motives and evaluate her behavior. She had to be reassured again and again. She had to understand that she had buried her discontent because she could see no escape from it. She had to confront the only two alternatives open to her: either adjustment to her marriage—or slow suicide.

She made her choice. Obviously a pattern followed for fourteen years, especially one which has traced the path of least resistance, could not be reversed overnight. Between visits she was filled with self-doubt; her courage often wavered. But the truth of what she had learned about herself was compelling.

Once she could recognize her many ills as the many-headed forms of self-destruction, she knew the direction she must take to escape the specter of suffering which had haunted her for fourteen years. Armed with understanding, reinforced by modern medicine's resources, she persisted, and she began to see results. After three months she felt physically stronger and better.

Little by little, creative energies began to flow. In her duties toward her husband and her children, which before she had performed as a burden almost beyond her strength, she now saw a vista of new opportunities.

"I can meet situations which used to upset me," she said. "I am finding ways of making my marriage work."

Some time earlier, I had called her husband in, to enlist his help. We discussed what mutual interests he and his wife could develop, what ways they could find to build a better companionship.

"For the first time, we are beginning to have something like an enjoyable family life," he confessed, and added significantly, "I am losing my fear of coming home."

2. SOME LIVE ON LOVE

In 1940 I was called to see a patient occupying a small suite in a fashionable hotel. The patient, I was informed, was suffering from an advanced tuberculosis of the lungs. She was under the care of a reputable specialist. But a new symptom, a recurring pain in the abdomen, had led her friends to consult me as an internist.

A nurse ushered me into the bedroom. My patient was a young woman in her thirties, plainly emaciated. Her face seemed withered by pain, the lips livid, the light freckled skin pallid. She had thick red hair and lively, observant eyes.

She answered my questions thoughtfully but without apparent reserve. Her speech revealed intelligence and education. I gathered that within the year she had gone through a divorce, her second. Her first marriage, entered on the rebound from an earlier attachment, had lasted only a few months, giving her a daughter.

She had never been ill except for the usual children's diseases. Her parents and one sister were well. There was no tuberculosis in her family.

Her present illness had begun less than a year ago while she was living in California. The symptoms of coughing and tiredness were first diagnosed as a bronchial catarrh resulting from nicotine poisoning. When she continued to complain of her unusual fatigue, the physician attributed it to an inflammation of the genital organs and hinted that a gynecological operation might be unavoidable.

22

Alarmed by her rapid loss of weight, her friends insisted that she be X-rayed. The films revealed an extensive tubercular process in the right upper lung, with two cavities, signs of complete tissue destruction. A consultant was brought in who at once admitted her to a hospital for pneumothorax treatment, the injection of air into the chest to collapse and rest the diseased lungs.

At first she improved; her temperature subsided, her coughing lessened, her appetite increased. After a few months, however, the treatments became increasingly painful and also lost their efficacy. Her temperature rose once more and coughing and sputum grew worse. New X-rays showed that the infection had not been arrested, that indeed a third cavity had developed. She was advised to have an extensive operation in which several ribs would be removed to force a collapse of the infected lungs. Now she faced a long convalescence, and because her recently divorced second husband and other friends were in New York, she was permitted to fly East for the operation.

The New York specialist confirmed the California doctors' opinion, and after a few weeks passed without change in the patient's condition he insisted that the operation must be no longer delayed. A date was fixed.

The night after that decision was reached, the patient suffered an attack of abdominal pain which the doctor was able to control only with a hypodermic injection. From then on she was more or less in constant pain. At that point I was summoned.

I found no pathological condition other than the active process in the lungs; the abdominal pain was apparently of a psychogenic or "nervous" nature. It was routine to assume that in the absence of any other evidence, the new stomach symptoms must be due to anxiety about the prospective operation. At that time the thought of some deeper connection between conflicting emotions and organic illness did not occur to me.

Patients in a state of distress generally reject a diagnosis that their pain is the result of psychoneurosis. "Your pain is just nerves," sounds like a scolding, as though the doctor were accusing you of being a poor soldier. Yet the suffering is real. The patient becomes suspicious that he is not being taken seriously, and at the same time he feels himself accused of having caused a sort of false alarm.

Therefore I explained to the patient that purely physical pain is comparatively rare, and that it is fear which causes most pain.

The young woman accepted my explanation with surprising readiness, and then she burst out in a tirade against her own doctor. She declared that she had no confidence in him, that he lacked personal interest in her, that he was a cold scientist. She pleaded with me to take over her case. I told her I could not, because the rapidity and destructive character of her disease required a very experienced specialist. There were also the usual ethical reasons. I promised, however, to meet with her doctor.

I met him the following day. He showed me the chest films, including the latest series. They spoke an unmistakable language. A third cavity was visible and there were signs of a fourth one beginning. The doctor took a grave view of the situation, predicting that unless the lungs were immobilized (that is, collapsed) by surgery, the patient would probably not live six months longer. Even the operation offered her comparatively little chance.

The specialist's pessimism was not unjustified. For clinicians generally agree that if a cavity shows no evidence of closing by itself after six months it is unlikely to do so at all. Its resistance to treatment and to the natural healing processes of the body is proof of the malignancy of the disease—or of the patient's lack of recuperative powers.

Thus on my next visit I advised the patient that the operation seemed to hold the safest and probably the only promise of recovery. She received this advice quietly.

But she pleaded eloquently for time. She said she was feeling very much better. She had just begun to catch her breath. She needed yet a little time to get "mentally" ready for such a far-reaching decision—this despite the fact that she had come to New York for the express purpose of an operation, and had already allowed some weeks to go by. Finally she persuaded me that a delay of a week or two more would not matter.

The next morning her former husband called on me, bringing with him two friends. At the sick woman's request he had arranged matters with the specialist, most amicably, he assured me. Would I now take the case? Again I declined.

But the ex-husband had another question. He and his friends had observed the patient's sudden and unforeseen change for the better. One of his friends was a Columbia professor, the other a research man. Men of trained and critical minds, they were puzzled. How did I account for the reversal against all clinical predictions? I answered truthfully that I had no clinical explanation.

We agreed that another specialist should be consulted. The patient was outwardly cooperative but it was soon evident that she was fighting a stubborn battle for delay. When the consultant was at last able to examine her, we had X-ray and other physical proof that the tide had in fact begun to turn.

Against all odds and all predictions, the hitherto precipitous course of destruction had come to a standstill. The final objective proof came when the sputum repeatedly failed to show tubercular bacilli. The operation which had been so urgent was now indefinitely postponed.

With the first warm days of spring a new problem arose. The young woman became uneasy at the prospect of a summer in New York's humid heat. I proposed Saranac Lake. She feared a change in treatment might jeopardize her progress.

Good fortune came to our rescue. For some time I had nursed a plan for a little country clinic accentuating a more individual approach to the patient. I had found hospitals, as a rule, reserving to surgery an undue priority over the medical division. Also the impersonal atmosphere of a large institution dedicated to efficiency is often depressing to a sensitive patient.

Pursuing my idea on a modest experimental basis, I succeeded in leasing a country estate large enough and suitable for my purpose. Since my tubercular patient had become non-infectious, I could take her there with about a dozen other patients for the summer season. Her former husband, with his present wife and a friend, rented a cottage nearby, so that she would not find herself entirely alone among strangers.

Some six difficult weeks went by, difficult because of our efforts to fit this rebellious and moody patient into the routine of an institution.

Then one evening, driving back from New York, I saw her walking lightly along the country road. She recognized my car and waved. Exuberant joy radiated from her face, a face amazingly transformed. Her hollow cheeks had filled out and a fine tan had smoothed away the lines of bitter resignation. She confessed that she was crazily happy.

It seemed that our patient had fallen in love again. The man was a celebrated artist who had come to the little country clinic for a convalescence. Whether it was his physical charm, his fame, or his sympathy, in any event to the lonely woman living the life of an involuntary recluse he represented the fulfillment of all her longings.

I could not have found a mightier ally in our battle against illness. Three months later, when the time came to close the little clinic, our patient seemed cured, restored, filled with hope and confidence in the future.

But after a few months in New York she protested that she was bored with her restful life. She missed the companionship of the other patients in the clinic and their open admiration of her as an attractive woman. Most of all she missed her new love, who had moved to California. Perhaps to make up for lost time, or perhaps to conceal from herself the growing suspicion that he was becoming indifferent, she plunged into more active living. She took a part-time job. She began to go

COMING SOON

June 18. YOU SHALL KNOW THEM by Vercors.
The author of "The Silence of the Sea" explores the infinite possibilities of the age-old question: what is man? His sophisticated fable for moderns is amusing, sardonic, fascinating in its implications. Little, $3.50.

June 19. THE SINGER NOT THE SONG by Audrey Erskine Lindop. Two men, a Mexican bandit and an Irish priest, clash dramatically over the fate of an isolated Mexican village. The fact that they grow to like and respect one another in the process adds considerably to the tension and excitement. Appleton, $3.75

June 22. LIFE AMONG THE SAVAGES by Shirley Jackson. Putting aside the macabre overtones of her unique fiction, Shirley Jackson writes irresistibly of her own entertaining home life as wife and mother of four children "in an old, noisy house full of kids, toys, and books." Farrar, $3.

June 25. OUR VIRGIN ISLAND by Robb White.
The author and his bride built a rare and adventurous happiness on a tiny island in the Caribbean. Their life of subtropical domesticity reaches its climax in a terrible hurricane. Doubleday, $3.50

June 29. BING CROSBY'S OWN STORY, CALL ME LUCKY. A colorful and heartwarming self-portrait in which Crosby reviews his fabulous career from Spokane days to the present. S. & S., $3.95, $1.

June 30. THE GOOD-FOR-NOTHING by James Yaffe. The story of two brothers in a well-to-do New York Jewish family, one a charming wastrel, the other a little too good for this world and destined to be his brother's keeper. Little, $3.50

Please send the books whose numbers have been encircled below:

Order Form

1	2	3	4	5	6	7	8	9	10
11	12	13	14	15	16	17	18	19	20
21	22	23	24	25	26	27	28	29	30
31	32	33	34	35	36	37	38	39	40
41	42	43	44	45	46	47	48	49	50
51	52	53	54	55	56	57	58	59	60
61	62	63	64	65	66	67	68	69	70
71	72	73	74	75	76	77	78	79	80
81	82	83	84	85	86	87	88	89	90
91	92	93	94	95	96	97	98	99	100
101	102	103	104	105	106	107	108	109	110
111	112	113	114	115	116	117	118	119	120

☐ *Charge my account*   ☐ *Check enclosed*

NAME _____

ADDRESS _____

_____

June

out socially, and to stay out late at night. Her visits to my office became increasingly irregular.

Until this time, X-rays and other tests showed consistent healing of the lungs. Then one night of blizzard, after an unsatisfactory evening at a concert, our young woman was unable to find a taxi and walked home through the snow in silk sandals.

The next day she had the grippe. It was her first temperature in six months. A bladder complication prompted me to take her to the hospital. I feared a relapse of the tubercular infection, but the urologist found the infection nontubercular and her bronchitis showed no evidence of her old disease.

Recovery, however, was slow, and again I urged her to try Saranac. But the man who had become the keystone of her life was in California. I warned her against Los Angeles, which did not have the high altitude she needed. She compromised for a point between, a sanitarium in Colorado.

But soon she wrote to me, complaining about the sanitarium. After several weeks she wrote again, saying that she had coughed up blood. She sent me her new X-rays. They showed a beginning process on the right side and a new cavity on the left.

She continued to write, one day in despair, the next with renewed hope. She left the sanitarium, but was undecided what to do next. She took a cottage and engaged a nurse.

She went rapidly downhill. She contracted laryngitis, an ominous symptom.

At last she had a visit from the man she loved. "I held out until you came," she told him exuberantly, unaware of how shockingly emaciated she had become. He stayed with her a little while, and then he left the room.

Almost immediately the nurse called him back. When he reentered the sickroom the patient was dead.

The Emotional Dynamics of Illness

A closed case invites critical analysis. Usually this means a comparison of one's own findings with those of the pathologist, a study of the autopsy to find wherein it sustains or disproves one's diagnosis.

But let us make our analysis from another point of view. Let us review this case to discover, if we can, how this tragic young woman miraculously conquered her malady. Let us also try to see why, after she had regained her health and had nearly as good a chance, medically speaking, to live out her years as any one of us, she succumbed once more. Let us try to penetrate the double mystery of miracle and martyrdom.

A medical chart records any illness a patient has had in his life. Everything from whooping cough to German measles is duly registered there. But events of striking force, such as the birth or death of a love, the beginning or the end of a life's work, all of what we might now call manifestations of the creative or the destructive instinct, are considered too unscientific, too irrelevant to be noted.

Yet these are the events which turn and twist a life. Indeed, the wider our experience, the more certain we become that these are the verdicts of life and death.

Let us recall my first visit to the tuberculous patient in her hotel suite. She had answered the routine questions about the beginning of her illness: the approximate time, the initial symptoms, the first erroneous diagnosis. Then, apparently under the impact of revived emotions, she revealed something really important: she knew the very day when "it" began.

She said "it" in a half whisper, as if she were talking to herself or suffering embarrassment at voicing a deep feeling. Perhaps it seemed useless to try to convince a physician of a connection of which she was herself only half aware, only half convinced. The "day" was not the day of her divorce but the day on which she felt the full significance of her divorce, the day when her former husband married his secretary.

A few minutes later she made another of these almost involuntary revelations. She was speaking of the first X-rays and the extent of the lesions in her lungs which they revealed. She ridiculed the doctor who had treated her for nicotine poisoning. She said, with a flash of anger, that she knew all along how sick she was.

"I did not demand X-rays earlier, because I did not care," she said. And she added, with quivering lips, "Because really, I did not want to live."

Did she want to die? Or did she want to be sick, to frighten her former husband, to make him feel sorry for her, to punish him for abandoning her, like a child who fancies himself dead and his parents sorrowing?

Words are sometimes used to hide rather than to reveal. On later occasions the patient talked freely about her husband's shortcomings, about her good fortune in being free and financially secure. She protested too much, I thought, as though she were trying to convince herself of the advantages of her new life, when what she really saw before her was loneliness, emptiness of purpose, gray nothingness.

I did not then, as I do now, see an acute illness as a sort of protective act of nature, a defense against an attack which, unless the victim is forced to rest, may lead to total collapse. Or as a needed period of withdrawal during which a patient may come to a decision on some deep-reaching problem or make peace with a difficult situation. At that time I did not realize either that illness might be a cover for failure, an escape from an unendurable position, a gesture toward suicide.

In brief, the thought of emotional factors possessing any causal relationship to illness had no practical significance for me. Despite Thomas Mann's *Magic Mountain* or Dumas' *Camille,* despite lectures by various psychoanalysts, I would have rejected flatly any suggestion that a disease like tuberculosis could have been brought on by emotional conflict.

The intimations of poets and writers I dismissed as "interesting" but fictional and therefore incompatible with the demands of scientific reality. Psychoanalytical theories also seemed too far-fetched for serious consideration. My approach differed in no respect from that of a majority of physicians: that tuberculosis is, after all, an infectious disease, that it is caused by a specific bacillus, and that it is transmitted by contact.

We have known this since 1882 when Koch presented his epochal discovery of the tubercle bacillus at a short and dramatic meeting of the Berlin Medical Society. In the last seventy years a mass of research has been accumulated on this disease, but little change has been made in the conclusions drawn by Koch from his original investigations.

Obviously then when my patient suddenly confounded the clinical evidence and made her about-face toward recovery, I was just as baffled as her friends. True, I had experienced miracles in medicine, and had learned to rate them somewhat higher than merely the exception to the rule. I had not, however, experienced the healing power of words. I did not suspect that the words one speaks as a release from an intolerable burden, in those rare moments when one feels one is understood, are not like the words of ordinary speech. I did not know that words of explanation and reassurance, born out of compassion, may be as healing as potent drugs.

To be sure, I had had intimations of something like this. And the idea again came to mind when I discussed the case with the specialist. But a fleeting—and unscientific—glimpse of truth could not stand against the force of X-rays, plus the knowledge that a patient in advanced tuberculosis releases from one and one-half million to four million bacilli every twenty-four hours, plus the probability that she could have brought the infection home on her shoes, or petted a dog, or inhaled the bacilli on the street, in a department store, or riding in a railway car.

And added to all this was the well-known fact that almost every child or adult living in a city experiences a tubercular infection, recognized or unrecognized, at one time or another. And finally statistics show that some twelve per cent of the world's population die of this universal scourge.

But how did science explain this phenomenon, that one individual survives the infection with no apparent bad after-effect, and another becomes ill and dies?

Predisposing factors have been named, a long list of them, with environment near the top of the list. Poorly ventilated dwellings and work shops, slums, asylums, damp and dark tenements have been described as breeding places of the bacillus. Constitutional factors have been named. Hippocrates long ago portrayed the predisposed victim of the disease as "the smooth, the whitish, that resembling the lentil; the reddish, the blue-eyed, the leuco-phlegmatic, and that with the scapulae having the appearance of wings."

But my patient did not have scapulae, or shoulder blades, like wings; she was well built. And her environment had never been dark and damp. She had grown up in sunshine and had always enjoyed the good things of life.

Later, when I had gained more insight into the emotional dynamics of disease, it was as if a curtain had been raised. Rereading the medical literature, I found much to question, much that was contradictory, much that seemed one-sided, even superficial.

For example, a classical medical textbook says of the predisposition to tuberculosis of one sex rather than the other: "Women are perhaps somewhat more frequently attacked than men, possibly from the fact that in a more sedentary, indoor life they are more liable to infection." Could one not just as readily deduce that women should be less liable to infection because they are less exposed to it?

All authorities agree on the theory of lowered resistance. The parable of the Sower is quoted by Sir William Osler: "In a large proportion of us, the seed falls by the wayside. In others, the seed falling upon a rock or on stony ground withers away as soon as it springs up. In the last group, in which the seed falls on good ground and springs up and bears fruit a hundredfold, are the cases in which the disease progresses and the unfortunate victim dies of tuberculosis."

But in spite of the generally accepted theory of lowered resistance, modern statistics agree that tuberculosis is more frequent during the adolescent years, and that the years between twenty and forty show the highest mortality.

Are not these our best years? Are not men and women in their prime between twenty and forty? If lowered resistance means that of the body alone, why should the disease be more often fatal during the years when the body is at its peak? May there not be factors other than purely physical ones, which act upon the body during these years?

We speak of the adolescent years as the most difficult in our lives. Parents dread them, expecting the sunny child to change overnight into a moody, difficult, unstable youth or young girl. We know these years as years of confusion and emotional restlessness, years when all the disturbances of childhood may raise their heads again. They are the years in which we must at last accept the realities of life in an adult society; no further postponement is possible.

Consider the years that immediately follow adolescence. Are not those the period of grim and relentless struggle to succeed, to make one's place in the adult world, to achieve economic and emotional security? Are not those the years which to the less ruthless, to "the smooth, the whitish," often bring defeat? Cannot defeat shatter the inner man? Cannot defeat lower the body's resistance?

Still another factor, that of environment, is supposed to play an important role. If this is true, then the children of tubercular parents would be greatly endangered. But the medical literature reports that infants from a tubercular milieu show no higher mortality during their first years of life than other children. Older children living in a home where tuberculosis exists also show the same rate of infection and mortality as children of healthy homes, no more. Perhaps the suggestion that these parents take special care may adequately explain the contradiction. Or perhaps there are other reasons.

In apes and monkeys in a wild state, tuberculosis is unknown. In confinement it is the most formidable destroyer with which these creatures must contend.

Among men, North American Indians show a proneness to this disease more than double that of white Americans, and Negroes in the United States are second to the Indians. The unhygienic living conditions to which these two groups of Americans have been generally subjected are given us as the reason. But these minority groups are also subjected to other depressing conditions, of a social rather than a physical variety.

Scientifically—that is, studying the evidence critically on a wholly materialistic level—we have no absolute explanation of what causes the predisposition to tuberculosis. All we have are hypotheses. We seek the answer in laboratories, concentrating on tissue, studying the serum reactions of guinea pigs, trying the same techniques on human beings. But reports of research projects often betray their disappointment at man's refusal to act like a guinea pig.

No Life Without Love

We will go back now to our suffering young woman. During the first phase of her illness she asked in detail about the technique of the operation which was so urgently recommended. She was only curious, she said, and I thought no more about it at the time. But another case threw new light on this facet.

A young woman, a fashion model, came to me with an obvious malignancy of the breast. An immediate operation was necessary, but instead of the surgeon I suggested, she chose a plastic surgeon. The night after the operation she collapsed. With blood transfusions and medication she rallied, but soon afterward she collapsed again. She had chosen the plastic surgeon in the hope that he would merely remove the tumor. Instead he had removed the entire breast.

The patient had suddenly awakened to the realization that she had been "mutilated." To her this meant that she had ceased to be a competitive female. It would be futile to attempt to evaluate her reaction objectively. The depth of this shock can be understood only from the subjective point of view of a woman.

Within a year this patient died of metastasis in the brain. Now statistics show that a patient has a good chance if breast surgery is properly performed and done in time. Perhaps in this particular case the operation was not performed with the necessary skill; possibly all axillary lymph glands were not completely removed. As a matter of fact the plastic surgeon did operate a second time after a few days.

But today we can imagine another, more significant possibility: feeling that she was no longer a desirable woman, the patient did not wish to live.

Our latter-day Camille had, I believe, the same fear. Her initial improvement from tuberculosis may have been a heroic effort to escape what she too would have considered a mutilation. She fought a delaying action against the second specialist, needing time to make enough progress so that he would not doom her to the operation. Her summer love affair gave her new confirmation that she was again a desirable woman. By finding a man who wanted her, she had achieved a victory over the husband who had rejected her. The future glowed again. New hope drowned out the clicking of time.

Sir William Osler declared: "What happens to a patient with tuberculosis depends more on what he has in his head than what he has in his chest."

Thus we can understand that when the tragic woman approached the end of her renascent happiness, there came the relapse. She had to face reality once more.

She was a quiet sufferer. Hers was not a positive, not a fighting spirit. She was at the same time rebellious and submissive. She day-dreamed vengeance, but she retreated into martyrdom. She was without direction, without inner security, without the belief in her own worthiness of love which would spur her to fight for love. Instead she surrendered not only love but life itself.

3. MAN DIES WHEN HE WANTS TO DIE

LIFE holds many doubts but only one certainty, the certainty of death. This is the one certainty which all human beings share. Although animals too must die, as far as we know they cannot foresee their own death, and therefore they do not fear it. Man, however, can envision his own end. His fear of death is one of the prices he pays for the intellect which entitles him to call himself Homo sapiens.

The fear of death seems to be universal, at least in our culture. Most of us make our first acquaintance with death in some form quite early in life. A pet dies. An animal lies dead in the road. Or, more disturbingly, there is the dark hush which falls over the house because of a death in the family.

These experiences take deep root in childhood. They are a lightning glimpse into an awesome secret, an instant of revelation instantly cloaked again in darkness. The silent mystery with which death is fearfully shrouded for us in childhood may haunt us all our life.

When we fear death, what are we afraid of?

Do we fear the pain of dying? Physicians know that most people suffer far more pain, both physical and mental, in living than in dying. Death is characteristically serene, and the face of a dead man is peaceful.

"Calm and gentle is the death of every good person," wrote Schopenhauer. "Come, sweet death," sang Bach. And the great physician Sir William Osler testified:

"Most human beings not only die like heroes but, in my

wide clinical experience, die really without pain or fear. There is as much oblivion about the last hours as about the first, and therefore men fill their minds with spectres that have no reality."

Perhaps what we really fear is that life may end *before we are ready*. Standing in the midstream of life, full of the things we have only begun and the things we have yet to begin, do we not fear that we will be cut off before we have finished with living and doing?

If this is what we fear, then there is a single answer to banish fear: it does not happen that way.

We die only when we are ready to die. We die when we want to die. We die because unconsciously we want to die, although rationally we may profess that we have everything to live for.

If we truly wish to live, if we have the incentive to live, *if we have something to live for*—then no matter how sick we may be, no matter how close to death, we do not die. We live, *because* we want to live.

But the incentive must be one in which we inwardly, utterly believe. It is not the "everything to live for" in the eyes of the world, which keeps us alive, but the something which meets our own uncompromising measure of what is worth living for.

A very old lady, one who had accomplished a pioneer work in education during her lifetime, once told about a dangerous illness she had suffered in her middle years. She lay hovering between life and death, in the twilight of half-surrender, when she overheard two of her co-workers talking just outside the open door of her hospital room.

"If we could only reach her! If we could only make her understand," one of them said passionately, "how much we need her!"

Such a message may resurrect the will to live. It is not one single factor which brings an individual close to death, nor one single factor which rescues him. But when the balance of many factors hangs undecided, one significant word may swing the weight of a complex decision. The words this woman overheard concerned her life work, for which she had made many sacrifices. In a moment of discouragement and wavering faith, the intensity of her colleague's plea reassured her and gave her courage to take up the struggle again.

Something to Live for

Doctors are aware of many "miracles" of healing, of patients snatched back to life against apparently hopeless physical odds. Biological medicine alone is at some difficulty to explain these "miracles." I had such a case in my earliest days as a physician.

One night I was called to attend a man who lay dying in an apartment across the street from my brand-new office. His regular physician, who happened to be my chief at the hospital, was out of town. The patient was in his sixties, a pharmacist who enjoyed a very fine standing among the top doctors of the city.

His brother met me at the door with a frantic plea. "Doctor, you must keep him alive until morning"—he pursued me breathlessly—"until we can get a marriage performed. He must not die until he has legitimatized his son!"

Then I learned that this ultra-respectable man had been living with his housekeeper for more than twenty years. But he had never had the courage to publish his transgression of the proprieties by a marriage. True, he had provided well for his son, who was even then studying at the university, preparing to enter his father's pharmacy. But without legal status, the young man could not succeed to his father's name in the business. The patient had postponed the necessary formalities until there was little hope that they could be performed at all.

I struggled through the night against a myocarditis in its last stages, until the threatening rattle of fluid in the lungs subsided. When a minister finally arrived, the dying man had gained consciousness enough to take part in the ceremony.

Then came the "miracle." My former chief met me some time later and asked, "What did you do? That fellow was a dead man! And just now he waited on me himself in his pharmacy!"

The druggist lived two years longer and saw his son graduated from the university. The old man was not in very good health, but well enough to spend a few hours almost every day watching over the business. He lived another year or so, introducing his son to the clientele, especially the distinguished medical customers. Then, peaceful and content, he died.

I was much abashed by my chief's excessive praise. Actually I was unable to claim any technique beyond those outlined in the text books, plus the zeal of a young doctor who cannot bear to lose a patient. Now, after many such wrestling matches with death, some won and some lost, I think I can understand why that sick old man was first willing to die, and then determined to live. He had doubtless been torn for years by his inability to overcome a rigid social code. Deprived of the satisfaction of acknowledging his son, he must have suffered from a deep sense of failure.

Once the decisive step was forced on him by his brother, he found he had a new and happy task to fulfill. He had to live to participate in his son's graduation, and to give the boy a good start in the business. Obviously medicine helped to keep life in his failing body. But medicine alone could not have brought him back to life without the powerful resurrection of his will to live, by that formal act which blessed his union and gave him a son to carry on his name and his work, that promise of immortality for which most men long.

To Each His Own Goal

Each of us has a goal, conscious or unconscious. The goal may change, or become confused. Other purposes may arise which conflict with it. At such periods we may be in danger, as will be seen in later chapters.

Deep within every living thing there exists the will to live, that inborn dynamic principle whose purpose is to preserve the individual as well as the race. It is the keystone of every organic existence. So strong and passionate is this force, that man and animal alike will battle desperately when life is endangered, however starved, wretched, and deprived that life may be.

Yet this biological will to live seems not enough to support us through the increasing complexities of life in a civilized world. We need a moral and emotional force to make the struggle endurable. The will to live in civilized man is a combined biological and psychological drive. As long as we have something to live for, the will to live carries us through the moments of crisis which are inevitable in every life.

The poet Goethe expressed the belief that every extraordinary man has a mission which he is called upon to fulfill. Once he has fulfilled it, Providence no longer requires him on earth. Demons trip him up again and again until he succumbs. The composer Mozart and the painter Raphael, both of whom died at thirty-six; Shakespeare and Byron, even Napoleon who pursued his destiny through a lifetime of heroic exertion without fatigue, were among the extraordinary men whose death, in Goethe's theory, came when they had accomplished the purpose designed for them.

Goethe himself was a living example of his own hypothesis that man dies when his work is finished. He began *Faust*, his masterpiece, when he was a youth of twenty-four. He wrote the last line of Part Two fifty-eight years later, in 1831. In 1832 he died, without ever seeing it in print.

Philosophers and poets often express intuitively what science, with its more cautious methods, later confirms. We can restate Goethe's comment in modern psychological terms.

For his "extraordinary man" we may consider the ordinary man and woman, you, myself, the neighbor to whom you just now said good evening. For Goethe's "mission" we can understand the self-assigned goal of each human life. His "demons" we can translate to mean that unconscious drive to destruction which balances the will to live in each of us, Freud's destructive instinct.

Let us put it this way. From birth and through the years of struggle toward maturity, each human being aspires toward some achievement, clear or clouded, conscious or unconscious. Toward this he strives, through the entanglements of life, its successes and defeats, until he reaches his mark—or until he becomes convinced that he can never reach it. Then he dies.

Exceptions leap to mind. The fulfillment of a great task does not necessarily mean the end of life. With each new eminence which a man may reach, new perspectives may beckon him to new endeavors. One man may exhaust himself with a single great effort. But another gains conviction in his purpose, and continues onward.

There are apparent exceptions at the other end of the scale, for example the pauper who lives to a ripe old age in an institution, aspiring to nothing and accomplishing nothing. Such a man, however, has resigned from the struggle to achieve, and asks nothing of life but a vegetable existence. Presumably we could all live longer if we were content with less. Many a farmer lives long and in good health, creatively busied with the succession of the seasons, measuring his aspiration to the harvesting of each year's crop. Those who drive themselves to a premature grave might well be found to be people whose goals were from the first unrealistic and unrealizable.

For it is within ourselves that we set these goals. We weigh ourselves in scales of our own devising. Each of us is his own judge. The world has laid its highest tributes at the feet of some men whose ambition was never satisfied, men who still strove to achieve some greater position, some mightier power, no matter what they had already won. And by the same token, many a man or woman has lived in modest content with little that the world would hold desirable, but for them it was enough.

Most of us fall somewhere between the man with insatiable

ambition and the man with little or none. But with all of us, the deciding estimate of our accomplishment is not society, nor any group of persons or set of standards outside ourselves.

Too often it is not even our critical or reasoning mind which passes judgment on us. Unless we strive toward that maturity of mind which makes these judgments conscious and reasonable, they remain unconscious, and they remain the immature judgments of childhood. To keep our goal clear, and to judge it by rational standards, is the task of our conscious, reasoning mind.

Conscious or unconscious, we make our own choice. No human being is spared the struggles of life, but each human being has his unique way of reacting to them. The pain of adjustment, the awareness of the world's misery and inequity, cry out in a Beethoven symphony. Throughout the ages there have been those who grieved over the bitterness of life but felt themselves helpless to improve it. Yet in each age some individuals have rebelled against what they would not endure, and have exerted themselves to change it. When the dynamic energies of the rebel have been translated into action or teachings, the world has found another of its great leaders and reformers.

Whether the individual accepts life with its inexorable conditions, or rejects it, will determine his course. If, revolted at the world and at the same time despairing of his ability to better his lot, he rejects it, then his very negativism leads him to frustration. But the individual who accepts life, whether he protests or not, strives to adapt himself to situations which he cannot avoid. He begins in infancy a long series of adjustments, and the more readily and easily he adjusts himself the more he is recognized as "normal."

Each battle in this lifelong struggle of adjustment takes him nearer to his goal or further from it. Sooner or later in every man's life, and perhaps not once but many times through the years, there comes a moment when he despairs of ever reaching his goal. Occasionally, like Goethe's extraordinary man, he becomes aware of having reached it. He has achieved his utmost. He cannot surpass himself. There is nothing left for him to do.

These are the moments in which we may become battle weary. We may yearn to withdraw from a struggle which can have—or so we believe—no satisfactory outcome. At such times the body begins to lose its ability to make adjustments, or its resistance to disease. When the longing for peace outweighs the joy of battle, when the determination to seek peace becomes irreversible and conclusive, then we die.

This is what is meant by the statement that man dies when he wants to die, that he dies *because* he wants to die. Death can no longer be looked upon as a visitation, coming without warning, before we are ready.

A Medical View

Traditionally we have considered death from disease to be death from "natural causes," as contrasted with death by violence or accident. Now there is medical authority for believing that death from disease is not natural, and that the only natural death is from old age.

Pathology is regarded as the most exact and conservative branch of medical science, and it is from a pathologist that this interpretation comes. Dr. R. Roessle holds the same chair of pathology at the University of Berlin from which the great Virchow published his theory of cellular pathology, locating disease in the cell changes, a theory which has become a guiding principle of modern scientific medicine. In 1949 Dr. Roessle issued a study of longevity and physiological death which seems to lend the support of medical science to the poets and philosophers.

Dr. Roessle defines natural death as physiological death, the result of the aging of tissues. The long-lived, he points out, are those whose tissues wear out at a harmonious rate, so that no one organ or function of the body succumbs prematurely.

The long-lived are also possessed of a high degree of adaptability.

This interpretation of natural death deepens our understanding of the diseases of old age, and suggests new ways of prolonging life and guarding health in our later years. Traditionally, the family and even the physician strive to find an exact organic diagnosis of an aged person's illness, and are likely to treat the failing heart, for example, to the exclusion of other considerations.

But as Roessle points out, even when a person of advanced age dies of an infection, such as pneumonia, allowance must be made for his lowered resistance because of age, and the infection should not be regarded as the cause of death no matter what the doctor's certificate may say.

To prolong life, therefore, we ought to regard the whole person, his interest in living and his adjustment to life, instead of devoting ourselves exclusively to his physical symptoms. Indeed, in the new science of geriatrics, many of the traditional complaints of old people have been found to disappear when social activities, interests, and a generally happier adjustment could be provided.

Carrying the Roessle findings in longevity a step further, we may say that the individual whose tissues wear out at a harmonious rate is one whose destructive instinct does not take a toll of one or another organ of his body. The adaptable individual may be one whose acceptance of life makes him willing and able to adjust himself to the changing, and often none too favorable, conditions of life. One who fails to adapt himself is following a destructive trend.

This brings us back to the destructive instinct, and the time and the manner in which we choose to die.

The Triumphant Death Wish

How does the power pass from the creative to the destructive side? Why does the will to live weaken and bow before the wish to die? What are the reasons for those sudden events in illness which confound physicians, those lightning changes between night and morning, in which a patient on the road to recovery at evening is seen by the light of the next day to be marked for death?

One story, of the many which we might tell, may demonstrate this turning from life to death, this shift of power obscure in its origin and discernible only in its effect.

The man whom I was called to see, on a sweltering summer night, was no stranger to me although I had never met him. His name glittered with international renown. As a creative producer and director in the theater he had been an unrivaled genius for decades.

Before I entered his room that night, his son described to me the incident which had precipitated his illness. The day before, vacationing on an island some distance from New York, he had gone into a telephone booth to make an important call, setting a date to begin rehearsals for his new production. While he was telephoning, his Scotch terrier was attacked by a larger dog. The terrier sprang at its master to escape the attacker and, fixing its teeth in his arm, hung there howling while the larger dog locked its jaws on the terrier. Trying to separate the two animals in the narrow, dark, steaming telephone booth, the patient had become fearfully overwrought. When the excitement was over he found it difficult to speak.

He returned to New York the same evening. His difficulty in speaking had increased and his right arm felt heavy, as though paralyzed. A doctor, sent by a friend, came immediately but the patient showed the physician the door. His son feared I might receive the same treatment, and suggested I give his father some excuse, such as that a city law required me to cauterize his arm against rabies.

I found the patient sitting in an armchair, reading a paper, a gray-haired man with penetrating eyes and a sharp-featured, arresting face. He looked at me keenly, holding his head in a characteristically proud way with his pointed nose high. Answering the question in his look, I merely said I was a doctor who had come to examine him. There was a pause during which he continued to fix me with his critical gaze. Then he mumbled inarticulately and his left hand waved me to a chair.

The right corner of his mouth was visibly drawn down, indicating paralysis of the facial nerve. When he answered my questions he tried to cover his partial loss of articulation by accenting the final syllable of every word. The right arm showed a mild motor disturbance. His blood pressure was rather high. His heart was normal in size and its function was good.

I explained to him that the excitement of his experience with the dogs had apparently caused a spasm in certain arteries of the brain, which rest and treatment would cure. His face disclosed the fear that he had suffered a stroke, and to erase any doubt I explained the meaning of "spasm." He seemed convinced and somewhat encouraged.

My report to his son was optimistic, depending on developments in the next few days. We decided against moving the patient to a hospital. He passed a quiet night, and after a few days he began to show signs of improvement.

But time began to press. My patient was on the threshold of a Broadway production, one of the elaborate, costly dramatic spectacles for which he was unequaled in Europe or America. He had important decisions to make. The rehearsal date which he had been about to set with his telephone call the preceding Sunday was already past. Urged to set a date when he would be well enough to begin his work, I strove to win time for him. I asked for a consultation with one of New York's most distinguished neurologists. The consultant corroborated the diagnosis of cerebral spasm.

A week later, noting his general improvement except for his speech, which was better one day and worse the next, the neurologist and I held a second consultation. As a result a specialist was called in to give the patient speech lessons. Far from successful, the lessons seemed to depress him, and presently I advised against their continuance. The patient visibly relaxed. He enjoyed listening to music. He took to writing little messages on slips of paper. He was pleasant and cooperative. He missed his cigars and his coffee but was cheered by the progress he was making.

One morning, taking advantage of his nurse's absence in the kitchen, he dressed to go out. The day was a religious holiday, requiring fasting and attendance at services. Our patient refused food and was adamant in his decision to fast and pray. The nurse, unable to deter him, called me. I tried to give him an intravenous injection of glucose, but for the first time in our relationship as patient and physician he resisted me. He went to attend services.

That night one of those inexplicable changes took place. In the morning the nurse, hearing a shattering of glass, hurried into the patient's room. He had prepared to shave, but with his first glance into the mirror he had discovered the extended paralysis of the right side of his face. The mirror had crashed to the floor.

As though to drive himself deeper into the realization of his disability, he set himself the very next morning to answer the many messages of reverence and respect which had come from all over the world on his seventieth birthday, some two weeks before he fell ill. He found that he could not write. The discovery excited him so that his speech, which had been much improved, deteriorated once more. He was gradually losing sensation and mobility in his right leg and arm.

When, a few nights later, he complained of a pain in the right side of his chest, I called in a cardiologist. This doctor found heart and circulatory system in "excellent condition," and blood pressure well down to normal. He shared the opinion that the patient was suffering a spastic disturbance, and agreed that the prognosis would have been very favorable if there had not been a recurrence of the initial spastic attack.

Out of consideration for the family's growing anxiety, a neurologist was summoned from Boston. Before this doctor began his examination I asked him specifically not to test the patient's ability to write. Nevertheless, as the specialist proceeded with a very thorough examination in an atmosphere of growing tension, I saw him place a writing pad before the patient. No doubt the neurologist wished to determine whether the damage had occurred in the sensory writing center in the brain, in the nearby motoric center of the right arm, or in both.

The patient took the pen. He hesitated, and one could see evidence of a rising resentment against the doctor's relentless pursuit of his symptoms. He began to write. He used force, bearing down on the pen. His face flushed. Again he hesitated, evaluating the distorted letters of the single line he had scrawled. Once more he tried, but in the middle of a frustrated upstroke and with a damning mumble he flung down the pen. Thus ended this examination.

The patient now sank into a deep depression. During the days which followed the nurse frequently surprised him in the act of testing his writing when he believed he was unobserved. The first neurologist now took a serious view of the situation. The paralysis in the facial nerve remained unchanged, and though the patient's speech had worsened into a completely inarticulate mumble, his bodily functions remained for a while in good order.

But it was obvious that the sick man was going through a series of strokes. There were two more consultations, but all medication, all suggestions, all efforts failed to halt the downward course of the disease. A difficulty in swallowing appeared and it became obvious that the entire anterior central gyrus, the area in the brain which harbors all these centers, was involved. We had before us the classic picture of cerebral hemorrhage.

The patient sank into a coma from which he did not awaken. Pneumonia developed, and on a Sunday night, just five weeks after the onset of the illness, he died.

"Death That Is the Cooling Night . . ."

As spectator to this man's struggle between his will to live and a wish to die which grew steadily to overwhelming power, the reader needs to understand not only his state of mind at the time but also his physical condition. Although, as we have learned, both are interwoven, we must know whether he had ever shown himself particularly susceptible to this or any other illness.

Actually up to the date of the initial attack the patient had been in perfect physical health. There were no symptoms of trouble, no storm signals of any kind. A clinician might point out that overindulgence in nicotine and strong coffee could have affected the condition of the arteries. Yet a cardiologist of great repute found, three weeks after the beginning of the illness, "the heart sounds are excellent . . . the heart itself not dilated . . . the electrocardiogram shows a normal tracing in every respect . . . blood pressure is normal . . . liver not enlarged." Physically, this man was in as good condition as a man can be at his age.

But now let us turn to the emotional picture. When he came to the United States for the first time in the early twenties, laurels strewed his path. He was acclaimed as an unsurpassed master in his field by both the press and the public.

He returned ten years later, a refugee fleeing the Nazi terror. The laurels had faded; the reverence had become perfunctory. The guest of honor was now a competitor, and his welcome accordingly diminished in ardor. One must weigh the effect of this on a man accustomed to live like an uncrowned king in his native land.

After a few years of moderate success he determined on a production which was to be his masterwork. I was told by his friends how much effort, enthusiasm, and devotion he put into his work. The opening night critics dealt him a crushing defeat.

One producer told me that this production was too far ahead of the times to be a success. The reason for its failure, however, is immaterial. The effect on the patient is what counts, and that was devastating.

Shortly afterward he had his seventieth birthday. If success had continued to shine on him he might not have observed that this birthday marked the end of his three score years and ten.

It is possible to imagine the emotion with which, following the failure of his crucial production, he greeted the significant day. Suddenly, and for the first time in a life filled with creative activity, he must have known himself to be an old man. People no longer understood him or, what was worse, he had gone beyond understanding them. There was no prospect of rising to a higher peak than that from which he had fallen. Every new attempt would be at best an effort to recapture a lost eminence.

He went to the seashore, brooding. He had every reason to believe that his show was over.

But he had financial obligations. His possessions and his very considerable fortune had been either confiscated by the Nazis or frozen because of the war. He was urged to revive a production which had been an outstanding success abroad. His name had great drawing power, and many people stood ready to back him in this venture. He let himself be persuaded.

Yet this was only a technical resurrection of showy craftsmanship which he was undertaking to produce. From his point of view it was bare of creative art; it was to be done only for the sake of money. He was a proud man. He was tired; he had no wish to resume the battle. He had abdicated.

When he went to make the telephone call, to set the date for those rehearsals which he surely wished might never take place, the conflict within him had doubtless reached its climax. The dog fight was really unimportant. Any ordinary occurrence, a loud voice in the street perhaps, might have precipitated the spasm. It might have come upon him during the night, or during rehearsals or at any stage in the preparation of the production. The emotional setting for illness was ripe.

The prospect of giving his talents to a work without creative possibilities was the death knell of his creative instinct. Significantly, the destructive instinct thrust its dynamic power against those centers in the brain where are located the skills of gesture, of motion, of speech, those very skills which had been the medium of this man's genius. Modern psychoanalytic psychology has gathered a wealth of evidence to convince us that the choice of the organ or organs to be attacked by illness is not accidental, but is related to the whole personality.

Now we can see why speech lessons upset him; he had been the acclaimed master of speech. Now we understand why the test of his writing threw him into a black depression. His whole life had been devoted to the arts of communication of ideas. Now he could communicate neither by speech, by gesture, nor by the written word.

But his constitution was strong, his will to live a powerful force. Only his pride was greater. He refused to continue life as an invalid, either in the physical or the artistic sphere. The outcome was inevitable.

The power of reason is formidable. It gives logical grounds for hope; it whips up new activity by revealing new possibilities. These were the days during which the patient showed outward improvement.

When reason and emotion are locked in battle, however, emotion eventually wins. There was the relapse, for which we physicians had no medical explanation. Coming the day after the patient's fast, the relapse might have been the result of physical exertion. He had chosen to fast against all the efforts of his physician and his nurse to dissuade him. That very choice was a self-destructive act, in unconscious obedience to his triumphing destructive instinct.

Later I learned that the holiday was also the anniversary of his father's death. I have observed that, just as a word of reassurance at a critical moment can inspire the creative instinct and raise a man once more to strive in his own behalf, so an alluring mental image can encourage the destructive instinct and cause the patient to succumb. Especially when a system has already suffered strain, the thought of one's dead father or mother, of a wife or other beloved person who has gone before, beckons one to follow.

The death instinct promises peace and surcease from struggle. But it does not rely upon lure alone, nor upon its power over the unconscious centers of the body. It pleads its case convincingly to reason too. No man lives forever. Why stretch a burdensome existence for just a few years more? The reward is not worth the effort.

And so a man shuts himself away from the outside world, not to hear the voices of those who love him, not to see the tempting glitter of fame which has already betrayed him, not to falter in his resolution to seek eternal rest.

The strange behavior of the sick, often so perplexing to their families and friends and even to their physicians, thus becomes understandable. When a man on his sick bed apparently fights with all his strength to recover, while his lips reiterate the assurance that he wants to live, the same man commits acts which are aimed directly at his own destruction.

We who stand at the sick man's bedside are handicapped in our effort to understand him by the very fact that we ourselves are well. We attempt to evaluate a sick man's subjective experience, his feelings and his desires, with a healthy man's calm and reasonable objectivity. But it is not what *we* would feel or desire, but the hidden inner resolution of the sick man, which will determine the outcome.

When death comes, it comes as a wished-for end. It comes as a natural event for which body and mind are prepared. It is a deliverance, as in the words of the visionary poet Heine, which Brahms set to music:

>"Death that is the cooling night,
>Life that is the sultry day.
>It is growing dark already—I feel drowsy—
>The day has made me tired."

How Not to Shorten Life

Can we guard ourselves against this shift of power away from the life-preserving force? Can we sustain the will to live?

The physiologist Rubner declared a generation ago that the best way to prolong life is not to shorten it. Today we are beginning to recognize that the first danger to length of life may not be the invading germ, nor any physiological process beyond our control. We are beginning to understand that the first line of defense is in our emotional health.

If we are emotionally sound, we will be physically sound. Body and mind are one. When we truly want to be well, to live long and in health, we have the power to do it.

If grown children, who have long left their parents' home to live their own lives, come to a parent's bedside and say, however sincerely, "Live for our sake. We need you," the parent may be touched, but not really convinced. A mother whose children are immersed in their own lives knows when she is no longer needed as a mother. If she has not carried forward into her later years an interest apart from her children, something which seems to her really important, then she will not want to live.

The same may be true of a man who has retired from his business or profession, if he has lived solely for his work. When his work is finished he may have nothing left to live for.

We need not come to this pass. Within the physiological life span of man—which modern research suggests may be anywhere between one hundred and one hundred and fifty years—we can live as long as we truly want to live. If we live to our full capacity, not merely as parents, not merely as workers, but as mature, well-rounded human beings, then we will have something yet to live for even when work and parenthood are ended.

There are two measures we can take, if we so desire. We can learn to guard our emotional health as we guard our physical health. And we can learn to develop our fullest capacity as human beings. These are our twin safeguards against illness and against premature death. They are the deeper roots of our will to live.

If we want to live, we can nourish the will to live at these roots. It is within the power of every normal human being to do this, sometimes alone, and sometimes with the aid of medicine.

If we are really working at living, we need not be afraid of dying.

Life is a continual adjustment
of internal relations to
external relations.

HERBERT SPENCER

4. WHY DOCTORS DISAGREE

WHY do doctors disagree?

If medicine is an exact science, why is there not a single scientific answer to an illness? How is it possible for a patient to go from one doctor to another and receive a different diagnosis and a different treatment from each for the same set of symptoms?

People talk about good and bad doctors. But we cannot dismiss the problem by saying that an individual doctor doesn't know his business.

The confusions and contradictions of practical medicine today have tempted many a layman to dismiss the whole profession. When a man goes to a doctor, he delivers himself into another man's hands for what may be his future good or ill, perhaps his life or death. He may be forgiven if, confronted first by one and then another opinion, he calls down a plague on all doctors and tries to get along without any medical help. Or even if he turns to quacks and fads.

The patient remembers that until a few years ago the medical profession issued grave warnings about "focal infections." Tonsils and adenoids were ripped out, teeth were pulled, and appendectomies were performed, all as preventive measures, to protect health, not only to cure disease. A man still in possession of his appendix was afraid to undertake a

55

long journey, and one who still had his tonsils was in a class with savages in primitive lands who resist vaccination.

A newspaper story of the late 1920's told of a young man and his wife who had decided to renounce civilization and were going to live on a romantic Pacific island. Before they went, however, both these young people had all their teeth pulled and dentures made, to be sure they would be safe from "focal infection" in their primitive paradise.

Today it is once more fashionable to wear your tonsils, and the surgeon who used to recommend an appendectomy as a health measure, like a circumcision or a good set of false teeth, has now become somewhat more conservative.

Fundamentally, however, little has changed. Instead of tonsils, the scalpels of today are harvesting gall bladders, fibroid tumors, sections of stomachs and colons, ovaries and wombs. Appendectomies are old fashioned but hysterectomies are high style.

Yet it is unjust to question the surgeon's good faith. It is unjust, and furthermore it solves nothing, to make the individual doctor the villain of the piece, be he surgeon or internist, gynecologist or any one of the dozen specialists we have today.

The doctor is no villain, any more than the patient with "imaginary" symptoms is a naughty child to be scolded and sent home with the injunction that he must be a good boy and stop bothering busy physicians. Doctor and patient are both victims, and while the patient suffers, the doctor's dilemma may be just as difficult to bear. The doctor stands bewildered, perhaps dismayed, and often on the defensive, at a crucial turning point in the history of medicine.

Technological Medicine

The technological revolution, which gave us engines to do the work of muscles and delicate machinery to replace the skill of hands, penetrated every lane of human activity, and medicine was no exception. While the nineteenth century was crowding farmers and cottage craftsmen into city slums and teaching them to run machines, and incidentally killing them en masse with infectious diseases, it was also transforming the art of medicine into a precise, disciplined science.

The century up to the First World War was one of stormy progress. When man turned the lens of a telescope upward against the heavens he knew himself to be no more than a speck of dust in the universe. But if he turned a similar bit of ground glass downward, in the tube of a microscope, he was a giant, and he made giant strides toward knowledge of the physical factors in illness.

In England, Jenner observed that milkmaids lived unworried and for the most part unharmed through devastating outbreaks of smallpox. Often they had had a very mild kind of pox; the cows as well frequently had a slight sickness of the same kind. Out of such reasoning, and without knowing that he was dealing with a tiny organism which caused the disease, Jenner gave the first vaccinations in 1796, and became a hero in his country.

Pasteur watched the growth of bacteria in fermentation, and pointed out the way to killing them in milk. Lister poured bacteria-destroying carbolic acid over his instruments and his hands and sprayed it on the patient's body during an operation, besides sterilizing with heat. This was the first great step toward modern aseptic surgery. Koch learned to stain tissue under the microscope and identify bacteria, and he identified the *tubercle bacillus,* the terrible killer of that time. Although Semmelweiss was derided in Vienna, he became, nevertheless, the savior of women from childbed fever.

At the beginning of the great century of progress Laennac invented the stethoscope, and Roentgen discovered the X-ray almost at its close. Halfway between, in 1858, Virchow stated his theory of cellular pathology which made the pathological branch of medicine into a fortress of scientific precision.

Now the giant bent over his microscope actually saw disease: he saw the changes in the diseased cell. And now the *cause* of disease was assumed to be this cellular change. "Illness," said Virchow, "is life under changed conditions." This is probably the shortest definition of illness in medical literature, and a masterpiece of scientific neutrality as between illness and health.

In infectious diseases the man with the microscope was fortunate. He could see the invading disease germ. But in certain diseases, such as cancer and arteriosclerosis, he saw tissue changes, but no germ. And the "functional diseases," the gastric disturbances, the asthmas, the heart seizures, were still more baffling. The microscope failed to reveal either germ or cellular change; the malfunctioning organ persisted in remaining physically normal and healthy.

Dedicated scientists hoped that they would one day discover the physiological cause of the tissue changes in the one group of diseases, and that with still more refined technique and still more sensitive instruments they would see tissue changes to account for the abnormal behavior of the organ in the second. But for the answers to these two physiological mysteries, the organic and the functional disease, the man with the microscope is still seeking in vain.

The infectious diseases, however, offered a ready battleground for the new scientific warfare on man's afflictions. The invading army of teeming microorganisms could actually be seen; the filterable virus, invisible under the optic microscope, came only later to baffle the researchers until the electron microscope was invented.

On every hand ancient superstitions began to dissolve before the searching light of science. Serums were developed against the plagues which had terrorized man for centuries, and principles of hygiene took the place of mystic signs and amulets to ward off evil.

Walter Reed with his heroic human guinea pigs proved that a mosquito carried yellow fever, and sanitary engineers attacked the breeding places of mosquitoes and showed how that curse of the tropics could be eliminated. Wassermann came forth with his serum test for syphilis. Ehrlich introduced its first effective cure. Schick produced not only an immunization for diphtheria but also a test for susceptibility.

Pharmacology labored to perfect scientific methods of testing old and producing new remedies, and a sort of alchemistic renaissance revived the medieval belief that against every ill there grows an herb. New drugs mushroomed out of test tubes, some of ephemeral value only, but others of enduring and even miraculous properties. Without these patient and precise men taking step after cautious step in the laboratory, checking and rechecking, and without the impressive pharmaceutical industry which has grown out of their efforts, we might not have today first the sulfa drugs, then the antibiotics, the antihistamines, and finally the synthetically produced hormones.

But as the mass of detailed observation and experiment, of theory and procedure, of scientific data, grew ever larger, the individual physician became dwarfed before it. No one man could absorb so much knowledge and put it to use. Specialties sprang up in research, and inevitably specialties sprang up in medical practice. With so much known and so much yet to be known, it was all a man could do to equip himself with the scientific knowledge we had gained of a single area of the body, and to keep abreast of the new knowledge which was every day being offered for his use in diagnosis and treatment.

Thus, as a logical next step, the family physician disappeared before the onrushing need for specialization. The man who had known all about his patient's life, his work, his family; who had perhaps delivered him into the world, had seen him through childhood measles and adolescent disturbance; who had received his confidences and who, more than any other living person except possibly the priest or minister, knew his patient's mind as well as his body—this man became extinct. He was sacrificed to the aseptic tidal wave of scientific data and scientific precision. The art of healing became a standardized scientific technique.

In the old-fashioned doctor it had been a virtue to make do with little, and to depend on his sharpened observations, his experience with people sick and well, and his knowledge of his patient in particular. The new scientific man, the specialist, approached a case with an arsenal of equipment. He saw not a sick man but a sickness. He concentrated on the diseased organ like a mechanic working on a worn or broken part of a machine. He treated an organ but not a suffering human being.

Indeed he had little opportunity to observe the human being. As more and more chemical and mechanical aids— blood tests, biological tests, basal metabolism tests, electro-cardiograms, fluoroscope and X-ray examinations—entered into a diagnosis, as more and more specialists were called upon for their special knowledge, the relationship of doctor and patient became increasingly remote. More than this, the doctor was sternly warned against allowing merely human factors, his own or the patient's, to corrupt the purity of his scientific data.

And so we have the picture of the patient ushered in and out of a doctor's office as though on an assembly line. He gives his history to an assistant or a crisp nurse with a printed form, perhaps, which provides blanks for only physical information: age, height, weight, previous illnesses, operations, symptoms.

He is prepared for examination, again by a nurse or assistant. The doctor himself, held to a schedule of appointments as tight as a railroad time table, comes in only when the patient lies stretched on a table under a sheet, a completely dehumanized, deindividualized object for examination.

The patient is asked to breathe, to grunt, to sit up, to lie down, but never, on pain of breaking the doctor's scientific concentration, to talk. And when the time comes for discussion of the case, for diagnosis and a survey of the treatment to come, it is the doctor, not the patient, who talks.

The doctor, surrounded by his charts, graphs, chemical analyses, specialists' reports, undertakes to tell the still mute, still dehumanized sufferer what is wrong with him and how he is to be cured—or that there is nothing wrong with him and he must go home to live with his pains and his fears as best he can.

If the patient enters the hospital he is likely to be still further stripped of his human individuality. Case Number 1040 protested for them all when she wept, "I'm *flesh* Number 1040! When my doctor finally gets here, he is followed by his retinue—the bigger the doctor, the longer the tail!"

The examination is public, with hardly a word to the patient. Then comes the bright, "And how are we today? Feeling better? That's fine. Take it easy." And the doctor is gone.

Busy as he is, important as he may be in the profession, the doctor would make time for the few minutes of private conversation for which the patient longs, if he believed it would help the case. But all his training is against permitting the variable, unreliable, *unscientific* human element to confuse or sway his handling of the illness.

Dr. Carl Binger describes the traditional "grand rounds" of the hospital in his book *The Doctor's Job:*

"We would assemble in our white coats around some hostal bed with a chart hanging at the foot of it so that the patient could not read it. There usually was learned discourse about livers and lungs and respiratory quotients, serum proteins and urea indices. Much of it did not need to be said at the patient's bedside, but it was and is the tradition to talk about patients on rounds in their presence. Of course, the patients did not understand. What does a red-faced cop off his beat, lying in bed in a short white-cotton nightshirt tied in the back, know or care about hemoglobin? The less he knows the more he will misinterpret. . . .

"Is it *scientific* medicine to consider his liver or his bone marrow and not him?" Dr. Binger asks. "Actually one has to consider both and one is not less of a scientist but more of one for doing so, because the first task of a scientist is to observe and describe phenomena as they occur in nature. And a cop's emotions, even when off his beat, lying in bed, are none the less natural phenomena."

The Surgical Approach

Above all, in the race for more and more refined specialization to deal with the growing accumulation of physical
data, surgery triumphed.

To enlightened people surgery was the most progressive,
the most rational and direct method of dealing with illness.
The question of what had brought on the illness was not
within the domain of the surgeon. The surgeon's business
was to do a clean-cut job of removing the offending organ.
And that he did.

All around him, technicians came forth to support him
with better tools for his exquisite skill. Blood chemistry,
anesthesia, drugs to prevent and to combat infection, drugs
to encourage and to discourage blood clotting, painstaking
procedures for preparing the patient before the operation,
for keeping him alive through it, for hastening his recovery
after it, were developed—and are still being developed—by
battalions of single-minded scientists.

An entire branch of medical science grew up around the
surgeon, to perform like a symphony orchestra in a concerto
of which he was the virtuoso. Hospitals focused their most
concentrated attention on the drama in the operating room.
Even the human body cooperated, demonstrating that a man
or woman could get along minus a kidney or a gall bladder,
with half a stomach, one set of lungs, or part of the sex organs.

In Europe one woman was reported to have had twenty-
three major abdominal operations. *Furor operaticus passivus*
—passive operative madness—was the ironic name the report-
ing physician gave to the craze for surgery. A story went the
rounds of the hospitals a few years ago about a man with this
plea tattooed on his belly: "Don't take out my appendix. Was
taken out twice."

No one questions the incomparable skill of hand, eye, and
brain which surgeons develop for the performance of their
stellar role in the climax of the drama, when they are called

upon to do a precise violence upon a living body under pressure of the time clock.

But one can question a development in medicine when the physician becomes so engrossed in technique that he sees nothing but the area of operation. One can question a science, presumably dedicated to healing and the preservation of life, which could complacently accept the terse verdict at the end of a report: "Operation successful, patient died." This was, to many, the logical absurdity at the end of an uncompromisingly "scientific" mechanization of medicine.

Toward the end of the great century of mechanistic progress in medicine, resistance to this rigid formula began to grow. Doubts were expressed whether the sharp line between body and mind, between "scientific medicine" and neurology's younger brother, psychiatry, could be maintained.

Psychiatry was the scorned orphan of medicine because its area, the diseases of the mind, stubbornly refused to give physical evidence of their presence. Psychiatrists endeavored to find the cause of mental disease in brain tissue, but all their brilliant anatomical research came to nothing except, for example, in general paralysis resulting from syphilis, and in senile dementia, the deterioration of the brain in old age. In these, at least, some physiological damage was discovered. Otherwise the most serious psychotics were found to have brains physiologically as sound as any normal man.

But if brain anatomy proved to be a blind alley, progress was being made in the psychological research laboratories. Pavlov demonstrated scientifically by his conditioned reflex experiments that physical functions originate in a psychic impulse. Neurologists sought the nerve pathways by which the subjective idea in the mind is translated into physical action.

In France, Charcot brought order out of the chaos of nervous disturbances. His pupil, the young Freud, followed him through the chambers of the Salpêtière, observing the many unhappy human beings whose illness was not understood, because it was of the mind.

From the neurology of his day Freud set forth in new directions to explore the dark world of the unconscious. For all that he was hooted at in the streets of Vienna, the early teachings of psychoanalysis had a dynamic impact which could not be ignored for long.

In 1914 a brilliant cure of toxic goiter (hyperthyroidism) by psychotherapy was reported in Germany. This was a case in which surgical treatment had been completely unsuccessful.

Signs of a change in medical thinking began to emerge, especially in gynecology. Freud's revelations of the depth and power of the sexual impulses gave pause to thoughtful medical men.

"There is too much minor gynecology and too little etiological [causal] thinking," wrote a leading professor of gynecology at the University of Berlin.

". . . Their illness is a psychic conflict sailing under a gynecological flag, which has escaped the attention of the quacks," declared the director of the Woman's Hospital of the University of Tübingen.

Elsewhere, and in other branches of medicine, the same questioning voices were heard. In such prevalent ills as heart diseases and gastrointestinal disorders, a literature began to grow on the possibility of psychic causes of physical illness.

The years between the two world wars were full of insecurity and indecision, and in medicine as in politics and economics, the ideological issue was not resolved. Suffering people, misunderstood or scornfully called hysterics, neurotics, hypochondriacs, were driven into the arms of cult healers. It was an era without faith, hungry to believe anything. Little apostles found ready followers. Charlatans everywhere rejoiced in a gold rush.

Practicing physicians continued to have neither time nor sympathy for the "nervous" patient. They clung to the comforting distinction of scientific medicine between physical and mental, between "organic" and "nervous" illness.

But the neurologists and the physiologists drove on along

the pathways between psychic and physical, and the psychologists in their laboratories studied the physical manifestations of emotion. The connection between anger and rising blood pressure, between fear and acceleration of the heart, between the desire for food and the secretion of juices in the stomach was not new. But the physiological reactions began to be probed with an eye to how these mechanisms could be related to abnormal states, or in other words to illness of mind and/or body.

A tremendous amount of work along these lines was reported in the 1920's and the 1930's. It is remarkable how little it has penetrated into medical practice until very recently.

Both in this country and abroad, some doctors were even then in rebellion against the often unnecessary resort to surgery. The gynecologist Dr. Ernst Graefenberg wrote in a medical journal in 1929:

"Correct recognition of psychogenic pains [pains of psychic origin] is of great importance because such pains often result in major operations. Many an appendix has been sacrificed to a harmless . . . pain [in the lower portion of the small intestine]. If the pain happened to be in the left lower quadrant, the left adnexae [ovary] were doomed . . . Back pains were at once associated with displacement of the uterus . . ."

Today we recognize that the victims of a surgeon's rash diagnosis are legion. Patients in a state of emotional as well as physical distress are poor judges of a situation. They and their families are ready to take the pain of the body for the cause of the illness.

A sick man will follow, though fearfully, anyone who promises a way out of his misery. And many a sufferer from emotional conflict, as Menninger and others have pointed out, will willingly, even eagerly, place himself on the altar of the operating table and sacrifice a part of his body to the terrible feelings of guilt which unconsciously dominate him.

Every doctor can draw out of his files cases of unnecessary operations. Here is one out of my own, a young woman who at twenty-six has already been deprived of her ovaries and uterus. In 1941 she had undergone an appendectomy which resulted in adhesions. In 1944, after a miscarriage, she had hemorrhages. A painful pulling in the lower abdomen led to the usual diagnosis, and an operation was performed, during which a small cyst on the left ovary was discovered. The ovary and part of the uterus were removed.

The patient recovered from the operation, only to find her pain still with her. In 1945 the other ovary, also revealing a cyst, was removed. With two operations and postoperative treatments, with nothing left of the organs which were presumably the cause, she still had her pain.

Uterine hemorrhages resulting from psychic trauma have been reported many times in medical literature. In this case the young woman had gone through the emotional shock of an unsuccessful marriage and a divorce.

The Problem Child of Medicine

Despite the growing knowledge of the connections between mind and body, the doctrinaires of medicine remained unyielding, and many of them do to this day. Some admitted a certain "mental overcast" in illness. But on the whole the practicing physician was careful not to become infected by the "mental" trend.

This is not surprising in the face of their medical training. One of my professors was a consistently objective, sober scientist, except in one lecture.

"Gentlemen," he said with unaccustomed emotion on this occasion, "if I have failed in having taught you anything else, I hope I have succeeded at least in implanting in you a critical mind. For that, gentlemen, is the only guarantee against mysticism, against all this metaphysical nonsense which whirls about us these days. I want you to believe in facts and facts only. I want you to believe in what you can see, what you can feel, and what you can demonstrate. In the making of a satisfactory diagnosis, I shall tolerate no escape into the nebulous realm of the mental!"

Words like this, spoken conjuringly over a pair of oval-shaped glasses, penetrate deep into a future doctor's consciousness. They give definition to a doctor's integrity. They set limits which he cannot overstep without betraying his medical honor.

To influence the mind or attitude of a patient is called "suggestion," unworthy of a good doctor. Dr. Flanders Dunbar illustrates this confusion in the practicing physician's mind:

"A colleague of mine once said, 'Of course I can give Mrs. X a sedative, but if I do so, I shall tell her that it will not do her any good because I don't know what is really the matter with her, and she has had all the tests I know. It will only make her feel better for a time.' . . . Another physician cured Mrs. X with the use of mild sedatives and sound advice, but was considered dishonest or at least unscientific . . . The scientific way is to tell the patient to 'buck up,' that there is 'nothing the matter except his imagination,' that he seems to have 'one of those troubles we do not yet understand.' "

Americans, in many fields the foremost apostles of technique, at first resisted the theory of emotional factors in illness, although Freud received an enthusiastic welcome here in 1909. In Europe, on the other hand, clinicians attempted to find ways of admitting the emotional side of illness into their practical work while at the same time rejecting its deeper significance.

Doctors of great repute lent themselves to this search for a way to let the new psychological approach enter scientific medicine by the back door. One distinguished European internist suggested that people could be divided into two types, the "depth" person and the "cortical" person. The depth person was moved mostly by glandular activity which produced hormones and enzymes within his body, and he would react almost exclusively to physical experience, such as muscular exertion. The cortical person was dominated by the cortex of the brain which is the seat of sensory perceptions, and he would react principally to the experience of his senses. This doctor carried his logic all the way back to the amoeba in an effort to explain the soul as a biological-functional expression.

Another clinician reported his observation that a disease looks different to doctor and patient. The "autoplastic" or patient's picture of the illness exaggerates the objective symptoms which the doctor discovers. But it also includes the whole imaginary complex which the patient forms about his disease.

Therefore, this professor proposed, the doctor must seek insight into the patient's personality. He must consider the individual beyond the diseased organ. He must be ready to act upon the mind of the patient when the need arises.

Tact, knowledge of human nature, a perception of the patient's feelings would as a rule suffice, he concluded, in guiding the physician to say and do the right thing. One of a physician's most important tasks must be to instill hope and courage in his patients, and if necessary to deliver a sound scolding to the sinful soul. Naturally the physician's character, his educational and cultural background, are of great importance.

"Let's have a little less chemistry and a little more of these qualities," he proposed, "and we will manage to *handle our medical problems without the need of employing psychic hypotheses of questionable value.*"

Thus, in an effort to keep psychiatry out of the doctor's examining room, this adviser returned full circle to the old-fashioned physician, the bedside manner, the *art* of healing which had flourished before the science of medicine had swept the doctor's personality, along with a good many of his humane practices, onto the junk heap.

The days when the doctor, after examining the patient, was invited into the parlor to have a glass of wine and talk things over with the family, were gone forever. But it was beginning to be felt that perhaps some of that old-fashioned doctor's ways with sick people were not altogether useless. Let the doctor be a little kinder, a little more sympathetic—or, when necessary, a little more of a Dutch uncle, making it clear, of course, that it was all for the patient's own good. Then the physician would not need to get involved with this vague, unscientific, unseeable and untouchable, mental stuff.

Other schools came up with other answers. But they were all a desperate effort to whittle down the new science, to take bits and pieces of it into their own practical handling of illness so that they would not be obliged to accept the whole. School medicine presented an almost united front against the mounting influence of the teachings of Freud.

Today it is no longer enough to restore a little of the art of healing into the practice of medicine. Today we have the mounting evidence of the neurologist, the endocrinologist, the very scientists themselves, to support the psychiatrist's plea that the mind be no longer excluded from the science of dealing with illness.

Dr. Franz Alexander, director of the Chicago Institute for Psychoanalysis, states the case eloquently:

"The fact that the mind rules the body is, in spite of its neglect by biology and medicine, the most fundamental fact which we know about the process of life. This fact we observe continuously during all our life, from the moment when we awaken every morning. Our whole life consists in carrying out voluntary movements aimed at the realization of ideas and wishes, the satisfaction of subjective feelings such as thirst and hunger.

"The body, that complicated machine, carries out the most complex and refined motor activities under the influence of such psychological phenomena as ideas and wishes. The most specifically human of all bodily functions, speech, is but the expression of ideas through a refined musical instrument, the vocal apparatus.

"All our emotions we express through physiological processes: sorrow, by weeping; amusement, by laughter; and shame, by blushing. All emotions are accompanied by physiological changes: fear, by palpitation of the heart; anger, by increased heart activity, elevation of blood pressure, and changes in carbohydrate metabolism; despair, by a deep inspiration and expiration called sighing.

"All these physiological phenomena are the results of complex muscular interactions under the influence of nervous impulses, carried to the expressive muscles of the face and to the diaphragm in laughter, to the lacrimal glands in weeping, to the heart in fear, and to the adrenal glands and to the vascular system in rage. The nervous impulses arise in certain emotional situations which in turn originate from our interaction with other people. The originating psychological situations can be understood only in terms of psychology—as total responses of the organism to its environment."

Thus the doctor, reminded every day that the mind and body are one, can no longer resist the next logical step in thinking: if mind and body are one in normal functioning, namely in health, cannot mind and body be one in illness?

That it can be so, and by what pathways it is so, we shall try to understand in the following chapters. Only thus can we grasp the true picture of what makes illness, and only thus can we find our way back along those pathways to the cause of illness. We must find our way, not as doctor alone nor as patient alone but as doctor and patient together, working toward an end deeply desired by both, the safeguarding of health.

5. WARNING SIGNALS

THE destructive instinct, as we have learned, is an ever-ready force lurking in the unconscious mind. When the climate is right—when, for example, we are caught in the toils of emotional conflict—then the destructive instinct can become an active threat to our health.

But if it is unconscious and inaccessible to reason, then how can the average man and woman recognize it? Is there any way to detect this plot against our health in time to save the body from harm? In a word, can we prevent illness?

Once we accept the fact that man wages war not only against others but also against himself, once we begin to look for the signs of this inner war, then we can find them. For the signs are there. We can say with conviction that illness does not come as a bolt out of the blue, a thief in the night, a visitation without warning. Even a heart attack sends its messages before, if we can only read them.

We moderns find these warnings difficult to read because we tend to think in mechanistic terms. We are accustomed to dials and indicators. For example, a man came to me recently, shaken by a friend's sudden death from a heart attack. What upset him most was that his friend had had an electrocardiogram taken only a few days before, and the findings had been negative.

"Now we can't rely on anything!" my visitor protested.

Many of the warning signals are subjective and do not register on dials, and therefore we ignore them as a passing depression, or as hypochondria. Let the pointer of our bathroom scale swing upward, or the mercury in the doctor's blood-pressure machine climb, and we pay attention. When the fever thermometer reading reaches the red mark, we are frightened. But when our inner feelings warn us that all is not well, we reject the warning as superstitious nonsense. We are almost too well educated in the scientific method. If a symptom does not meet the rigid standards of science we dismiss it entirely.

But what we thus dismiss may be an inner perception of danger. Why, for example, did this man's friend go to have an electrocardiogram taken? Had he perhaps caught a faint whisper of anxiety from his unconscious mind? Most of our actions are instigated or influenced by some inner motive. When we are baffled, it is because we are not trained to listen to these muted voices from our unconscious. But we can learn to listen.

The Riddle of Fatigue

Fatigue is one of the most frequent of these warnings from the unconscious. Fatigue without cause, without apparent physical reason, fatigue which often exists in the absence of any exertion whatever, is an experience which almost all of us have shared. Which of us has not known a moment of weariness, inertia, indifference—and which of us has not jumped up full of energy, our weariness forgotten, at the summons of a telephone call, provided it is the call we were waiting for?

We are on familiar terms with fatigue. The patient in a doctor's office speaks for millions with the words, "I don't know why, but I'm tired all the time." A man, giving his case history, says, "I was working too hard. I was overtired." Of one who succumbs we say, "He died of overwork. He wore himself out."

Yet we know both from daily experience and from laboratory experiment that a man or woman of normal physical development can carry on heroic exertions over long periods of time with little or no rest, and yet suffer no greater fatigue than a night's sleep will repair. We have only to think of rescue workers in flood or earthquake, carrying on around the clock, often with the added emotional strain of fear for themselves or anxiety for their families.

During the blitz over London, Winston Churchill writes in *Their Finest Hour,* it was feared that plague or epidemic must result in a population living under such strain, with little sleep, crowded together in shelters every night, struggling to keep home and work going under unimaginable difficulties. Meanwhile the shattered sewers were pouring possible epidemic into the Thames River.

"The fact remains," he reports, "that during this rough winter the health of the Londoners was actually above the average. . . . The power of enduring suffering in the ordinary people of every country, when their spirit is aroused, seems to have no bounds."

We can add that everywhere, every day, people go about their tasks without weariness if they are supported by enthusiasm and belief in what they are doing.

The chronic sufferers from fatigue do not have the excuse of unusual exertions. They are wearied by a day of normal activity. They are weary before they begin the day's work. They are weary whether they work much, or little, or not at all.

Medicine has tried to define the symptoms of fatigue but has immediately run into trouble. The objective symptoms, when any exist, are not exclusively symptoms of fatigue. Low blood-pressure, secondary anemia, loss of weight can be symptoms of numerous other disturbances. More often there are no measurable symptoms at all. The weary man or woman describes a subjective state, a feeling which pervades his mind and body but which rarely registers on a doctor's instruments. Yet the fatigue is none the less real because it is subjective. It is real, and it is a warning.

Think of it as battle fatigue, as a sign of inner war in which energies are being consumed which would otherwise be available for our daily living. If we probe for it, we find under the fatigue a state of anxiety. The man who drives himself at his work to the point of exhaustion, the point which we call overwork, is a man who is driven by anxiety, an inner, un-formulated fear. Fatigue is the symptom we are aware of because it is conscious. Anxiety is a deeper problem.

There is also a whole group of people who refuse to admit fatigue or anxiety. It is painful to their pride to admit such weakness. They want to be the captain on the bridge who never sleeps. They are the people who push themselves with-out mercy, often until illness strikes them down in earnest. Theirs is an unrealistic heroism, and wasteful. There is no shame in admitting weakness. We must admit and face it before we can take rational steps to deal with it and its causes.

Fear Without Cause

The word "anxiety" comes up often these days in any dis-cussion of inner disturbance. Freud, who gave the problem of anxiety careful study, defined it as "internalized fear." Fear is a healthy mechanism. It is an alarm bell, a warning of impending danger.

When an animal confronts danger, he pauses for an instant —Fight? Or flight? In that instant, in which he must make the decision on which his life may depend, he suffers fear. Not only does he subjectively feel afraid. The subjective feeling is at once accompanied by physical changes. The heart beats faster; the blood pressure rises. Impulses stream along the nerves. Messages race to the glands. The adrenal glands pour their hormones into the blood stream, energizing the body. The entire physical system is galvanized into preparedness. Whether the decision is to battle the enemy or run from him, in that instant of alarm the body is mobilized for action in its own defense.

Man, a more complex animal, does not need to confront present danger to feel fear. He may fear a hurricane many miles away as he reads the storm warnings. He may fear an employer, a teacher, the loss of his job, or an impending examination, or a war that threatens across the world. So long as the fear is justified by external circumstances, so long as there is an actual threat, his fear is healthy as the animal's fear is healthy, because it prompts him to preparedness.

When the danger is over, fear disappears and the body relaxes. Heart, blood pressure, glands and nerves return to normal. This is healthy, natural fear, a mechanism of self-protection.

But when the danger does not exist in reality, when it dwells only in the fantasy of the sufferer, when it does not subside with the passing of its apparent cause—then the fear is no longer healthy. Then we have morbid fear, that internalized, destructive fear which we call anxiety. We have a diffuse state of uneasiness, a general feeling of worry, of pressure, of tension.

All these subjective feelings are real, though the danger which arouses them are not. They can lead to such physical symptoms as higher blood pressure, faster pulse, without apparent organic cause. The body is in a permanent state of preparedness to meet danger. Because it is not related to reality, this is a neurotic state.

The causes of anxiety vary with the individual, his innate self, the environment into which he was born and grew to maturity, the fortunate or unfortunate circumstances of his life. Usually these causes are buried deep within the unconscious. To unearth them, psychiatrists often must probe for many months. The psychiatrists speak to us of infantile dependency, hostility, aggression; of feelings of inadequacy and inferiority; of guilt.

Why guilt? What has the average, decent, law-abiding citizen to reproach himself with? Most of us can say, with justification, "I have done my best to be a good son, a good husband, a good father, a good member of society—why should I feel guilty?"

The answer is, conscience. Conscience is the voice within us which tells us what is right and what is wrong. Freud called it the superego, the part of the self which sits in judgment on both the conscious intelligent self—the ego—and the deeper, instinctual self, the self composed of instinctive needs and desires, which Freud termed the Id.

It is not necessary to discuss here all the varied and sometimes desperate struggles of the inner man with his superego, his conscience. It is important to understand, however, that the pattern of that conscience is laid down in childhood. Its judgments and evaluations of right and wrong are often a child's judgments and evaluations. And the sins for which our conscience castigates us in maturity are often sins only according to the limited, inexperienced, sometimes grievously mistaken interpretations which as children we may have made of the adult world and of adult standards.

Here is an example of guilt with which psychiatrists often have to deal: Suppose a child has been naughty, and a father has spoken harshly to the child; the child has rebelled against the rebuke. Shortly afterward the father may fall sick and die. For the rest of his life, the child may carry buried within him the conviction that it was he, by his naughtiness and rebellion, who killed his father. Coupled with the unfortunate sequence of events, the child in his deepest self may have wished his father dead; this is not unusual, and at some stages of growth it is normal.

This is only one simple reconstruction out of many possible early experiences which may instill an underlying guilt feeling. Guilt may grow out of a child's interpretation of sin or crime. It may result from any of the violent impulses and unsocial acts of childhood. It may be born of a misunderstanding of any innocent childhood experience which was accompanied by emotional shock.

Whatever the forces which conspire to bring it into being, the guilty feeling is there. It is a burden which the superego lays upon the individual throughout his life, unless it can be exorcised by understanding and emotional maturity.

Guilt implies punishment, and the superego is relentless. The individual expects punishment, fears punishment, and at the same time longs for punishment to expiate his "crime" and free himself from his guilt. We have cases of neurotic criminals who commit crimes in order to be caught and punished; the punishment which society visits upon them assuages in some measure the guilt they feel for some inner crime. The relief, even eagerness, with which these men accept their sentence is a source of wonder to those around them. In prison they are model inmates.

Of course these neurotic criminals are abnormal, but abnormality is only the normal to an excessive degree, and almost everyone carries into his adult life some remnant of guilt from his childhood struggle to adjust to the rules of society. In extreme cases we have suicides, those who come to a point where they can no longer endure their guilt and their fear of punishment, and who at a stroke free themselves by giving life itself in expiation. Less dramatic are the martyrs who punish themselves throughout life by making undue sacrifices for others.

Most of us carry our burden of guilt more easily. We give ourselves the friendly advice which is given and taken many times in adult life: "Forget it." Yet we do not really forget anything; we only bury it. Some day, when we are under pressure, our feeling of guilt may raise its head again as anxiety.

We have pointed to the pattern of guilt only because it is a very common cause of anxiety, but there are many others. Suppose an infant's craving for love has been met by a cold, unresponsive parent. Throughout his life that individual may be anxiously seeking love, with the bitter conviction that he can never succeed, that he is forever unworthy of love because even his mother could not love him.

Feelings of inadequacy drive him to set impossible, perfectionist standards for himself: he must be ever richer, more successful, more worthy of love. Feelings of hostility creep between him and those from whom he craves love; they cannot love him, says his inner voice, and therefore he dare not love them.

And so on into the infinite variations of which the theme is capable. The infant, struggling to live and grow, strives from the moment of his birth to adjust himself to a real world which is at best no paradise. He must learn to curb his desires, to make friends with his environment, to meet the standards of his parents so that they may love him and continue to care for him in his helpless, dependent state. His tiny personality takes on the shape determined by his innate strengths and weaknesses in this struggle to survive. It is no wonder that he takes with him into manhood some burden of conflict and misunderstanding, and that this should emerge at some time during his life, generally in a period of crisis, as an undefined anxiety.

Anxiety is thus a predominant underlying symptom, an accompaniment of most illnesses and complaints. Whether the complaint is fatigue, insomnia, indigestion, colitis, constipation or diarrhea, or allergy of one sort or another, anxiety generally lies behind it.

To Eat or Not to Eat

The list of ailments which are now recognized as arising from emotional distress grows every day. "Headaches as Much Psychological as Physical," "Life Stresses Tied to Osteo-Arthritis," "Love Conquers All—Even an Ulcer;" "Tooth Health Tied to Emotional Tone" are a few of the headlines gleaned from the newspapers over several months. All are reports of studies made by physicians and psychiatrists of high repute; the paper on the emotional basis of tooth decay was presented before a meeting of the American Academy of Dental Medicine. In our search for the warnings of inner stresses which may lead to illness, let us look at the advance signs of some of the more common ailments.

Obesity is now widely considered a consequence of emotional disturbance. The craving for food, for sweets, is interpreted as a sign of insecurity, a craving for love or a gratification in place of love.

There is no reason to wait until we have actually arrived at what the doctors call obesity, to take notice. We can draw the inference that we are inwardly troubled while the scale still tells us that we are only "putting on a little weight." Real obesity is difficult to cope with, and physicians regard it as a serious threat to health in itself. We can cope with the tendency before it goes that far, if we are willing to seek the inner cause.

People who are gaining weight generally protest that they eat very little. Their inability to keep track of all the guilty nibbling they do is part of the same picture, an inability to face the real problem which plagues them. Doctors often find a gland disturbance, and offer this as the cause of the overweight condition. The patient gratefully accepts this physical explanation, since it relieves him of the necessity of facing the real problem. But the gland disturbance is in fact only another symptom, an earlier step in the chain reaction set off by emotional stress.

Too careful eating, like overeating, is also a sign to heed. In any restaurant frequented by business men for luncheon we often see at least one man studying the menu not for what he likes, but for what will not disagree with him. Luncheon conversations are as likely to be about digestion as about business: "You still take Carbo-Seltz? I find Tum-Aids much better!"

Health foods, health farms, food fads of all kinds flourish as a consequence of the widespread nervousness about eating. It is well to understand that we are careful about food not because we have a delicate stomach, but because an inner disturbance is actually causing the delicate stomach and the nervousness about food, either one at a time or both together. In many people, food fussiness may be a harmless safety valve for emotional tensions. But the prevalence of digestive ailments, up to and including gastric ulcer, leads us to believe that the safety valve is not really safe, and that illness may be the end result of food fussiness.

Trouble with Love

Sexual difficulties of many kinds are evidence of the destructive instinct at work. These disturbances are widespread; Kinsey reports that sexual maladjustments are a factor in perhaps three-fourths of the upper-level marriages which end in separation or divorce.

Occasional or chronic loss of sexual power in a man is sometimes caused by diseases of the nervous system, but these cases are rare. Except for these cases, sexual impotence is given a variety of familiar explanations. A man is told that he is run-down, that he is preoccupied with pressing problems, that financial difficulties or family worries are the cause.

These superficial explanations may be true as far as they go. Specific pressures may have brought his inner difficulty to the surface and caused impotence. But the real trouble goes deeper and has existed long before.

A youthful fear of venereal disease instilled by a fearful parent; a childish belief in the immorality of sex, engraved on the immature mind; an attachment to a mother which was never properly outgrown; even a fear of impotence itself; these and other factors may unconsciously check or suppress entirely the normal capacity for a pleasurable sexual relationship. Whatever its cause, impotence is a form which the destructive instinct may take.

Frigidity in women, a similarly self-destructive sign, is astonishingly widespread. The accepted estimate has been that fifty per cent of women are frigid; Kinsey found it to be seventy-five per cent.

Frigidity, which one authority calls the "hateful response," can scarcely be other than psychological in origin, and it has been so reported in countless studies, including a recent one in the *Journal of the American Medical Association* by Kroger and Freed. "Psychological factors are solely responsible for the symptom complex of true frigidity," these doctors write.

Why is a woman frigid? She may be suffering from the same fears which bring about impotence in men, plus the added fear of pregnancy. She may be thus unconsciously expressing her acceptance of the role of a martyr who must submit to masculine aggression. She may be showing her hostility toward men in general, or toward her marriage partner in particular.

Certainly the large number of women who are sexually dissatisfied demands attention, considering the possible illnesses which may result. Perhaps this is the real explanation for the current frequency of hysterectomies. Most so-called "women's troubles" can be traced to an emotional origin, of which frigidity may be an advance sign.

Some Like Splints, Some Like Scalpels

The accident habit has lately received wide attention as a menace to life and property. The National Safety Council's report for 1950 lists 90,000 persons killed, nearly nine millions injured, and a loss of nearly eight *billion* dollars' worth of property in the one year.

The German psychologist Marbe was the first to observe, a quarter-century ago, that having accidents was a habit, that a person who has had one accident is more likely to have another than a person who has never had an accident. Dunbar found in a study of accident cases that eighty per cent of fracture patients had had two or more accidents.

The psychiatrist suggests that there is a broken-bone personality: healthy, happy-go-lucky, cavalier toward sex and family, with a planless, live-for-the-moment philosophy. The accident type has a cousinly resemblance to the juvenile delinquent. Both are in rebellion against society, we are told, but while the criminal breaks the law, the other breaks his leg.

A patient of mine, an actor, is never seriously ill, but every year he has an accident resulting in one or several fractures. One season, in a play which he had performed hundreds of times, he broke a bone in his foot. The next year he fell and broke his leg. The third year he fell out of a third-story window onto a paved street. By the law of averages he should have been killed, but this debonair young man leads a charmed life. He suffered multiple fractures, but he will probably be in shape again for his next accident.

Sometimes accidents have what appears to be a significant target in the body. Almost any woman remembers days on which she suffered a series of minor mishaps in her kitchen, when things spilled and dishes slipped out of her hands. Sometimes the accidents turned on herself, and she cut her finger or burned her hand.

Another sign of emotional disturbance is the addiction to surgery. The man or woman who has not just one but many operations to talk about sometimes seems to enjoy not only the memory of past operations but actually to welcome the prospect of more such experiences in the future.

Recently I received a telephone call from a patient who had seen me a few months before. On that occasion she listened for nearly an hour while I explained about a gall-bladder condition that she was then developing. After that I took great pains to point out to her exactly what changes she should make in her way of life. She asked me then whether she needed an operation. My answer was an emphatic negative.

But now on the telephone she said, with a note of triumph, "You never told me about the gall bladder. I need an operation."

"I don't think you do," I repeated.

"Oh, I must have the operation!" she exclaimed, alarmed and indignant that I might try to forestall it.

Similarly on another occasion when I was examining the dowager of a distinguished old family, I expressed astonishment at the number of surgical scars which crisscrossed her abdomen like the map of Europe. She took my comment for a compliment, and enumerated her operations with pleasure, labeling each scar with the name of one or another eminent surgeon. She had forfeited to the scalpel every organ which it is possible to live without.

Menninger interprets this repeated submission to the surgeon's knife as an expression of unconscious guilt. The sufferer, anticipating punishment for his unknown crime, repeatedly offers a part of his body in expiation, hoping that life itself will be spared to him. After the operation, Menninger points out, there is a marked period of relief and wellbeing, as though the criminal were enjoying a reprieve. Whatever the unconscious reasons may be, it is certain that the almost aggressive demand for surgery is a symptom of the self-destructive force on the rampage.

Sometimes an operation seems to be necessary for a sick person's emotional comfort, and sometimes we emerge from the hospital with some serious problem solved or some needed adjustment made. How much better, if we can, to attack the problem and make the adjustment without sacrificing an organ in the struggle!

Older Than Your Years

Premature signs of aging present us with another group of warnings that the destructive instinct is at work. We age, not by years, but by events and our emotional reactions to them. One man loses his money and becomes gray overnight. Another man suffers reverses, struggles for a period, and then finds a new direction and forges ahead once more. He may show the scars of his bout with adversity, a few new lines in his face, but he has refused to accept submission to a triumphant destructive instinct. Instead he has exerted himself to put forth new creative efforts.

Among our millions of widows in the United States we have ample opportunity to observe the effect of the same experience on different women. Chronological age seems to have little to do with the difference in reactions. One woman who loses her husband regards her life as ended, and gives outward evidence—in her gradual withering, her graying hair, her shrinking posture, the querulous tone creeping into her voice—that she is preparing for death. Another woman, actually older, begins to blossom. She may enter into the competition for a new husband, or she may embark on a career in business, or she may do no more than busy herself with interests for which perhaps she has not had the leisure until now. In any or all of these creative ways she is expressing her vigorous will to live and enjoying its fruits.

When graying hair, coarsening skin, the shambling walk and stoop of age come before their time, we may be sure we are confronted with a man or woman wearying too soon of the struggle and willing to submit to the lure of self-destruction. Sometimes the retreat into old age is clearly a defense against what can no longer be borne. A very sick man, stooped, shuffling, with trembling hands, came to me for treatment, and I incidentally asked him when he became deaf. He gave me the approximate year.

Was he married then? Yes, he was. Did his wife complain a great deal, perhaps loudly?

"Oh, it was intolerable!" he exclaimed.

A European doctor reported an experiment he tried some years ago on a deaf patient who liked to sing. Once while she was singing a song the physician accompanied her softly on the piano. At the change from one verse to the next, he suddenly began to play in a different key. The woman, giving no sign that she noticed the change, continued to sing, but in the new key.

The doctor in this case expressed his doubt whether the patient was really deaf. But such doubts are irrelevant, merely because she seemed to hear only what she was interested in hearing. Many of us have known deaf persons who can hear nothing which is said to them directly unless it is shouted, but who catch even a whisper if it is something about themselves. It is too easy to smile at such deafness as a sly device, an escape from responsibility or a mischievous way of causing inconvenience and trouble to the family.

While all this may be true, the deafness itself cannot be dismissed. It is real. It is a warning that the sufferer is in the toils of the destructive instinct and has already sacrificed part of himself, his sense of hearing, to the ravaging force.

The physiologist Rubner observed that peasant women who work as cheap labor in the fields in some parts of the world are given to early withering of the face, but they suffer no loss of physical strength and endurance. Here is an example of specialization in aging. We can reason that these women have relinquished their competitive role as women. They have resigned themselves to the life of the working bee, which needs no beauty of face but only physical competence.

A witty friend of mine once said, "Nobody is responsible for his face up to the age of thirty. From then on he shapes it." Emerson remarked: "A man finds room in a few square inches of the face for the traits of all his ancestors, the expression of all his history, and his wants." Rubner, whose approach was not philosophical but scientific, wrote that aging of the features depends on facial expression.

Facial expression is, of course, an expression of the inner self. It is the barometer of the emotional climate in which we live; it is the record of our most private life. Effort, grief, worry may leave their indelible marks even on a comparatively young face. There can be no question that behind a face which looks older than its years an emotional struggle is being fought, and perhaps lost. The marks of defeat and surrender to age are a warning.

At Odds with Work

There is a whole group of minor ailments which might be called occupational, like the waiter's flat feet. A medical textbook (Von Mering-Krehl: *Internal Medicine*) mentions a sickness dating from pre-typewriter days, called mogigraphy, the inability to write. Students, clerks in business firms, and others who spent long days pushing a pen across paper were its victims.

With the characteristic medical approach, the text suggests physical reasons for the disability: probably the penholder was too thin, or the pen itself was too sharp or too blunt. Not for a moment was it suggested that the victim might be protesting against his dreary lifelong task.

After much research, in the course of which he only rarely found a periostitis (inflammation of the bone) or a neuritis (inflammation of the nerve) a leading neurologist of the time came to the conclusion that "these individuals are neurasthenic" and probably worry and grief were involved and some such "psychic influences" as embarrassment and excitement. His verdict, by the way, was: incurable.

The same textbook talks of "occupational spasms" which affect pianists, violinists, flutists, tinsmiths, and watchmakers. But in the case of milkers, in whose hands there was only rarely found a neuritis or other anatomical cause, the condition was called an occupational neurosis, and the milker a "man of neuropathic condition."

The neurologist Moritz adds, parenthetically and with a question mark: "(Anxiety may be primary?)"

The annals of great creative workers are full of tragic evidences of the self-destructive drive. Renoir, plagued by gout at the prime of his life, withdrew from Paris to Provence where he spent his last years painting with his brushes strapped to his crippled hand. He doggedly persisted against the unconscious destructive instinct, defeating himself and yet painting, displaying himself to the world in the heroic role of a martyr to his work.

Sometimes the destruction has a creative end result. Lovis Corinth, the German impressionist, at fifty suffered a stroke from which he rallied, and afterward achieved his finest work. Beethoven's deafness ended his career as a virtuoso, but he went on to write his great symphonies.

Still the destructive signs are there and must be heeded. We cannot count on great symphonies emerging from deafness and great paintings from a paralytic stroke. The conductor who has neuritis in his arm, the singer with his sore throat before a critical performance, the teacher with laryngitis—all give evidence of the self-doubt which every normal person occasionally suffers. When the disability becomes frequent, or chronic, it may be more than an occasional self-doubt. It may be a sign of conflict taking a destructive direction.

Inner Fear Turned Outward

One more group of warning signs remains to be included. Sometimes an anxiety of which we are not conscious may become externalized in the form of an unreasonable, baseless fear. One wakes in the night, certain there has been a noise and convinced an intruder is in the house. A patient told me of such an experience, one night when she was alone in her Connecticut farmhouse. She awoke, got out of bed, grasped an ax, and walked through the house, following the sound of footsteps, only to discover that the sounds were those of her frightened heart. She was able to laugh at the picture of herself, a very tall, thin, sophisticated city woman stalking through the empty house with an ax in her manicured hands. The cause of fear was all within herself.

Inner fear, or anxiety, may be turned outward and fixed on some external object or condition; we call this a phobia. We speak of acrophobia, the fear of heights; agoraphobia, the fear of open spaces, and claustrophobia, the fear of closed spaces; astrophobia, fear of thunder and lightning; dromophobia, fear of crossing streets; cynophobia, fear of dogs and rabies, and even triskaidekaphobia, fear of the number thirteen. This list could go on and on; the unconscious mind seems endlessly imaginative, and human beings in trouble find any number of outward causes, relevant and irrelevant, on which to fix their fears, including phobophobia, the fear of fear itself.

A real phobia is a sign of deep disturbance, and most of us settle for less. But we do externalize our inner anxiety; we do fix it on trivial causes. We worry about a business appointment the next day, or a dinner menu, or next month's bills (or perhaps last month's bills). We worry about anything, and then we worry about losing sleep worrying. The worry habit is definitely a sign of inner anxiety, and it is destructive.

Dangerous Crossings

In our campaign to find the danger signals before illness strikes, we can be helped by a knowledge that there are also dangerous periods in life, and dangerous seasons of the year.

Troubled people have a narrower margin of safety than those who are at peace with themselves, and the more troubled, the narrower the margin. An individual may go along for years without apparent difficulty while environment and circumstances are favorable; he may give no outward sign that he is carrying on a war within himself. But at a time of crisis or pressure the personality must call upon its reserves, both physical and emotional. If these reserves have been depleted by continuous inner conflict over the years, the individual discovers that when he most needs his strength it is not there.

This is why we have breakdowns over a death in the family, a defeat in love or work, or the varied illnesses growing out of war, either during the pressure of war itself or in the readjustment to civilian life afterward. One who is already teetering on the edge needs only the push of circumstance to topple him over.

Therefore it is well to consider those periods in every human life which are likely to provide the push. We have said that no man, woman, or child can avoid the pain of growing up. Adjustment is struggle. The need for adjustment is continuous. One must adjust oneself to environment, to family, to society, to the responsibilities of adulthood, to the realization of one's own limitations.

At certain ages this struggle becomes intensified. These are the dangerous periods. Medically speaking, these are actually the times of life when we find more people falling ill.

Adolescence is known to be a difficult time. The young person in adolescence is confronted not only with the changes in his own body and personality, the new demands made upon him by his need for independence, by his awakening sexual appetites. He must also face for the first time his responsibilities as a member of the adult world. He will soon be called upon to choose a career, to choose a marriage partner. The thousand demands of maturity are now just ahead of him.

As he emerges into his twenties he may have found the work of his choice or he may not. Some decisions may have been made for him. In any case his need for adjustment is now pressing. Rare is the fortunate young man or young woman for whom the path of the twenties is smooth. We may even question whether a smooth path is fortunate, for a struggle to mature at this age may avert more serious difficulty later.

Adolescence and the early twenties are the years of our freshest strength, our most abundant physical vigor. They are also years of great emotional pain and stress, years of anxiety and indecision and fear. They are the years in which a number of acute illnesses—among them tuberculosis, rheumatic fever, and pneumonia—are particularly likely to strike.

Let us say that our young man and young woman have made their adjustment in the twenties and embarked on the career and the family life of their choice or as close to their desires as they could achieve. Now comes the danger period of the mid-thirties.

Whether we accept the Bible's three score and ten as fact or symbol, the concept of a lifetime of seventy years has all the power of tradition. Most of us consciously or unconsciously approach the thirty-fifth birthday as a milestone; some begin to meditate even earlier. At this accepted halfway mark we take stock of what we have done with half our lives.

If the accounting falls short of our ideal or desire, we become frightened. Time presses. Half of life is gone, the stronger, better half. From now on, our anxious self reminds us, we are on the downhill side. In the distress of hurry we ask, can we do what remains to be done? Can we overtake the success, the love, the happiness which is still just out of reach? The mid-thirties are a time when many functional disturbances begin to emerge.

Time moves on. The young man and young woman who have weathered their thirties are now in their middle or late forties. Climacteric and menopause are either upon them or in the near future, a physical reminder that one aspect of life—in the woman, the physically creative aspect of child-bearing—is ended.

For a man, and for a woman whose career or profession is important, this is also the time when success should have been achieved. Most people feel that if they have not reached the peak by the time they are fifty, they are not going to get there.

This is the time of the greatest number of breakdowns and the most serious. Especially in women, the belief that life is over, that they are now old and useless, no longer competitors in the sexual race, no longer physically productive, is often overpowering. In men the crisis is more subtle, but the number of men who suffer their first heart attack at this time is impressive.

Stormy Weather

The idea that two seasons of the year, spring and fall, are dangerous periods may sound fanciful, more in the realm of poetry than medicine. But every doctor knows that he has more sick people to take care of in the fall. As for spring, it has for centuries been the time for blood-letting and dosing, the traditional brimstone and molasses season.

Hellpach, a professor of medicine in the University of Frankfort who later became minister-president of Baden, wrote extensively on what he called "cosmic influences on the psyche." He was one of the first, some twenty-five years ago, to seek a connection between the change of seasons and the sudden increase in pregnancies, sexual crimes, suicides, and admissions to mental hospitals which occurs between the thirty-fifth and the sixtieth parallels from April to June, and below the Equator from October to December. Among both school children and working adults, he observed, physical activity increases and intellectual activity declines.

He described the species of intoxication which seems to infect the human race in the spring, the increase of instinctual activity and the submergence of rational considerations and inhibitions. But he confessed that the physical explanation was not clear. He suggested that the physiological effect of the increasing warmth of the weather was "intellectually paralyzing, the increase of light motorically stimulating." Science takes the long way 'round to define what any schoolboy knows is simple spring fever.

In normal persons, basal metabolism reaches its peak of the year in the spring, and thyrotoxicosis—the disease of overactive thyroid—is most frequent in spring, least in fall. We also know that hot or cold temperature can change the basal metabolism by fifty to one hundred per cent.

If the resurgent blossoming time of the earth is, as Hellpach says, instinctually stimulating, its opposite season is depressing. Troubled souls are inclined to be despondent in the autumn. The end of growing things in the fall carries their spirits down to depression and often has a noticeable effect on their physical condition.

Years ago I had a neighbor, a hard-working farmer who in the spring and summer was a most responsible and respectable citizen. But on the day his field work was finished, his tools and machinery cleaned and put away, his sheds and barns made secure against the winter, this man began to drink.

"Why," I asked him once, "do you do this? Why do you give in to this weakness, year after year?"

"Just wait till spring," he said. "I'll go on the wagon in the spring."

The explanation of his conduct is, of course, obvious. In the spring and summer, when he is creatively occupied, his inner conflict is stilled. But when the fall comes and creative work is ended, when he has nothing but the dull winter months of routine chores to look forward to, then his dissatisfactions rise to plague him, the destructive instinct takes the reins, and he escapes via the alcohol route.

Certainly, as creatures of nature, we are affected by natural phenomena. Dogs bay at the moon, respectable house cats refuse to come home on moonlight nights, and somnambulists walk in their sleep under a full moon. Cattle become restless before a storm, and wild herds actually stampede. It was observed during World War II that fliers became drowsy and listless at high altitudes, and this phenomenon was explained by the decreased functioning of the adrenal glands.

Arrhenius, the Swedish chemist who was director of the Nobel Institute and who won the Nobel Prize for his theory of electric ionization, gave medicine the scientific connection between electrical charges and the autonomic nervous system. Efforts have been made to find a relationship between changes in static electricity in the atmosphere and in the nervous system which controls the visceral organs and the ductless glands.

Whether or not the exact train of psychic reactions to physical phenomena will some day be explained, we know pragmatically that as the earth turns in its course it brings changes in our natural environment to which we are vulnerable. At such times those who are at odds with themselves may see the signs of inner struggle. The symptoms are there for them to see—that is, if they wish to live in health.

6. THE CHAIN REACTION OF ILLNESS

THE NATURAL world presents to our senses an infinite variety
of detail. We know also that there are worlds beyond our own,
both too great and too small to see with the unaided eye. Yet
despite this labyrinthine complexity, there arises one day an
Einstein whose penetrating intellect brings harmony out of
massive chaos and reveals to us a universal majestic order.

So with man, nature's most complex and contradictory
child. The apparently unrelated patterns of illness, of which
we have sketched some of the advance symptoms, also fall into
a revelatory orderliness. Chaos does not exist in nature, but
only in man's imperfect understanding.

Physiologists, endocrinologists, and psychiatrists, working
in their separate fields, have been converging toward a single
theory. The human being, they tell us, reacts to stress—that
is, difficulties in life—in one of two basic ways. Either he
deals with it aggressively as an animal deals with an enemy,
by fight or flight. Or else he evades the difficulty, turning like
a child for help and protection to a parent or the equivalent
of a parent.

Whichever way he chooses, he may be blocked by an obstacle, either external or within himself. If he sets out aggressively
to deal with his difficulties he may be stopped by circumstance,
or he may be stopped by his own fear—of failure, of punishment, of some unhappy consequence of his action. If he seeks
parental protection, he may be rejected by the person from
whom he seeks it, or he may be halted by his own pride and
guilt since he is aware that he is no longer a child.

But in each case a series of reactions has been set in motion in the body. These, blocked, now turn aside from their original goal, which was to act in some way on the difficulty.

The aggressive impulse, fight or flight, sets up a chain of reactions which when blocked may lead to one group of diseases. The regressive impulse, the retreat into infantile dependency, may lead to another set of diseases.

Thus we see emerging two great groups of illnesses resulting from the two basic emotional responses to stress.

The aggressive personality is susceptible to heart disease, high blood-pressure, arteriosclerosis and other circulatory disorders, migraine, rheumatoid arthritis, hyperthyroidism. Diabetes and some skin diseases also possibly belong here.

The regressive personality reacts with fatigue states, functional disturbances of the digestive tract such as indigestion, diarrhea or constipation, colitis and a whole train of gastrointestinal complaints including peptic ulcer, plus certain allergies and respiratory diseases.

So far we have in bare outline an explanation of why energetic, dominating Aunt Martha has migraine while Uncle Henry, meek and timid soul, suffers from a chronic dyspepsia. We mention Aunt Martha and Uncle Henry as symbols for the many couples whom all of us know.

Take Mr. and Mrs. S for example: Mrs. S, a strong personality, is a public speaker and a leader in community-organization work. Mr. S is the conservative, cautious vice-president of a corporation. Mrs. S suffers from migraine. Mr. S has chronic gastro-intestinal disturbances and bronchial catarrh.

Mr. and Mrs. T are in business together. She is outgoing, at ease with people, active, enthusiastic. He is somber, heavy, easily irritated, withdrawn, and in private depends on his wife for every trivial decision. She has rheumatic pains in her neck. He has persistent stomach trouble.

And Mr. and Mrs. N. She had a hyperthyroid condition and he had a stomach ulcer—until they separated and both illnesses disappeared.

Two Reactions to Emergency

To grasp the full promise of this approach to illness not only for cure but also for prevention, we must trace the course of the chain reaction of the emotions through the physical mechanisms of the nervous system and the internal glands.

We have within us three nerve systems, the central, the peripheral, and the autonomic. The one of which we are aware, and by which we walk, talk, laugh and cry, eat when we are hungry, cover ourselves when we are cold, is the central or voluntary system; that is, it is controlled by our conscious will. The peripheral system deals with the sense organs.

The autonomic nervous system is the one with which we are now concerned. This system is involved entirely with internal activity. It controls the so-called smooth muscles, those of the visceral organs, the veins and arteries; its branches reach into every tissue and every cell of the body. Our heart beat, our breathing, the expansion and contraction of blood vessels, the mechanism of digesting food, storing it, and releasing it for the body's use—all this is the business of the autonomic nervous system.

This system cannot be commanded by our conscious will. *But it reacts automatically to our emotions.*

The autonomic nervous system has two divisions, both essential, which must function in harmony for us to remain in health: the sympathetic system and the parasympathetic system. They work in opposition to each other. One dilates and the other contracts; one stimulates and the other inhibits.

The parasympathetic system (also called the vagus system) runs a steady conservative course, preparing food, storing sugar, protecting the body against cold by contracting the blood vessels, making you cough in a smoky room. The parasympathetic system is the peacetime governor.

The sympathetic system deals with emergency conditions. Let us say you hear a burglar entering your home. Alarm sends its message through the sympathetic system, and the organs are at once activated to war production. Blood is driven out of the abdominal cavity to the lungs, the muscles, the brain, bringing them their needed increase of energy for action. The blood pressure rises. Carbohydrates are moved out of storage in the liver and muscles and converted into fuel. The adrenal glands, the fighting glands, pour their stimulating hormones into the blood stream. The body is made ready for a fight—or for flight.

Since these systems work in opposition to each other, whichever is in control—depending on the emotional state of the individual—determines the condition of the body. Under the dominance of the parasympathetic system the body tends to withdraw into a vegetative state: after eating we rest; after working we sleep. The body conserves and prepares itself for the demands of living. The sympathetic system is for action. When it is in control the peaceful upbuilding functions of the body are arrested. All is mobilization, production, the spending of reserves and resources.

Now we begin to see once more the outlines of two personalities within the one human being, two possible basic reactions to life. In a well-integrated, well-adjusted individual these two systems function in harmony, each assuming control as the situation demands. But when the individual is in conflict emotionally, this harmonious cooperation is disturbed.

Let us again create an emergency, a situation demanding decision and action. A burglar is entering the house.

Aunt Martha, the energetic, the aggressive, whose sympathetic nervous system is the dominant one, leaps out of bed, seizes whatever weapon comes to hand and descends to meet the intruder. Uncle Henry, a parasympathetic type, covers his head with the bedclothes and lets Aunt Martha handle the emergency.

So far so good. If there is a burglar, Aunt Martha's highly energized heart, muscles, and brain have their outlet in action, and Uncle Henry enjoys the protection he craves.

But suppose there is no burglar. Suppose the situation is not such an absurdly simple fiction as we have concocted, but one of those complex, emotion-tangled snarls which form the real pattern of human living.

Suppose that, instead of a burglar, Aunt Martha must face, day in and day out, the truth of her marriage to a timid, indecisive man. Suppose that Uncle Henry must confront through the years his inability to make an outstanding success in business, to achieve the stature of a man in his own and his wife's eyes.

Aunt Martha, driven by the need to deal aggressively with life situations, is in a state of continuous preparedness for action—and cannot act. It is contrary to her ethical standards to act on her dissatisfaction with her husband; she can neither abandon him nor accept him as he is, and her efforts to change him into a more aggressive personality are frustrated by his inability to change, as it were, from the inside out. She is caged, filled with thwarted drives, with the rage and hostility which are the products of continuous frustration and which she buries in her unconscious because it is wrong to have such feelings toward one's marriage and one's husband. When her inner tensions become too great, she has one of her violent migraine headaches.

There are people who go about in a state of perpetual preparedness for a battle which—because of fear, of conscience, of family obligations, of social standards—they can never fight. The repeated rise in blood pressure may lead to hypertension and possible embolism or stroke; the disturbance in carbohydrate metabolism may tend to diabetes; the chronic muscular tension may cause rheumatoid arthritis; the constant state of vigilance may bring on toxic thyroidism.

Uncle Henry meanwhile lives in unconscious longing to withdraw entirely from the struggle into a state of childish dependency. He cannot meet the demands made on him by the world and by his ambitious wife, nor can he in reality creep back into his mother's arms. He wins some comfort and protection from his wife's stronger personality, but at a price.

Pride castigates him, guilt tortures him, and indigestion is his fate.

Why indigestion? Why do dependent personalities react with digestive disorders?

The infant's earliest sensations of comfort and protection are related to food. His first physical discomfort is hunger, his first satisfaction is eating, and both the hunger and the relief of it are identified with his mother. Hence the infantile pattern of seeking relief from emotional discomfort through food.

In nature, an animal first fights and then eats, dining on his victim. But a dependent personality, figuring there's a tough job ahead, says, "We'd better have a bite first." Frustration and guilt in seeking relief through a dependent pattern take their toll on the same organs. The digestive system is the target.

Before we are misled into dividing the human race arbitrarily into two categories, however, let us keep in mind that man with his complexities does not lend himself to simple classification. Each of us has his differences from every other. To press any of us into a preconceived, rigid scheme, however logical, is an affront to our uniqueness.

Any man or woman may be both aggressive and regressive. The body may be mobilizing to fight while the child within whimpers for protection. We can use our knowledge of the two types of emotional response and the two groups of illness as a guide, but we must be prepared to find the line between them crossed and recrossed, and symptoms of both reactions existing in a single individual, even at the same time.

The Meaning of ACTH

This interpretation of illness—that a given disease falls into one of two groups, arising from one or the other basic emotional response—is offered by the Chicago psychiatrist Franz Alexander in his excellent book published in 1950, *Psychoso-*

matic Medicine, Its Principles and Applications. It is drawn not alone from psychiatric findings but from a vast array of clinical and laboratory research by biological scientists, especially Doctors W. B. Cannon, George Draper, and E. Moschcowitz.

The truth of this approach is being daily confirmed, most compellingly by the endocrinologists, whose field of study is the ductless glands. This group of scientists is making medical history today. It was of the endocrinologists that Freud long ago warned his students, remarking that this biological next-door neighbor was close on the heels of psychoanalysis and might one day overtake them.

In October, 1949, scientists gathered in Chicago from medical and research centers all over this country, for the first conference on ACTH. Out of this meeting came the story of what appeared to be a miracle: arthritics who had been helpless for years rose up out of their wheel chairs and walked; some of them danced. There were films to reassure the skeptical that the wonder was a fact. Newspaper headlines trumpeted the hope that sufferers from rheumatoid arthritis, of whom there are seven million in this country alone, could be cured. Doctors Philip S. Hench and Edward C. Kendall of the Mayo Clinic were awarded the Nobel Prize in 1950 for the isolation of the hormones ACTH and cortisone, together with the Swiss scientist Reichstein who developed a similar hormone independently.

Since that October day the brilliance of this news seems to have dimmed. Relapses of arthritic patients after treatment have been reported in a percentage of cases. Doctors have suggested that the miracle hormones might be of benefit only to a limited group of people and only if administered periodically, like insulin to diabetics. Dr. Hench himself has declared that ACTH is only a treatment of symptoms, *not a cure.*

At first glance these reports seem discouraging. We remember the excitement generated by Steinach and Voronoff's work with the sex glands, and the latter's famous "monkey-gland" operation which first sent a wave of hope across the world that the secret of youth had been found, and then became a popular joke. Is the miracle of ACTH dwindling too under the critical eyes of the experimenters and clinicians?

Not so. The significance of ACTH and cortisone is not so much whether they cure. Their significance is that they reveal to us a most important link in the chain reaction of illness.

What Are Hormones?

The system of the internal or ductless glands, functioning with the sympathetic and parasympathetic nervous systems, is constantly engaged in meeting the changing conditions to which the individual is exposed. It does this by means of glandular secretions, which are called hormones.

The sex hormones were for a long time the hormones predominantly used in medicine, and for this reason people have a tendency to identify hormones with the product of the sex glands only. They say, "My doctor gave me hormones," but this is like saying, "My doctor gave me capsules." There are probably hundreds of different hormones produced in the body.

Hormone is a general term, meaning the secretion of any one of the ductless glands, and there are a number of these glands. We call them "ductless" to distinguish them from the glands which have ducts or canals. Sweat glands, tear glands, salivary glands all have ducts and empty externally, on the outside of the body. Other glands, like those in the digestive system, empty within the body into an organ. The ductless glands empty directly into the blood stream.

The theory that inner fluids regulate the functions of the body goes back to Hippocrates, who named four cardinal fluids responsible for health or illness: blood, phlegm, yellow bile and black bile. The four humors, as they were called from the Latin word for moisture, survive in our language as descriptive of four types of personality. A cheerful, confident person we call *sanguine,* from the Latin for blood. A stolid one is *phlegmatic.* A man easily angered is *choleric,* a word derived from the Greek root *chol* for bile, and a gloomy man suffers from *melancholy,* which is *chol* plus *mela* meaning black, or "black bile."

The theory of the humors dominated medicine through the Middle Ages and into modern times, until it was abandoned in favor of Virchow's cellular pathology. The French physiologist Claude Bernard, studying the digestive juices, discovered the functions of the liver and pancreas, and stated his belief that health depended on the *milieu intérieur,* the inner condition, by which he meant the balance of these fluids.

This idea was carried forward by the American physiologist Cannon, who coined the term "homeostasis" to describe the tendency of the body to maintain balance. Thus the theory of the humors returns in a new, scientific form and becomes the basis of the most promising biological research of our time, endocrinology.

Among our ductless glands are the sex glands, the thyroid, the pancreas, the thymus, the pineal, the adrenals, and the pituitary. Each of these produces its specific hormone or group of hormones. We know the functions of *some* but not of *all* of them.

The adrenal glands, which lie just above the kidneys, produce a powerful hormone under conditions demanding physical action. We have long known that that area of the body was a source of physical energy and courage. One of Shakespeare's characters calls out for "strength in my kidneys." The familiar adrenalin is the trade name for this adrenal hormone, and is used medically as a stimulant.

The pituitary is the master gland, the switchboard through which impulses are directed toward the other glands. For all its importance, it is a small gland, seated at the base of the brain in a protective bony cradle called the Turkish saddle. It has three lobes. In the anterior lobe are tiny centers of specific hormones which go out to stimulate the other glands. The sex glands, the thyroid, the adrenals do not go into action unless the pituitary sends to each its specific activating hormone.

The word *tropic,* from the Greek word pertaining to turning, is used to describe these anterior pituitary hormones which turn toward or are directed at specific glands. What Hench and Kendall isolated in the anterior lobe of the pituitary was the hormone directed at the cortex or outer layer of the adrenal gland. They called it the adrenal-cortico-tropic-hormone or, briefly, ACTH. Cortisone is one of a group of twenty-eight hormones in the adrenal cortex which are activated by ACTH.

The physiological chain of reactions appears to follow this course: a stimulus is carried through the hypothalamus (a part of the interbrain between the cerebrum and the medulla) to the anterior pituitary, which then sends out its tropic hormones to the glands.

Stress Gives the Alarm

Stress is the term now used in medicine to cover all the conditions—external or internal, physical or emotional—to which the body is exposed. Professor Hans Selye of the University of Montreal, in his book *Stress,* lists three diseases as outstanding examples of the effects on the body of our modern stressful life: thyrotoxicosis, a disease resulting from excess activity of the thyroid gland; duodenal ulcer; and hypertension, or high blood-pressure, of the variety which comes from causes other than diseased kidneys. He groups these three under the name, "stress diseases."

Under the continuous strain characteristic of civilized life —because these diseases are comparatively rare in primitive society—the stress diseases are often described as "wear-and-tear diseases," and medicine adds several more to the list: obesity, underweight, diseases of the heart and blood vessels, and some others.

Stress, whether an emotional disturbance or a physical one such as injury, exposure to cold, fever, in short any noxious condition, sets up an alarm reaction in the body, a chain of functions designed to meet the condition. Selye calls this series of reactions the "general adaptation syndrome," a syndrome being a group of related symptoms. A continuance of this syndrome eventually brings about one of the stress diseases.

Selye demonstrated by experiment that any stressful experience, physical or emotional, as well as an overdose of certain hormones, can bring about the same diseases.

Working with rats, Selye reproduced in terms of rat experience the equivalent of the stressful conditions which man must endure in his society. The rats were subjected to surgery. They were fed large quantities of salt. They were exposed to cold. They were exhausted in whirling cages. They were worried with the shrieking of air-raid sirens, the jangling of bells, the flashing of lights. And they were given excessive doses of certain hormones.

The rats rapidly developed symptoms of the various stress diseases: rheumatic, allergic, and hypertensive disorders, especially severe arteriosclerosis and persistent high blood-pressure.

Then the rats were given ACTH and cortisone. The symptoms subsided. The diseases were checked, and actually reversed.

Dr. Selye concluded that the body has a unified defense mechanism which operates by way of the ductless glands and their hormones. Health seems to depend on the balance of these hormones, or what Cannon called homeostasis. When stress continues too long, a breakdown may occur in this integrated defense system, at the point of production of one or some of these hormones. Thus when we supply these hormones medically we restore the broken link, and the defense system can again function.

"They are the first natural agents," the *Journal of the American Medical Association* points out, "by means of which it is possible to demonstrate the potential reversibility" of a number of diseases which up to now have been considered incurable.

ACTH and the Two Basic Reactions

Further experiments with ACTH and cortisone seem to lend support to the theory of the two groups of illnesses proceeding from the two basic emotional reactions, the aggressive and the regressive.

ACTH is now an established treatment for rheumatoid arthritis, rheumatic fever, certain skin diseases, certain allergies including hay fever, and others; the list is still growing. All these diseases, as we have learned, belong to the group stemming from the *aggressive response* to stress.

On the other hand, three cases of peptic ulcers were treated with ACTH. The ulcers, far from improving, became much worse. Peptic ulcer is one of the leading diseases in the list of those belonging to the *regressive response*.

A still more significant development was reported in January, 1951. Experiments conducted by Dr. G. Shwartzman, at Mount Sinai Hospital in New York, revealed that cortisone increased the susceptibility to infantile paralysis. This seems to indicate that a breakdown of the glandular system opens the way to *infectious* diseases, as well as to diseases of "wear-and-tear."

This report throws new light on one of my own cases of several years ago. A young man, whom I had treated some time previously for stomach disorders, came to me and asked to be examined for polio. He showed no symptoms, and I was obliged to tell him that we know of no way to test susceptibility to the disease, of which he was extremely fearful.

The following year he went to another physician and again demanded to be examined for polio. Again he was reassured that he did not have the disease.

The third year, he contracted an acute case of polio.

Any explanation of this curious and disturbing case would be purely hypothetical. Yet Selye suggests that fear may bring about an overreaction of the body to stress. If we follow the theory of the two basic emotional patterns and their disease groups, it may be assumed that the fearful, regressive personality probably produces too much ACTH or its allied hormones. Thus the system becomes susceptible to illnesses like peptic ulcer, and infectious diseases like polio.

Much more research along these lines is needed, and is being done, to set us firmly on the track of this new, and perhaps revolutionary, approach to illness by way of endocrinology, which dovetails so closely with the theory of the emotional background of illness.

A patient of mine had suffered intensely from headaches for many years and was totally blind in one eye, when the other eye began to fail. The optic nerve of the second eye was found to be inflamed and badly damaged. This man had an old case of syphilis which had been treated unsuccessfully with the classic medications, plus massive doses of penicillin. Five injections of cortisone restored vision in the failing eye, and in the seven months since, there has been no recurrence.

Why Not a Cure?

Yet these powerful hormones are not a cure. Hench has explained: "Both agents (ACTH and cortisone) affect not the cause of a disease but the reaction of the tissue to the irritant or cause."

ACTH and cortisone come close to a cure. They restore a broken link in the body's effort to maintain or regain balance, at the point where continued stress has caused a breakdown.

But obviously, hormones cannot cure, if the underlying emotional pattern remains unchanged. Hormones, impressive as their brief record has already become, may still do no more than repair what the inner conflict will again break down. We cannot expect a cure if the individual continues a course of self-destruction.

It is not enough to repair the link in the body's system of defense. We must get at the source of stress which is forcing the body to make this continuous excessive effort.

We have a fair chance of avoiding physical stress, except in abnormal situations, because we are aware of it. Of emotional stress we may not even be conscious, or we may evade or seek to escape the necessity of becoming conscious of it. But there is no substitute for the rational effort to deal with emotional stress. Hormones are a weapon against disease, but the preservation of health remains, and must still remain, within ourselves, because it depends upon the individual's own specific way of reacting to the stress of living.

We now know that the body can restore itself if we will only allow it to do so. The body is not a feeble, perishable weakling; we can have faith in its strength. It can be pushed far, very far, and still find resources to recover. If the body has exhausted these resources we can supply medically the help which will restore it. This restoration is, however, only temporary. It is a lift on the way back to health. The true recovery is still in our hands.

In Philip Barry's play, *The Second Threshold,* young Doctor Wells muses, "Wonderful stuff, these new drugs. But in many cases, if I had to choose between them and the will to live, I'd take the old original . . . All the same, it's nice we have both."

There is a conscious, rational role which each of us can play in the defense of our health against the stress of living. The body is constructed to endure this stress. The human organism is the product of thousands of years of selection and adaptation, and it is built for hard usage. From the stress of living we have nothing to fear.

It is when we permit stress to continue indefinitely, or repetitiously, without taking rational steps to relieve it, that we suffer damage. It is when we permit ourselves to follow a neurotic pattern, that we ourselves defeat the body's resiliency. When we fight the same battle over and over *in fantasy,* when we fear disaster *in fantasy,* when we run for protection *in fantasy,* then we wear out the body's mechanisms for maintaining balance.

This we must remember: whether we fight the battle in reality or only in dream, whether we labor physically or in the mind, the demands on our body are equally real.

Once we make a decision and set a course, once we take action in the world of reality, then we relieve the body of that emotional stress which is as real as physical stress. Positive decision, realistic action in the direction of adjustment, are steps on the road back to health.

The infantile dependency pattern is not an effort at adjustment; it is an evasion. The aggressive pattern, on the other hand, is an effort at adjustment. But it must be carried through. We must deal with the real difficulty by means of real action, either fight or flight.

Fight means changing the situation, or changing oneself; that is, positive adjustment. But flight from the situation is also normal and therefore healthy. It can be, not cowardice, but self-preservation.

The choice is ours. A chronic state of indecision is an expression of the destructive instinct. By true adjustment— which is not the same as compromise or resignation—we can achieve the satisfactions of healthy living.

7. WE SELECT OUR ILLNESS

WE HAVE examined the two basic emotional reactions to stress. We have seen that two groups of diseases emerge according to these two emotional patterns. But within each group of diseases, what brings on one disease rather than another?

Out of the research of physicians exploring the relationship between mind and body, a formidable truth appears: within the framework of our individual constitution, we ourselves choose the time of illness, the kind of illness, the course of illness, and its gravity.

Of course we do not make these choices consciously. We do not *reason* ourselves into illness. The decisions are made in the unconscious court of judgment which sits, waking and sleeping, within us. They are arrived at by way of involved and turbulent argument without words, the language of the emotions. Also we must remember that these decisions are not irrevocable. We can and do change our minds. We can and do reverse our course, and turn back from illness to health.

But the important new knowledge we have gained is this: that while the choice for illness or health is made emotionally, it is carried out through the physical mechanisms of the body.

Against doubts, questioning, and ignorance, against the natural resistance of the reasoning mind which is reluctant to believe what cannot be seen or touched, it is necessary to repeat, time and again, that we poker-faced civilized people are moved by impulses and inspirations, by feelings and emotional drives which our clear reason can never understand so long as we employ only physiological methods to examine them.

Physiology describes subjective experiences such as hunger, fear, rage, pain, in physiological terms. Psychology studies the motivation of these emotions. With our present methods, psychological study depends on verbal communication. We can penetrate another person's subjective experiences only if he can be led to talk about them. Only by inviting him to communicate, by giving him freedom to talk, can we gain insight into the dynamics of emotion, idea, fantasy. Those are the inner drives which lead to physiological and eventually to physical changes; in other words, to functional and at last to organic illness.

We must learn to understand and respect the elementary forces within us if we wish to understand what makes illness. Love, hate, fear, guilt, pride, vengeance are the values by which we are moved. Also, as Cicero said, "There is something so penetrating in the shaft of envy that even men of wisdom and worth find its wound a painful one." Our emotions fill us with dynamic power to deal with the problems of living, or they block our intelligence, paralyze our will, and hypnotize our consciousness.

The need for a way out, for escape, sacrifice, or self-punishment, drives us to single out an organ to destroy by illness. According to our emotional standard of values, we make the choice for a determined suicide or a half-hearted one, or for merely a gesture. The emotions have their own compelling logic. A man with sickness in his body follows a chosen route which the high command of the destructive instinct has determined.

Medicine speaks of tissue memory. A part or organ which has been injured in the past is said to retain a memory, and that is the part which will give the first sign of trouble when the individual is under stress. Medically this is explained by the principle of the point of lowest resistance.

Now we may seriously consider whether it may not be a case of returning to the attack on the same part or organ as, under stress, we attacked before. The same emotional pattern which fixed on that organ in the past fixes on it again. An obvious example is that a man who gets a stomach ulcer is likely to have a history of gastric disturbance. But there are less obvious ones. If you hurt an arm once long ago, it is in that arm that you are likely to have neuralgic pain in a time of stress.

The first time that a part of the body was involved in difficulty may go back to childhood, and we are not likely to remember too clearly what the emotional situation was then so long ago. But all indications are that the part of our body which suffers attack from injury or illness has a specific emotional significance within the framework of our whole personality.

Mrs. De S, for example, is a city woman of highly cultured background who married and went to live in an Indian village in the high Andes of South America. Her husband brought her back to the United States after a few years, very ill. She had a blood pressure of more than two hundred, pain in the neck and temples, a choking sensation in her throat. In particular she was almost blind; she had developed cataracts on her eyes.

When she came into my office she was near collapse. An old friend, she stayed to dinner. In the next hour or two she became young, animated, charming, telling witty anecdotes of her life in South America. The transformation was astonishing. In the course of the evening's talk she let fall, not once but several times, the remark, "I couldn't bear to look at that wall of mountains."

The cataracts were removed, the patient's health became better, and then the time came to return to the Andes. Now her blood pressure suddenly shot up again to two hundred forty. But because her relationship with her husband was a close one she would not remain in the States without him. She barely made it alive to their mountain home, and in less than a year she was back in New York, this time with a detached retina.

She spent months in the hospital and underwent an operation which was unsuccessful. Meanwhile her husband began negotiations for the sale of a large tract of his mountain land.

Gradually she improved. The eye began to heal itself. When they flew back she was hopeful that with the sale of the land they would at last be able to live again in New York where she could once more enjoy the life she longed for, the music, theater, and friends she had missed.

With the promise that she will one day be able to scale that mountain wall and enjoy the world beyond it once more, my patient is able now to look at it, and enjoy the beauty of the majestic peaks. She no longer needs to make herself blind.

We Choose the Time of Illness

I have said that we select the time of our illness. A high-spirited Irishwoman of forty-three came to me with a variety of complaints. She had been well and *strong,* she told me emphatically, until she was twenty-two. She was happily married, loved her husband and her two children, loved living in the United States.

But since the age of twenty-two she had been plagued by a series of physical miseries: infected tonsils, inflamed gall bladder, pains, nausea, a virus infection, an eye infection, an infection in her arm. Her tonsils had been removed, and both her children had been born by Caesarean operation. She had been a healthy, robust girl—why should she be so troubled by illness, she demanded.

I asked her in turn, what had happened when she was twenty-two. She said at that time she had left her home in Ireland, left her mother, her village, her youth behind. Memories, longing for places and people of her girlhood, and perhaps some unconscious protest against adjustment to her new life, not only in a strange land but with the responsibilities of adulthood—all these were present in the background of her many illnesses. Actually her real disease was homesickness.

The time we choose for illness may have symbolic significance. A man and his wife were celebrating the golden anniversary of what had been an apparently perfect marriage. Standing at his wife's side, accepting the congratulations of his friends, the man was all at once aware of something amiss within his body. Later he discovered that he was suffering an internal hemorrhage. He had never been ill in his life. The urologist diagnosed an inoperable growth involving the prostate gland and the bladder, probably malignant.

Under questioning this vigorous and highly respectable man confessed that his wife was frigid, and that he had had a mistress during his younger days. His wife had known it and reproached him with the fact through the years. As he grew older and more dependent on his wife, she used her increasing power over him to torment him with his offense.

Menninger tells us that feelings of guilt are especially strong in connection with violations of the sexual conventions, and it is not surprising that organic lesions should occur in the genitourinary organs.

Symbols too have a potency over us. So in this particular case the golden wedding, a significant milestone, brought to a critical stage a condition which must have been developing over a period of years.

Treatment with opposite sex hormones had here, as in many similar cases, a deterrent effect on the tumor, and the old man lived in comfort for nearly seven years.

But the death of one whom our superego tells us we have injured brings a new access of guilt. So when the patient's wife died his disease became suddenly reactivated. A biopsy—that is, a laboratory examination of a section of diseased tissue from the patient—showed that he did indeed have a malignancy, which had been held in check until the new crisis occurred. Then medicine could no longer countermand the verdict of the superego, and the destructive instinct carried out the sentence.

The following story suggests how infectious disease also may be purposefully, though unconsciously, sought.

Two men friends were celebrating a reunion after one of them had been absent overseas. At the end of the evening they dropped into a bar, and presently noticed an attractive young woman alone. The more aggressive of the two men, on the insistence of his timid friend, invited the young woman to their table and afterward to his home. Both enjoyed her favors.

The timid man came later to be treated for a venereal infection. He complained bitterly that his friend, who had taken no more precaution than himself, had got off scot-free.

Says Menninger: "I am convinced from my observations that even venereal disease is sometimes acquired partly because the victim invited the infection not only by his behavior (e.g. carelessness) but also by some unknown subtle modification of tissue resistance."

Significantly it was the timid man, the one with the stronger inhibitions and hence stronger guilt feelings, who suffered punishment. The germ which attacks the cells of the body is no more accidental than the tree in the path of the speeding driver who is unconsciously toying with suicide.

The Man Who Needs His Ulcer

How determined is the wish for self-destruction?

We have said that it might be half-hearted, or in earnest, or merely a gesture. A record of 2,030 deaths in Manhattan, covering a period of seven years, shows that forty-five per cent of all "natural" deaths were due to heart disease, twenty-three per cent respiratory, eighteen per cent caused by nervous disorders, and only six and one-half per cent digestive.

Digestive disorders are rarely fatal. A man may live in sorry discomfort with his stomach ulcers, but he is not likely to die of them, without the assistance of other troubles.

This bears out Franz Alexander's description of the digestive disorders as resulting from the infantile dependency pattern. These people do not want to die. They want to live—and to be loved. They long to be cared for. When love is denied them—or when out of pride and guilt they cannot accept love —then they suffer pain, and eventually damage to the tissues of the digestive system.

It is only when guilt and anxiety are overwhelming, or when hostility is acutely sharpened by the denial of love, that more dangerous processes enter in and the tendency toward self-damage becomes a drive toward self-destruction. Otherwise theirs is likely to be a repetitious nagging self-torture rather than a struggle to the death.

An elderly man, a grandfather, came to me with peptic ulcers which he had been suffering for thirty years, the major part of his adult life. If he could only be rid of them! It was all he asked of life, he said.

"Suppose tomorrow you woke up cured—what would you do?" I asked him.

"Why, I would enjoy life," he answered.

"How would you enjoy it? What would you do?" I persisted.

'Why—" he floundered, "I would enjoy it—like other people."

He could not be more specific. He had no plan, no purpose, no driving desire to be well in order to accomplish something which was important to him. For thirty years he had built his life around this illness. His colleagues in business catered to him, praised him for his devotion to his work despite his handicap. His family at home cushioned him with attentions because of his "condition." The bowl of hot soup was always waiting for him when he got home from the office.

To take away his ulcer would at one sweep deprive him of the special position he enjoyed, and of all the attentions which served him in place of mature relationships of mutual affection and responsibility. Take away his ulcer and you take away the bowl of hot soup, his substitute for love. No, he could not say how he would enjoy life without his ulcer, because he could not even imagine life without his ulcer. He needed his ulcer.

So often this is true of chronic sufferers from digestive disorders. Ulcers are frequently cured by medical means, but too often they do not stay cured. It takes a genuine effort, a profound galvanizing of all our forces, to overcome the ulcer-producing responses of the digestive system. And most patients of this kind are not prepared to make such an effort.

Their need for love, or for the attentions which are their recourse in the absence of love, is stronger than any need to be well and to function at full capacity in the world of adult responsibility. With all possible sympathy for these sufferers, and with all possible understanding and tolerance for them as victims of adult domination in their childhood, we must still recognize the average chronic ulcer patient as one who suffers from emotional immaturity first and from ulcers second.

To say this is not to judge or blame him, but rather to understand and help him. Often it is beyond his power to help himself, since his growth into emotional adulthood is blocked by a power stronger than himself.

A youth of twenty once came to me with an acute ulcer of the stomach, for which he had been medically discharged from the navy. Going back through his history, I learned that he had had a series of accidents: a football injury to his knee at school, an injury to his foot at work, and finally an accident on shipboard during his navy service in which he suffered a concussion as well as injury to both knees. Then he revealed that he had already had his first ulcer at the age of fourteen.

This early start on the ulcer route is not average, but this boy's future as a chronic ulcer sufferer had better than average preparation. His father had chronic ulcers. When I visited him at home, I saw an environment which might have been contrived as a laboratory demonstration of what makes ulcers.

The mother, a dominating woman, was also restless, neglectful, apparently without the slightest impulse of warmth or a wish to care for her family. Though they were better than well to do, dinner was a hastily assembled mess from the delicatessen store because she had spent the afternoon at a card party—food out of cans and paper bags, food which required no forethought and no preparation, and an overabundance of it, as though to make up for the time and care she had not spent on the meal. Too much food and too little love is often the background of an ulcer patient's childhood.

The house in which this family lived was handsome and expensive, but it certainly was not a real home. There was, in fact, no permanence about this family's living arrangements. Every second year they moved. When the father bought a suburban house and furnished it, the mother tired of it in a year, expressing a longing to be back with her friends in the city. So they sold the house and moved back to town. A year or so later she wanted to get out of the city again. The father bought a house in another suburb. At the time when the boy became my patient the mother was already tiring of this second country place.

Eventually the father also became my patient. From him I learned that he was comparatively well all week. But almost invariably after each weekend he suffered a violent attack of ulcer symptoms.

What deep discontent drove this woman to behave this way to her husband and son it is not our business to consider here. The very need for maternal domination which determined this man's choice of an aggressive woman as his wife sealed not only his own future fate but also that of any children born of such a marriage. The son was only a strikingly typical product of his parents.

The typical ulcer sufferer is likely to be aggressive rather than dependent on the surface. The last thing he wishes to reveal about himself, or to recognize in himself, is his need for love. Consequently he overcompensates with forceful, self-confident behavior. The father in this family was energetic, driving, a very good provider. He demanded recognition, and was inclined to be boastful about his business success. Away from his work he was a fish out of water. He talked about liking to have interesting people around him, but actually he was inclined to withdraw into a corner of a room, avoiding the necessity of extending himself socially.

This sort of individual characteristically does not gamble

at cards or the races. He most needs to be the center of his wife's attention and feels deprived by her rival interests.

Hunger for Love

Ulcers can also be an acute, sudden development in a specific emotional situation, provided the contributing factors of personality are present. An individual with a tendency toward dependence may go along for many years without trouble until a crisis occurs which finds out his weakness, his short supply of mature resources to deal with the difficulty.

A report from a Swedish clinic in 1950 gives the results of a psychiatric examination of 108 ulcer patients: fifty-four were found to be suffering acute mental conflict; twenty-nine showed chronic mental conflict; twenty-two had psychopathological symptoms without conflict, and only three revealed no psychological factors whatever.

That ulcers, of the whole long list of man's ills, have an emotional origin has been accepted for some time with little argument. What we are newly coming to understand is the nature of this emotional background. The general statement that ulcers come from worry is no longer enough.

Clever and skillful as we may be in our medical treatment of ulcers, the emotional setting of the patient's life, his need for love and care will balk all our efforts until we can awaken in him an understanding of himself, and an active, purposeful will to lift himself out of the dependent pattern which makes him ill. He will not live for his ulcer if he can find something better to live for.

Rebuke, reproach, rejection of his inarticulate plea for love will not help him. On the contrary, it will only drive him deeper into conflict with himself and perhaps despair. An attempt to "make a man of him" by force, without understanding, can change a mild illness into a serious one.

We must recognize, too, the pressures of our society which drive less sturdy individuals backward into this immature emotional pattern of dependence. H. R. Hartman, writing on "Neurogenic Factors in Peptic Ulcer," observes that Chinese coolies and Latin-American Indians never have ulcers, and suggests that the explanation may lie in their attitude toward living. They are free from the straining, driving ambition which characterizes Western white civilization. The coolie expects little of life, and when the day brings him his bowl of rice he eats it zestfully. He does not complicate his body hunger with other hungers since these other hungers, as far as we know, do not exist for him.

But we Westerners, under the pressure to achieve individual success, to "make good," need continuous confirmation of our value as individuals, continuous recognition of our worthiness to be loved. To us a bowl of rice is not merely food for the body but also a reminder of the parent who first provided us with both food and love. It becomes a symbol of love and also a weapon when love is absent. Feeling rejected, we reject in turn, refusing our food to punish the parent and ourselves.

In Indonesia I observed the coolies who worked as long-shoremen. They habitually spent half the day's pay for food, and the other half to enjoy the night with a girl. Each day provided the whole answer to that day's needs, no more and no less. Another day would bring another day's pay; if it did not, one went hungry. A simple life, without many things which make life meaningful—but also without ulcers.

Allergy, the "Strange Disease"

Among the attempts at self-destruction which may be termed half-hearted, we may also rank the allergies, those assorted afflictions which are rarely fatal but which give both patient and doctor so much trouble. (Asthma, however, cannot be called half-hearted, since it may take a serious course.)

The idea that the allergies may have emotional origins is

as old as medicine. Even Hippocrates related attacks of asthma to violent emotions.

But then about 1915, bronchial asthma, hay fever, and skin eruptions like urticaria and eczema were grouped as sensitivities to foreign substances. They were called the "atopic group," from the word *atopy*, meaning "strange disease."

In the next several years, serum sicknesses, contact dermatitis (that is, irritation of the skin from contact with certain substances) and hypersensitivity to certain medications were added to the group of "strange diseases," and since then they have been treated with the allergist's vast array of medical techniques. The word allergy itself means only altered energy or strength to react.

Today we are beginning to take a new direction in the understanding of allergies. More accurately, we are finding new signposts pointing back to Hippocrates' ancient direction. In one report in the *Journal of the American Medical Association* during 1950, thirty unselected cases of urticaria were studied to determine if there was any relation between a "stressful life situation" and the skin processes which caused eruption.

The attacks of skin eruption were found to be "highly correlated with an emotional disturbance of a particular kind." Contradicting the assumption of half a century, the researchers found "no relation between exposure to the allergens and the attacks of the disease." In other words, the foreign substance to which the patient was supposed to be allergic, the hair of the pet dog or cat or the vase of roses, had no effect *unless there was an underlying emotional disturbance.*

What "particular kind" of emotional disturbance was found to be present? "The traumatic life situations responsible were almost exclusively those in which the patient felt resentment because he saw himself the victim of unjust treatment about which he could do nothing."

To put it crudely, the patient could safely stroke his dog

unless at the same time he were having an argument with his wife.

Intuitively, people have related their emotions and the sensations of the skin. Expressions in our every-day language bear this out. While the allergists labor painstakingly over their scratch tests, we tell a friend, "I feel like jumping out of my skin," and our skin may actually break out in an ugly rash. We feel like tearing someone—or ourselves—to pieces, and we may really be plagued by a maddening itch. Many an itch can be traced to confused emotions in sex; one seems to be saying, as Flanders Dunbar suggests, "Love me but don't touch me."

In an allergy case among my own patients the woman's Siamese cat was named as the villain. She protested angrily, "How can you get sick from anything you love so much?" As it turned out, she was right. We had clear proof that her asthma was due to a frustrating emotional relationship. In the eight years since that relationship was resolved, she has not had a single recurrence of her asthma.

Do we unconsciously select among the "strange diseases" the particular one which suits our emotional situation? There is evidence that we do. The skin disturbances seem to occur where hostility and resentment are the dominating emotional factors. The asthmatic attacks are most frequently traceable to situations of emotional dependence. Psychiatrists explain the asthmatic wheeze as an aborted cry of the infant for help.

A young woman in her thirties, a chronic asthma sufferer, described her childhood. "I was an only child and always had the best of food and care. I used to envy other children because they were allowed to eat hot dogs, jelly apples, cheap candy, and I was not. Later I thought I would have been better off if I had been permitted to eat any kind of junk. My play-mates were never sick, while I always had these so-called 'colds.'"

She remembered, once as a child, testing her father's love for her by a trick. At the hour when he was expected home in the evening she lay down in front of the door, pretending to be dead. Her father, first frightened, then furious, gave her the first and only spanking of her life. She remembered the long and deep unhappiness she suffered over the loss of her first pet dog. She remembered " 'way back, always being afraid that something would happen to my parents, especially to my mother."

Clearly this was a child marked by insecurity in her parents' love, and by the overprotectiveness of her mother.

This young woman's asthma was variously attributed to different kinds of dust, and to the hair of her pet dog which she loved. I asked her to keep a careful record of the time and circumstances of her attacks.

One report she gave me thereafter is typical and striking. By this time she was married, though she and her husband lived with her mother, now widowed, and they had no children.

On this occasion she was out for the evening with her husband. She was dancing, enjoying herself thoroughly, when suddenly she was seized with a violent asthmatic attack. The time was half-past ten in the evening.

What, I asked her, had happened at about that time?

Nothing, she said; she was having a wonderful evening. To explain the asthmatic attack she seized on the first plausible physical explanation. Probably she had overexerted herself with too much dancing and laughing.

What had she been thinking of?

She struggled to recall, and then it came back to her. She had thought of her mother, wondered if she were all right at home alone, wanted to telephone home to make sure, rejected the idea because it was late and her mother would be awakened by the call. A few minutes later, when she had presumably put her mother out of her mind and gone back to her friends, she suffered the attack. Though a grown woman, she still had not gained freedom from her emotional attachment to her mother.

He Who Does Not Wish to Breathe

In general the respiratory diseases are a determined expression of self-destruction, at least at the moment of illness. We have been quicker to discover cures for these diseases than to understand their causes. Pneumonia is no longer a first-rank killer, now that we have penicillin. The miracle drug gives a man a better chance to change his mind and decide in favor of life.

The normal organism reacts protectively to an unwholesome atmosphere. Coughing in a smoke-filled room is the autonomic nervous system's protest against the irritating smoke, its effort to protect the bronchial tubes and the lungs by expelling the smoky air. Stating it another way, we say that the cough is caused by the physical or chemical irritation of the soft tissue in the bronchial tubes.

But how shall we explain the coughing spell in an air-conditioned room, or outdoors on a clear, fine day without wind or flying dust or pollen? Isn't the cause in this case due to an unwholesome psychological atmosphere?

On a visit to one of the General Assembly sessions of the United Nations I listened to a speech by a delegate defending his country in what was, on the known facts, an indefensible position.

This man had proved himself on previous occasions an able and eloquent speaker. Yet on this day he was hampered by a continuous, racking cough which he could not control no matter how many glasses of water he poured for himself. He could scarcely be heard, choking through his speech, and all over the hall the nervous tension increased until at last he finished his address and sat down.

On the assumption that the man merely had a cold, I watched him assiduously through the remainder of the session, but in vain. He used his handkerchief only to wipe his forehead. If, trained orator that he was, his voice was for some reason strained by use that day, surely he should have coughed at least a little when he sat down, or when he talked with his colleagues, which he did frequently in the course of the day. But he did not cough again that afternoon.

We identify life with breathing. Life begins with the first breath and ends with the last; in legal medicine an infant is considered to have been born alive if its lungs have contained a single breath. The question of infanticide has in many cases been determined on this test alone. We are safe to take the next logical step and assert that a person who does not wish to breathe does not wish to live.

A statesman, who had been a courageous leader of his nation during the war, was to open an international conference on which much depended. On the eve of the conference he was laid low with bronchial pneumonia.

An actress, who had struggled long and unsuccessfully for recognition on Broadway, accepted a modest Hollywood offer and overnight became a movie star. She returned to Broadway for her first starring role in the legitimate theater. Just before the opening, she came down with pneumonia.

The path of retreat which an individual chooses in a stressful situation depends on his characteristic emotional pattern. The man with a profound self-doubt may fall victim to tuberculosis. One with only a momentary panic may be stricken by pneumonia.

In pre-penicillin days laymen and doctors alike used to observe that it was often the vigorous, healthy man, the strongly physical type who had scarcely suffered a cold, who would fall prey to pneumonia and succumb with shocking swiftness.

We did not ask, in those days, whether the patient faced a more critical decision or a more challenging task than usual at the time he became ill. These individuals usually impressed those who knew them as being equal to any situation. Today we are more observant of emotional forces, and also more likely to preserve the victim so that he lives to talk about it. Perhaps in time we may learn exactly how the ever-present *pneumococcus* suddenly receives the signal to attack.

8. FIGHT OR FLIGHT

IF THE BREATH is our symbol of the body's life, the heart is the symbol of that inner life which, for want of a better word, we may call emotional. A valentine is heart-shaped, and we give our hearts when we love. We call a brave man lion-hearted and a coward chicken-hearted. Our heart is heavy or it leaps for joy. We know warm-hearted and cold-hearted people, we are touched to the heart, we wish a friend happiness with all our heart, and we speak with a full heart.

A story is told of Toscanini, that man of fiery temperament who puts so much heart into his music. He was being examined when he was eighty, and his physician commented cheerfully, "Maestro, your heart is exceptionally strong."

"No wonder—I never use it," Toscanini replied.

We say, cynically, that no one ever died of a broken heart. But we know in our hearts that people do. "Break, heart; prithee, break," pleads the faithful Kent to Lear before Cordelia's body, praying his tragic master to find release from his woes in death.

Everyone, sometime, has felt heartbroken, and at such times we imagine that the heart does actually hurt. Now the belief is growing that under certain circumstances, people may die of a "broken heart." It is not surprising that science often finds confirmation of a popular belief. A great deal of folk wisdom may be nonsense, but a great deal of it is rooted in experience. The doctor observes a patient for a short, concentrated period, but the lore of the people is the sum of observations handed down through the generations of man.

124

Thus we have a cardiologist, Dr. Franz M. Groedel, writing in a report to the Rudolf Virchow Society: "The close correlation between psyche and body . . . is nowhere as evident as in the circulatory apparatus. Under agreeable emotions the heart becomes accelerated; disagreeable emotions, even dislike, slow the pulse rate. The heart beat is influenced by music, accommodates to the rhythm."

If the heart is responsive to such mild experiences as like and dislike, no wonder that it may become the target of stronger, potentially destructive emotions.

A case comes to mind, a widow of sixty-nine, a remarkable old woman. She lives alone, until recently above the small factory which was her pride. She had built the factory with her own earnings years before in order to set up her five sons in business.

When she first came to see me she thought she had suffered a heart attack, but there were no organic signs of an attack. Still, she did not feel well. She was weak, dizzy, depressed, had stomach pain and indigestion. Her blood pressure was high.

She was fighting the city, she told me, which had condemned the neighborhood in order to build a highway. She would have to move. Worse than that, the factory was going to be torn down.

Two years later I was called again to see her. She "felt like dying," she said, weeping. Her heart ached so that she could not breathe, could not sleep. The factory was gone, her boys could not find another location, and meanwhile one of her sons had died of a heart attack. "It's God's will—but as a mother my heart hurts," she said. Her heart was in fact greatly enlarged, and her blood pressure had gone up alarmingly.

Sometimes we can stave off the destructive process and gain a little time. In this case cortisone proved an effective medication, and the woman's sturdy will to live regained strength. Three weeks later she was well enough to come to the office for a check-up. Her blood pressure had gone down to normal.

Since then her sons have built a new factory, and again she

lives in the same small building with the shop. Her hostility against the city, against fate, has abated. She wants to live, now, for the sake of her four remaining sons.

Love and the Superego

A first heart attack is often reported after an emotional shock, a sudden death in the family (especially if the death is from a heart attack), a fright, or an experience of physical over-exertion. But these are the immediate precipitating causes. We usually do not know what emotional conditions may have prepared the heart beforehand for an attack or, in other words, what long-continued emotional stress had already brought the heart to the point of "breaking."

A night call summoned me to a man whom I had known for some time, a healthy man who in his fifty-three years had suffered nothing worse than a cold. He was in intense pain, breathing with difficulty, perspiring. There was every sign of a severe coronary thrombosis. From what he told me it was apparent that he had had a first attack two days before, which he had dismissed as indigestion, something which had only lately begun to trouble him. The present attack had begun during the afternoon, when he had gone to play golf. He had delayed calling a doctor until the pain was unbearable.

He was a most rebellious patient, and the next two days were an unremitting struggle to keep him from killing himself outright by disobedience to orders. He wanted to be moved to a hospital, though a move involved some risk. He insisted upon getting up to go to the bathroom, though he had been expressly ordered to remain in bed, and a nurse was present to care for his needs. He refused to accept the diagnosis by a leading cardiologist, though the case proceeded through the several stages with textbook precision; he telephoned his friends, not physicians, to reinforce his stubborn belief that he had nothing more than indigestion and that doctors very often mistake indigestion for a heart attack.

Most of all he wanted to be moved out of this apartment, if not to the hospital, then at least to a hotel. If a man had the money, he insisted, he should be allowed to spend it. The apartment, he swore, was a stinking hole.

Fortunately I knew this man and understood the reason for his rebellious behavior. Normally friendly, jovial, cooperative, he was at the moment a man in a state of overpowering rage.

He was a successful business man, unmarried, who had fallen in love three years before with a very beautiful young woman and wanted to marry her, but had refrained from doing so out of love and respect for his elder brother, who did not wholly approve. In the three years that had passed, the man had twice tried to give up the girl of his choice, without success. On the other hand, he had come with her to my office on two occasions for blood tests preliminary to marrying, both times when his brother was out of the city. In this man's inner judgment, his elder brother apparently represented that stern, conservative conscience which we call the superego.

What brought the patient's rage against me, himself, and fate to the boiling point was that he had gone to this young woman's apartment at the first attack of pain that afternoon. That was where I had found him, and now that I proposed to keep him there for four or five weeks, that would be where his brother would find him.

During the two periods of his separation from the young woman, this man had looked aged and unhappy. Yet he had been unable to take the decisive step of marriage in the face of what he understood to be his brother's disapproval. Now, when I rebuked him for his bad behavior, he told me that he "didn't care" whether he lived or died. It was clear that, having twice tried to defy his superego and marry the girl, and twice tried to get on without her, he had reached the point where he could find no way out of his dilemma.

From time immemorial, a physician has said to himself at a patient's bedside, "He has no will to live." In this case I would have gone a step farther and said, "He has a violent wish to die." So in desperation I telephoned the elder brother, described the situation, and told him that he could do more than the physicians.

When I visited the patient that evening there was a marvelous change for the better. The man had lost his harassed look. He was serene, cooperative, glad to be in "this nice apartment" instead of in a hospital. His brother had visited him for a long time that afternoon.

Four weeks later, a marriage was performed in the sick room. Several years have gone by and it has been a most successful marriage. Our patient attends to his business, goes fishing, plays golf, has not had another heart attack and insists he has never been ill in his life.

On the surface this was an average case. The man was a typical heart sufferer, successful, healthy, the type who does not complain, disregards warnings, refuses to accept the physician's diagnosis that he is actually suffering a heart attack.

But, significantly, not one of the factors generally offered as the cause for coronary thrombosis was present here. There was no evidence of arteriosclerosis; the patient's blood pressure was low rather than high. There was no history of rheumatic fever, the second most important cause of heart disease. Nor was there obesity, diabetes, myxedema, or syphilis, which are listed in that order as causes by clinical medicine.

Nor could the high pressure of life in our times be blamed in this case. The man was under no particular pressure. He was successful to the point where he could virtually neglect his business if he chose. If anything, he suffered not from pressure but from boredom.

The Man in His Fifties

We talked in a previous chapter about dangerous periods in life. The age of fifty is one of these, widely recognized in women because of the physical manifestations of menopause, but more obscure in men since male menopause, or climacteric, reveals no physiological changes as far as we know. We have said that at fifty a man feels he should have reached his peak of achievement, and if he has not, he begins to despair that he ever will.

But so many heart sufferers in their early fifties are men who have achieved success by any standard, often as a result of their own efforts, starting at the bottom. What shall we say of them?

Consider a man of fifty, who has achieved his material success, has sowed his wild oats, has enjoyed fully the venturesomeness of youth. All that is now past. What has he to look forward to?

His life has been one of action, not introspection. He is by inclination neither scholar nor philosopher. For most such men, there is nothing left but to grow old, and they have not taken time in the course of an active life to develop the reposeful arts, those which contribute toward growing old gracefully.

Fundamentally such a man would rather end life at its peak, while he is still in full possession of his powers. He wants to die with his boots on.

I have suggested that the man who suffers a heart attack is likely to be struggling not with business or money troubles but with, as the French put it, an affair of the heart. So often we find a man in his fifties falling in love with a young girl. We say that there is no fool like an old fool, that no good can come of such a bootless effort to recapture our lost youth. If such a man suffers a heart attack we say that he is killing himself trying to keep up with a young wife.

In its unsympathetic way this verdict can be the truth. To a man in his September years, love for a much younger woman is filled with anxiety. He cannot relax for fear that he will lose her, or be unable to content her. He is continuously mobilized to fight for her love.

Yet I have known cases in which not love for a young wife is involved, but sexual rejection, with the consequent damaging effects of stress. A business tycoon who came to me for a minor ailment confessed that he had an unhappy reaction in his sexual relations with his wife. A few months later he succumbed to a fatal coronary. In another case a wife came to me in tears after her husband's sudden death of a heart attack, and confessed that she had been rejecting his sexual advances.

A rejection in love can happen at twenty or twenty-five without fatal consequences. Youth is resilient, we explain. By this we mean that the heart muscle is physically young and can stand punishment. But we may also mean that to a young man life still lies ahead and there are more fish in the sea. In his fifties, a man may feel that he is losing his last chance for love. Without love he may not want to live.

Attack Without Warning?

We are repeatedly told that a heart attack comes without warning. It may be true that the patient has not complained about his heart. But so often we find that the victim of a "sudden" heart attack has been consulting his lawyer about his will, or has recently taken out a new life insurance policy. "Don't you remember, you gave me the keys to the vault the other day, and told me about those securities?" our patient's fiancée reminds him.

True, we all experience premonitions of sudden illness, of death. We say this is because we all carry within us the fear of death.

Shall we say that a premonition of death means that we are in fact going to die? Not at all. But it indicates that deep within us, at that moment, a dialogue is going on with our destructive instinct. We think of making a will, of taking out more life insurance, because we are concerned for those whom we may leave behind. We are concerned with our responsibilities. Is it not possible that we feel, at such times, burdened by these same responsibilities, actually tempted by a momentary desire to escape from them?

Like Columbus' crew we all wish now and then that we could turn back. We all have our moments of weariness, of dwindling hope or courage. For example, one day a man walked into my office in perfect health, medically speaking, and remarked, "At this moment I am worth more dead than alive." A few months later he was dead.

By the same token, the unconscious debate can reach an affirmative conclusion. We can take new courage, and go on. Between those who unconsciously decide for life, and those who give up, the difference seems to be one of purpose. The typical heart victim apparently lacks a continuing purpose which would carry him safely through this fiftieth-birthday pause for self-identification.

Heart and blood vessel disorders, the cardio-vascular group of diseases which Franz Alexander places on the competitive-aggressive side of the emotional scale, rank first by far in the list of man's afflictions today. They are responsible for more deaths in the United States right now than the next five most common causes put together.

Curiously, up to the age of five, diseases of the heart and blood vessels are present in four times as many girls as boys. But the proportion soon begins to swing to the other side, and by the age of thirty to thirty-four, men are five times as subject to heart and arterial diseases as women. From then on the greater susceptibility of men to heart afflictions increases steadily, reaching its peak in the age group of fifty to fifty-nine, principally with coronary thrombosis.

Why are men more subject to heart disease than women? Medicine has no clear answer. Perhaps an explanation can be found in the different roles men and women play in our culture. The man is typically the bread winner while the woman tends the home. True, more and more women are engaged in competitive activities in the business and professional world. But a man must still prove his manhood by his success, while a woman has always the open door of retreat behind her, the fact that she is after all a woman.

No matter what new attitudes we profess, no matter how far education may cease to differentiate between men and women, no matter how aggressively individual women may assert their equality and individual men accept it, the difference exists as a profound principle of our society. It is learned almost simultaneously with the knowledge of whether one is a boy or a girl.

We begin to understand the reasons why a man may take this path of self-destruction as soon as we begin to penetrate the protective armor of his noncommittal outward appearance.

The world demands of a man that he deal with it in an aggressive manner. He meets competition, aggression, hostility, and he responds in kind. When the going becomes too hard, or when he reaches a point where the game seems not worth the candle, he seeks a way out.

Such a man's habitual pattern of aggressive behavior can then take a morbid, destructive direction, and the organs which are active in this emotional pattern are the ones which come under attack. Of the group of diseases to which the aggressive pattern leads, an individual's choice of one rather than another depends upon his individual patterns of response, both physical and emotional. Individual differences lead to individual responses. One may develop diabetes, another a stroke, a third a heart attack.

Of arteriosclerosis, the leading physiological cause of a heart attack, clinical medicine still professes ignorance of the cause, and researchers still seek in vain the physiological reason why cholesterol is deposited in arteries, thickening them, causing rising blood pressure, and leading to possible coronary thrombosis.

Rheumatic fever, the second most frequent cause of heart disease, is even more of a mystery to the clinicians. When American medicine introduced the theory of focal infections some two decades ago, the explanation seemed especially applicable to rheumatic fever. Weiss and English suggest that it was because "medicine felt so helpless in dealing with this disease (rheumatism) and because there was often so much obvious indication of infection, that the concept of focal infection was eagerly grasped. European medicine never paid so much attention to the idea. Consequently Europe did not sacrifice quite so many teeth or tonsils on the altar of this concept."

Dr. George Draper in his work on constitution pointed out a relationship between physical and psychic factors. In rheumatic fever sufferers he found physical asymmetry, such as one eye higher in the face than the other, or one breast smaller than the other. He also found a striking disproportion between the mature size and development of the body and the "expression and gestures of extreme childishness."

Medicine has in the past been so desperate for a physiological explanation of what causes heart disease that it has grasped at almost any physical straw. As a young doctor-to-be I was taking my State Board examinations, and one of the cases I was given to diagnose was a heart disorder. I was presented to the patient and left there, to get the case history and all pertinent information. In this case there seemed nothing at all to account for the condition. The patient—it was a woman in her forties—had good teeth, good tonsils, no history that would give a clue. I was baffled, and frightened too, since so much depended on my working up a good case.

The woman smiled at me. "You're a nice young man—I'll tell you something I haven't told any of the doctors." What she wouldn't tell the doctors was that she had been smoking; she couldn't tell, because at that time it was not considered nice for a woman to smoke. Nor was it nice for a woman to buy cigarettes, so she had not bought them. She had taken the stubs of her husband's cigars, shredded the tobacco and rolled her own cigarettes. She had been doing this for ten or twelve years!

This was a very acceptable cause for a heart ailment, and I received an invisible pat on the shoulder for a good case.

Nicotine is one of the clinician's favorite villains in explaining a heart attack, along with caffeine and obesity. But shouldn't we look beneath the surface, and examine the tensions behind these excessive appetites for food, for coffee, for cigarettes?

Confronted with the Number One killer of our time, we

doctors no longer have the privilege of saying, "We don't know." Today we have the evidence of the endocrinologists and the psychologists, and serious students of psychosomatic medicine are constantly offering us new indications that heart disease cannot be laid to physical agents alone.

We are not likely to conquer this disease until we understand that the man who strikes at his heart is the victim of a struggle of which he is not conscious. He is in a state of mobilization for a battle which is never actually fought to a finish. He is wrestling with a situation which he can neither adjust himself to, nor withdraw from—except by death. A man of action, accustomed to sharp, quick decisions, may choose the sharpest, quickest decision to end his torture: a heart attack.

Concealed Hostility

"Whether a person falls ill somatically [physically] or socially [mentally] seems to depend on the quantity of guilt, anxiety, and hostility in his personality," write Doctors Edward Weiss and O. Spurgeon English. These two members of the Temple University faculty, whom we have already mentioned in connection with rheumatic fever and focal infection, have produced in their valuable study, *Psychosomatic Medicine,* one of the first collaborative publications by a psychiatrist and a medical man.

Hostility is an emotion which all of us experience, some more than others. None is spared it entirely. We differ only in degree. We pass a man in the street talking to himself, arguing furiously, with gestures and contorted facial expressions. We see a man behind the wheel of his car, angrily honking his horn when he is trapped in a traffic snarl. We suffer bruised ribs from a man or woman who pushes into a crowded subway or bus by the elbow method. Another person steps on our toes—and glares at us accusingly.

Some people, restrained by conscience from venting their

hostility on others, turn it on themselves. Often in traffic it is a tossup whether a man will dent another man's fender or his own.

In the ordinary struggle of life some hostility is inevitable. When we are frustrated, or treated unjustly; when we are disappointed in a reasonable expectation of a situation or a human relationship, we react with hostility. A burst of anger, an expressed protest, a counter-blow at the offender may relieve the hostile tension, and we go on about our affairs. It is normal to feel hostility on occasion, and it is healthy to express it.

But there are those who are chronically hostile, and who can never express their hostility. Congreve, who wrote so lyrically of love, also wrote, "Heaven has no rage like love to hatred turned."

We have been talking about the pattern of infantile dependency, of what happens to a child who has never had enough love and who grows into adulthood still hungry for love and for the parental protection which it implies. A more vigorous personality reacts not only with a need for love. He is also likely to build a pattern of suppressed hostility.

Such a person is a potential danger to himself and to everyone around him, even to society if he reaches a position of power.

The child learns early that open hostility is not acceptable. If he strikes his father or mother, if he breaks windows or otherwise damages property, even if he breaks his own toys, he is likely to be punished. And so he learns, in sheer self-protection, to mask his hostile feelings.

The jolly fellow who slaps your back, the hearty handshaker who crushes your bones, the sugar-sweet hostess who makes you uncomfortable by her extreme efforts to make you comfortable, all are expressing masked hostility. The seething hatred within them, so strictly censored that they will honestly deny its existence with their last breath, is completely disguised by surface friendliness, and the only clue to its presence may lie in the excessive quality of the friendliness. The innocent victim is baffled to explain the vague discomfort he feels in his relationship with such people.

A doctor brought me a letter from one of his patients, which had upset him. He himself was suffering from that recently fashionable ailment, a herniated vertebral disc, for which he had to wear a brace.

"This," his patient wrote him, "is how you show your overwhelming hostility toward your patients." There followed an acute description of the many little persecutions this man visited on his patients: how he kept them waiting long past the time of their appointments; how he stopped in the middle of treatment to tell lengthy stories, or to make telephone calls which presumably could not wait until he was free; how whenever a patient remarked that he had an engagement and must be out at a certain time, the doctor, though making apparently heroic efforts to be swift, always managed to be extra long about his tasks.

So many of these small tortures were administered under the guise of giving extra service to the patient, of showing extra concern. He would rush breathless to his first appointment, mentioning that he had skipped breakfast to be on time, but neglecting to mention that he had delayed getting up until the last moment. He would groan, bending over a patient, "Today I have to wear my *heavy* brace."

"What a wonderful fellow!" the patient was supposed to think, meanwhile suffused with guilt at forcing this suffering martyr to take care of him.

How did the doctor himself react to this sharp and uncannily just accusation? He reacted in a very characteristic fashion. "How bad people are," he sighed, "how lacking in consideration and understanding!"

Whether a man who suffers a rheumatic twinge in his arm actually wanted to strike his mother-in-law, we will let the psychoanalysts decide. But we know what effect emotional stress has on the body, what frustration and repression can accomplish through the unconscious neuroglandular system.

Mothers and Sons

We have seen how the impulse to fight mobilizes the body, and how, when the fight fails to take place, the tensions in artery and muscle remain. We can understand how hostility, the frustrated or repressed impulse to fight, may strike damagingly at a coronary artery, a muscle, or a joint.

Domination and dependence, and their consequent hostility, fear, and guilt, are clearly the background of illness in the following story of a mother and her son.

Robert G was tall, good looking, quick and fluent of speech, with graceful manners. He was in every way a charming young man, and he earned his living as a comedian. He had been troubled for some years with pain in his back and legs, and he gave his history in a normal, routine manner, an intelligent patient telling his troubles.

Yet it seemed to me that he stressed only the physical and medical side of his story, taking pains to avoid any reference to his personal life, to events or emotions in relation to his physical complaint.

A patient seeing a doctor for the first time is likely to be reserved about his personal affairs. But a reference to a marriage or a divorce or the birth of a child, a death in the family or a business reverse, almost inevitably slips out, if only as a jog to the memory in an effort to fix the time of an illness.

This young man made no such slips. Doctors are familiar with these patients, who talk about their illness on a determinedly physical level. They love the use of medical terms. They censor all personal information from their speech, as though they had something to hide. They are recognized as persons suffering from insecurity or from guilty fears. Sometimes the resistance to giving information is an expression of hostility, the wish not to oblige.

In an effort to break through the young man's reserve I

asked him to write down his history with whatever background of events he remembered. The neatly typewritten page and a half which he brought me on his next visit was a detailed account of his symptoms with precise medical explanations and the treatments he had undergone, but with his personal life still rigidly excluded.

He wrote that his illness began while doing hospital shows overseas, "which required several hours of standing on stage two or three days a week." X-rays showed "a wedge-shaped fourth lumbar and calcification of several vertebrae and both hip joints. Heat and manipulation plus the canvas support slowly caused relief of the pressure on the nerve issuing from the area of the affected spinal segment"—this is the patient writing, not a physician—"and cessation of pain. Treatment and canvas brace were discontinued after two years."

Some two years later, the account continued, "accidental tripping over an exposed tree root while walking in the woods caused an extreme twisting of the spine and severe impingement on the nerve—" and so on. This siege required perhaps a year and a half for recovery.

"It is my opinion," the patient suggested in conclusion, "that gentle exercise and the use of a hard mattress plus . . . a quarter-inch lift in the heel of the right shoe gave nature a chance to rebuild protective cartilage which insulated the damaged fourth lumbar thus prohibiting pressure on the nerve and providing complete relief. That and the determination not to be an invalid for life."

Yet a year later the pain returned and he again took to his brace. A year after that he fell ill with an acute stomach ulcer with hemorrhage and his life was narrowly saved by numerous blood transfusions.

Here is the background which the patient censored:

He had lived with his mother, a widow, until he married and established a home of his own. He was successful in his profession, but he refused to accept weekend engagements, which were the highest paid, because he needed the time to "rest up." He was making, apparently, a serious attempt to free himself from maternal dependency, but he overreached and sought to free himself from all dependency—that is, authority—such as routine work and fixed hours. He gave up most of his engagements, which he described as "immature and unsuitable for a grown man." He tried to earn a living in business but he had no success.

Let us go back to the beginning of his spine trouble. The "several hours of standing on stage two or three days a week" which he blamed for his trouble adds up to perhaps a day and a half of work a week. Compare this with a salesman's job which requires standing on his feet some six or seven hours a day five days a week. What happened at that time, after a year of unsuccessful, because unrealistic, effort, was that his marriage came to an unhappy end, and he admitted defeat in his aspirations toward independence and went back to his professional work.

The day on which he tripped over a tree root was the day when he learned that his mother had a malignancy. The pain in his back returned after his sister had come across the country to see him, and died in an accident. His ulcer was the climax of mounting guilt and resentment, first over his mother's death, then over his sister's.

His mother was an able woman who had carried on her own business for years to support herself and her son. Like so many competent women left alone to bring up a family, she was overprotective and dominating. She herself eventually realized this. About seven years before this history began, she quit her business, as she explained, "to give Robert some sense of responsibility for himself."

Robert professed to approve of her retirement. But several times when he talked of feeling overburdened by his own problems, the mask slipped and he said, "She could have kept on—it was a fine business."

The mother's own history makes us wonder how accidental an accident actually is. Thirty years ago she fell and broke her right arm. Six years later, in an accident, she injured her right knee. Six months after that, she tripped and injured the same knee. A few years later she tripped and again injured the same knee. Finally she developed a suspicious lump on her right thigh, which she dismissed as a bruise resulting from a fall. The growth was removed and a biopsy confirmed the suspicion that it was a malignant tumor. Despite all efforts the malignancy spread and a year later she was dead.

We have already learned that accident and coincidence need not be pure chance. Like a slip of the tongue, a slip of the foot may give a momentary glimpse into the vast and largely unexplored continent of the unconscious.

In her own words this mother revealed an emotional clue to her son's illness and her own. "He is a man, and should stand on his own feet. I am tired of standing on mine."

And later: "I thought he was a genius. He was always talking in millions. One day I realized it was all dreaming, not reality." And she added, in despair and defeat, "I have not helped him."

This man, haunted by guilt, torn between his need for the protection his mother too long provided and his pride which demands that he make his own way, cannot deal with these powerful forces beyond his understanding, without professional assistance. But when psychiatric help was suggested, he reacted as to an insult: "I'm not crazy!" He is making some effort at adjustment, but to seek medical attention is to him a sign of weakness and, unaided, his progress is slow.

A great deal of suffering of this mother and son might have been avoided with a better understanding of the emotional pitfalls which life presented to them. Over-protection in childhood, domination by a parent, and particularly the situation of a woman left to bring up a son single-handed, may cause misery in later years.

"So many laws argue so many sins," wrote Milton in *Paradise Lost*. We might paraphrase the line today and say, so many ills argue so many sins—of parents and educators.

9. ESCAPE INTO ILLNESS

THERE are times when we need to be ill.

There are times when we need illness as a respite from struggle: to regroup our forces, or to gain new perspective, or to mature a little. At such times illness is not a defeat, and the destructive instinct is not necessarily destructive.

We must not think of the creative and destructive instincts as antagonists locked in battle with each other. In health they work together to achieve the best of which we are capable. We thrive on the balance between the creative and destructive instincts. There is no conflict between them. The conflict, when it exists, is in the self.

Our conscious self, the ego, must represent our whole personality in our dealings with the world. The ego must weigh and judge external situations, and add up the knowledge gained by experience, for the protection and advancement of the individual. The ego must finally bring harmony out of the needs and desires of our instinctual self, the dictates of conscience, and the demands of society and the external world.

When conflict arises, the destructive instinct may become an ally of the ego in its attempt to restore harmony. There is the face-saving illness without which diplomacy or government could barely function. A minister resigns because of ill health; a conference is delayed because of the indisposition of one of the conferees. Behind the protecting façade of illness a new minister comes to the helm, a new policy is formulated, and the wheels are again set in motion in a new direction.

In its constant task of acting for the individual in his relationship with the world, the ego comes now and again upon an apparently insoluble problem. It encounters an inability to bring external conditions into harmony with inner need or desire. Or it meets a stubborn inner resistance to the adjustment necessary toward an external situation. The ego as secretary of state has negotiated a treaty abroad, but Congress —the home government, the inner self—refuses to ratify it. Hence the face-saving illness.

We get ourselves into these situations. We have acted on impulse or with poor judgment. We have not explored the full consequences of what we have committed ourselves to do. Suddenly we are trapped into doing something against our interest, or against our deeper wishes, or in violation of some standard of our integrity or honor. And we see no exit.

Then the destructive instinct may come to save us. "Reason is not the foe of the instincts, and illness not a curse," wrote the philosopher George Santayana.

A distinguished actress was rehearsing in a new play in London, when she collapsed with a sudden acute appendicitis. She was at the peak of her career; the play in which she had made her London debut had just concluded its run in an aura of brilliant success, with tributes from the press and a reception by members of the royal family. Now as the actress was hurried to the hospital for an urgent operation, colleagues and admirers deluged her with sympathy. What a pity that her new play had to be canceled, that her ride on the crest of success was brought to an abrupt halt. Her friends might have been surprised to learn that instead of mourning her lost laurels, she lay in her hospital bed in a mood of relief despite her pain. She alone knew that an appendectomy did not blight her career; it saved it.

During rehearsals of the new play she had become increasingly uneasy. The part, she felt, was wrong; instead of enhancing her first success the play might jeopardize or even destroy it. Her conviction grew, and she became desperate. To go on in the play would be disastrous; to withdraw during rehearsals, even more damaging to her reputation.

Walking the London streets she thought, "If I fell in front of a car . . . ?" But no—she might be killed, or maimed for life. To fall into the Thames? And be pulled out dripping— oh, no! Only in the theater could drowned heroines look glamorous, like Ophelia. And there was also the chance that she might really drown.

The opening was only a few days off when one night she woke in frightful abdominal pain. Hysteria, she told herself firmly, and tried to ignore it. But as the hours passed she grew frightened, and at last called a doctor.

There was no question about the appendix: the royal surgeon himself performed the operation. The appendix was not only inflamed but ruptured, and there were consequent complications. But the actress sailed through the physical suffering, happy to sacrifice her appendix for her career. She made a complete recovery, a new play with a satisfactory role was found, and her next opening confirmed the success of her debut.

Theatrical folk often live dramatic personal lives. We may think that only an actress could present such a clear demonstration of the interplay between mind and body. But everyday people have such experiences too, though the dramaturgy may be less professional.

A young woman in her thirties, a private secretary, was subpoenaed as a witness in a trial against a man to whom she was secretly engaged. As the date drew nearer she became nervous and harassed. Suddenly she developed a pain in her lower abdomen. She welcomed the news that she had to have a hysterectomy.

She was recovering from a successful operation at Columbia Presbyterian Medical Center, when news reached her that the trial had been postponed. "Then the operation was all for nothing!" she wailed, inadvertently putting her finger on the true connection between the trial and her illness. But the destructive instinct came to her rescue again. As she was about to be discharged, she developed a complication which required her to stay in the hospital several weeks longer. When she came out, the trial was in session. But since she was convalescing from a serious operation, the court excused her from appearing.

Illness in Self-Defense

An individual driven by an ambition which is not his own sometimes saves himself by unconscious measures. A son exerting himself to gratify his parents or a husband striving to meet his wife's standards of success may need illness in self-defense. I have as a patient a boy of sixteen whose mother is very proud of his mental capacity and constantly goading him to new efforts. Before every important examination he falls ill with an acute infection of some sort. He comes out a top student anyway, but still he approaches each test of his ability in a state of anxiety lest he fail to measure up to his mother's aspirations for him.

A store manager, whom I have known for some time, was strongly dominated by his ambitious wife. He liked his modest work but he kept doggedly trying to better himself out of fear that he might lose her respect. One Friday night he called me in great urgency. He was in excruciating pain from a sudden sciatica, so extreme that he cried out when I gently moved his leg or even touched the skin. He told me that he had to be well by Monday. He had a crucial interview for an important business opening.

The drugs which are usually effective in such cases produced no results. He was slightly better Sunday but worse again on Monday, and of course he could not keep the appointment. At the end of the week he dressed, moaning with pain, and went to the store.

A few days later the opportunity he had sought was awarded to a competitor. He had definitely and conclusively missed his chance. The following day he came to my office. He did not limp; his pain was completely gone. All he wanted was a sleeping pill so he could get a good night's rest.

Emotional Blackmail

We come now to a curious love story with the destructive instinct as a somewhat dubious ally. The story began quietly enough when an attractive young widow sent me a friend for examination, to determine whether he had actually suffered a heart attack some three weeks before.

I knew this friend, who had been driving the widow to and from my office during her own course of treatments, and who had made good-natured jokes about his unsuccessful courtship. He was a big, hearty man of thirty, rather a slow-moving companion for the dynamic little Mrs. L who had successfully carried on her husband's business since his death from a heart attack about a year before.

The young man's supposed heart attack had occurred when he was driving his car, and the symptoms were the standard ones: pain in the left side of the chest, numbness in the left arm, shortness of breath. At the hospital to which he was rushed, he responded in the normal way to the traditional treatment for heart attack. The hospital diagnosis was "possible coronary thrombosis." All clinical examinations were negative, including X-rays and several electrocardiograms. At the time of my examination, three weeks later, he had no complaints except that he felt very tired. He confessed to smoking about fifty cigarettes a day.

I found no pertinent symptoms, especially no sign of arteriosclerosis which is concomitant to a coronary thrombosis. The cardiologist confirmed the fact that there had been no organic damage to the heart, and suggested nicotine poisoning, or "an allergic reaction to a considerable secretion caused by a chronic sinus condition."

Up to this point the case is in no way unusual. Medically we would make nicotine and perhaps the stress of big-city life the villains. In spite of the absence of organic confirmation, we would consider the attack a serious warning and would advise the young man to take it easy.

Then the charming young widow attempted suicide, and the whole strange story came out. I discovered that she had been secretly married to the young man before she had sent him to me for examination. It was she who had wanted to know whether his "heart attack" had been real.

We must remember that her previous husband had died of a heart attack; that marriage, she had told me more than once, had been a very happy one. She had resisted this suitor until he suffered a heart attack, and then she married him.

If I had been able to tell her positively that he had suffered a heart attack, would she have attempted suicide, or would she have repented of her marriage in more subtle ways? No one can tell. As it was, she found herself committed to a man she did not love. Unquestionably, whether consciously or not, she felt she had been blackmailed into the marriage. A year later she was able to admit that she could not forgive him for the device by which he persuaded her to marry him.

Did the young man have a heart attack? He was too simple a man to be capable of consciously simulating a coronary thrombosis; he was not the actor for such a performance. He would have had to deceive an experienced hospital staff, both in the original attack and in his physical reaction to the drugs and stimulants which they administered to him.

Consciously he could not have known that a heart attack was the one way to break down the resistance of the woman he loved. He could have had no understanding of her guilt feelings toward her dead husband, of her fear that she might be responsible for another death of the same kind if she did not marry him. This was not conscious, deliberate blackmail.

Yet it was emotional blackmail, though unconscious. Freud half a century ago pointed out that disturbances of the heart function could be brought on by anxiety. There is no need for the conscious mind to know and enact the symptoms of a disease. There is no necessity for the conscious mind to understand that a heart attack would succeed with the desirable widow where all other efforts had failed. One unconscious mind understands another.

Little children know, without knowing, how to penetrate the defenses of grownups and get what they want. Why shouldn't the child within the man have the same skill? And if the need is great enough, the destructive instinct finds the route to work upon the organs of the body and accomplish the desired purpose.

The Shock Therapy of Illness

Doctors have observed that people who have gone through grave illness in their youth are likely to live long and in good health. I had a friend, a respected writer, who in his seventies was in excellent health and mentally as keen as a far younger man. He had been a premature baby, always delicate, painfully aware of the contrast between himself and a robust older brother who was an officer in the army. As a child his chances of living even to middle age were considered poor. Yet at seventy he was in sturdier health than any of his contemporaries.

It is a familiar pattern, the sickly child who grows up to be a vigorous man or woman. There are biological explanations, such as the development of immunity. But there is also another possible explanation. Such an individual often makes a strong effort to overcome his bad start in life. The prospect of inferiority, of perhaps an early death, seems to galvanize the will to live in many small but significant ways. Such an individual takes better care of himself, conserving his strength for the things he wants to accomplish. He strives creatively to make his days meaningful since he may enjoy fewer of them than the average man. In time by these efforts he does in fact overcome his weakness, and he goes on to a life of normal length and better than average health and achievement.

Illness, itself a response to stress, may also have the therapeutic effect of shock. As a matter of fact I have observed over the years that either sudden, dramatic illness or accident has the effect of shock therapy, not unlike the insulin and electric shock which are recognized therapy in psychiatry.

A. C. is a gifted fashion designer widely recognized in her field. There was a period in her life when she was involved in a relationship with a brilliant but difficult man. The relationship was unsatisfactory. She was unable to attend to her work, her business ran down, and one day she said to me, "I deserve to be hit on the head."

A few days later I was summoned to the hospital. She had tripped in the street and struck her head against the curb. I found her with a dangerous fracture of the skull.

During her convalescence I told her, not joking, that she had given herself perfect shock therapy, but of too dangerous a kind to be self-administered. The injury had missed by a millimeter a vital sector of the brain. She made a remarkable recovery, broke off her relationship with the man and took up her life again with vigor and effectiveness.

Taking Stock

If illness is shock therapy, convalescence is a time for taking stock, making decisions, laying out a new course. Despite the weakness of the body, the patient who has resolved in convalescence the conflict which precipitated his illness may return to normal life able to embark with great resolution toward a new goal. A woman patient married to a hopeless drunkard could not break with him until after she had suffered a serious physical collapse. She has since remarried and had a child and her new life is a very happy one.

I was called at three o'clock one morning to the bedside of a man I did not know. He lay moaning in pain, struggling for breath. His wife, a handsome blond woman, stood in the doorway with her arms crossed.

"There's nothing the matter with him—just tell him not

to eat like a pig," she said harshly. I shut her out of the room and made my examination. The man was in critical condition, with every sign that he had an occlusion of a coronary artery. The tense home atmosphere prompted me to advise the patient's immediate removal to a hospital.

His wife refused to let him go. The next morning at nine an older man, the sick man's father-in-law, was waiting in my office. Quite overwrought, he at once began to argue that doctors are often mistaken, diagnosing simple indigestion as heart attacks. By repeating that I could not be responsible for the man's life if he were left at home, I finally succeeded in getting the patient to the hospital.

The sick man spent four weeks in the hospital and then went away for a long convalescence to a quiet resort. He returned, got a divorce, and later married for the second time. That was ten years ago. He has not had another heart attack.

More remarkable was a call I had one day from a woman whom I had never treated. "Please take me to the hospital for a few nights—*I don't want to break down*," she said on the telephone. There was nothing physically wrong, but she was in an extremely tense emotional condition. I gathered that she faced a critical situation in her marriage, for which she needed a little time, a little perspective.

After four days, calm, confident, she told me she was ready to go home, and I discharged her. I am certain she resolved her situation, whatever it was. A woman with the wisdom to run away and consider her problem *before* she became ill more than likely learned how to deal with it.

Dependent Children

The struggle for emotional independence begins early in life, and for many it continues long into adulthood. For some, indeed, it is a lifelong battle which is never really won. American mothers have been attacked for their supposed tendency to hold fast to their children. "Momism" is regarded as a serious factor among some sociologists writing of the American way of life.

Yet it is doubtful—and not for me to say—whether other cultures differ in that respect or whether American mothers actually keep their children more dependent. In other societies, perhaps, it was the authoritarian father who, in a less tender role, had an equivalent influence on the child. This problem is better left to the sociologists.

But we must agree that, whatever may be the pattern in other times and other cultures, in this country today we find a very large proportion of both men and women who either accept passively the bond of the silver cord, or else struggle far into their adult years, and at great emotional cost, to sever it.

A parallel observation is the great number of grown men and women who suffer from one of the dependency group diseases.

The pattern of infant dependence is the harder to dissolve because it is unconsciously maintained by both parties to it, the parent needing to dominate and the child seeking protection. We think of the tie as existing chiefly between mother and son. It is hardly less prevalent between mother and daughter.

I remember a family of five. In 1941 the father, a European diplomat, had sent his American-born wife and three daughters to the United States to protect them against the hazards of the war. He himself eventually lost his life in an air-raid attack in London.

First to come to my office was Annabelle, the eldest daughter. She was thirty-two, tall, slender, with a colorful, dynamic personality which however gleamed only occasionally throughout the first interview. She talked about herself through a glaze of cautious uncertainty.

She was tired, jittery; her hands shook perceptibly. Her natural slenderness was marred by a thickening of the hips and especially of the legs. Her ankles were swollen and puffy. She complained of feelings of weakness, weariness; of palpitations, prickling sensations in her arms and heaviness in her legs. She remarked that these sensations left her only when she went to the country.

Medically her most marked symptoms were a hyperthyroid and a chronic gall-bladder disturbance causing dizziness, nausea, and other related distress. The thickening of hips and thighs in women has been interpreted as resulting from a lessened glandular function, in this case probably a consequence of emotional stress.

Annabelle had just been divorced. She claimed her husband was "a mental case who led me a fiendish life . . . I was constantly ill until I left him." With one child, she had gone back to her mother. She was torn between her duties toward her mother, her own child, and a desire to find a happier relationship with another man.

At the moment, Annabelle was perturbed and depressed. She was being pursued by a social lion and was tormented by her inability either to accept or reject him.

During her visits Annabelle talked of wanting to get away from home. She hinted delicately that living with her mother in a twenty-room house fully staffed with servants was less than perfect happiness. She longed, she said, for a simpler life. And after several months when she felt much better physically, she went with my consent to England, whence she continued to report faithfully by mail.

Her letters, covering a period of nearly four years, are a record of growing strength and maturity. At first she was helplessly dependent on her hormone injections, administered by her English doctor according to my prescription. But she wrote: "I would use any excuse not to come back." A year later she said: "I have definitely put [her suitor] out of my life. I feel contented and years younger, a different person . . . Have been losing weight." Again, after three months: "I am happier than I have been since I was eighteen . . . feel an urge to do things which I haven't felt in years."

Two years after her departure Annabelle came home, but cut short her visit. "My symptoms," she laughed, "are all raising their ugly heads—I must hurry back!" Her beauty, her charm had blossomed in the two-year interval. She struck me as a woman who was now at last coming into the full realization of her capacities. She stayed only three weeks and hastened back to England.

Another year passed. "No medicine so far . . . feel marvellous." Six months later: "I am bursting with spirits . . . have fallen seriously in love."

Annabelle is still abroad. Her latest letter discussed the danger of war in Europe and the question of whether she ought to come home. "Things will probably be bad everywhere so I may as well stay here!" she concluded cheerfully.

Ariane came to my office a year after Annabelle's first visit, as a result of the elder sister's airmail persuasions. She was thirty, more classically beautiful but less dynamic than Annabelle, a rather passive personality, in her present condition almost lethargic.

She had recently recovered from a duodenal ulcer but still suffered the symptoms and feared a relapse. Her nails were brittle, she had frequent rashes and swelling about the body and face, and when she forced herself to entertain or go out socially she collapsed afterward. She was fatigued, "in a terrible state of nerves—I constantly feel like screaming." Lately she had noticed her hips getting heavy, her ankles swelling, spoiling her looks.

As a child, she told me, she was kept in bed by her mother for long periods because she ran temperatures easily, "probably all due to nerves." Between the ages of eleven and thirteen she refused to eat and her weight dropped to forty pounds. She was not conscious of any resentment against her mother; her only spoken comment was that her mother had overprotected her as a child.

She complained of getting upset over the most trivial problems. Medically she was in fact near a state of collapse, with a blood sugar of fifty-nine; the normal range is between eighty and one hundred twenty. She had a mild gall-bladder disturbance and her blood sedimentation rate was high, indicating that destruction of tissue was going on somewhere in the body and suggesting that she still had some ulceration of the stomach. We will recall that peptic ulcer is grouped with other digestive disturbances as emerging from the definite infantile dependency pattern of emotional stress.

Besides medical treatment, Ariane welcomed guidance toward an understanding of her involved emotional situation. Two months later she groped for words to describe "a feeling of inner strength, a new feeling of self-confidence." She was better able to endure the difficulties of daily life. As time passed she talked less of her troubles and more of her child. She had hitherto left the boy almost entirely to a governess, uncertain of her own influence, but now she was spending time with him, taking an interest in his activities: "I try to correct the mistakes of my own childhood." This implied criticism was the only reference she made to her mother in these days.

A year later Ariane was making a mock complaint about going out too much, where previously she had been too tired to go out at all.

She comes only rarely now. She has no ulcer symptoms, her legs have slimmed down, and her nerves are quiet. Her growing emotional stability has enabled her to make a better adjustment to problems that used to upset her. In regard to her mother she makes no comment. In that, too, she has apparently reached a way of living with more serenity.

Audrey, the youngest sister, came to see me upon the insistence of Annabelle and Ariane. She was a soft-spoken, gentle young woman, who appeared frightened and harassed. With great concern she had noticed that it was increasingly difficult to get up in the morning and get dressed, or go out and shop, or do any of the things that are natural tasks for normal people. She attributed all this to her lack of energy, about which she could do nothing.

In her appearance she had become neglectful. Indeed, her drawn face, stooped carriage, and slovenly dress made her look much older than her twenty-nine years. She came in with her hair blown, her coat flying open, breathless, disorganized, seemingly on the verge of exhaustion and as though she had just made it to the office.

She complained of feeling low and being depressed. Her metabolism, which on the record was always low, was now minus thirty and one-half. She suffered intestinal irregularity to a troublesome degree. She had had an infection in her sinus which had persisted for nearly three years despite treatment. At first it had improved with penicillin, but then it had returned during a period of great emotional distress when she openly rebelled against her mother's domination. Audrey had recently put on considerable weight.

Her bitterness against her mother was intense. She said she had been driven to the point of choosing between killing herself and breaking with her mother. The specific issue in dispute was her proposed marriage to a decent man making a decent living, but one whose social status was scorned by her mother. Her first marriage had been to a man approved by her mother; it had ended in divorce. She had a child by that marriage. It was a difficult delivery in which high forceps were used and which was followed by a series of other complications. The child died a few days later.

Audrey, like her sisters, was quick to see the relationship between her emotional and her physical suffering. Like them she made a conscious attack on her emotional difficulties while cooperating in medical treatment. Her physical symptoms began to diminish. Her weight came down gradually without strenuous dieting or radical medical treatment for obesity itself.

She went with her husband to the country for the summer, and when she returned I scarcely recognized her. She had become a beautiful young woman; Botticelli might have used her as a model. In five months she had lost sixteen pounds. She still suffers spells of fatigue but she traces them to emotional involvement, and finds that when she deals with her problem directly her fatigue disappears. Audrey, like Annabelle, is on the way to realizing her full potentialities as a mature woman.

When Mrs. T herself became my patient I knew a good deal about Annabelle, little about Ariane and nothing whatever of Audrey except what I gathered from remarks of her older sisters. Of the relationship between the mother and her daughters I knew nothing beyond Annabelle's reserved suggestion that she herself was happier away from home. What I learned of the mother's destructive grip on these three grown women, I learned from her own lips.

She was in her fifties, tall, thin, well-groomed, with a reddish complexion and protruding eyes. Her complaint was frequent headaches, a dull pain in her shoulders and neck, an occasional choking sensation, and dizzy spells. Most of these symptoms were due to her high blood-pressure.

Her specific complaints were an increasing pain in the joints of her left arm, which impaired free movement of that limb. She found it difficult to get dressed or to comb her hair or even to eat without help. She was afraid of becoming totally crippled.

The examination revealed mild arthritic changes, for which a favorable prediction could be given.

Her troubles she blamed on her daughters with a violent feeling. They hated her, she said. They wished her dead so that they could inherit her money. She swore that Annabelle was a fool and Audrey was a disgrace to the family, running around with low people. Mrs. T's language was excessive in talking of Audrey.

The only one to whom she granted any sense was Ariane, who had made a "decent" marriage. But she complained that even Ariane was selfish. And as she talked about unkind hearts, she philosophized about how her children would treat her if she were poor.

Gradually Mrs. T emerged as a woman full of hostility, all of whose actions were dictated by this drive, thinly covered by conventional motherly expressions. Living alone in her Fifth Avenue home with a butler, cook, and maids, she had trouble keeping even these paid servants.

That she was insecure and unhappy was obvious. She relied on money and position. She was unable to appreciate human values or maintain human relationships. Her only satisfaction seemed to be in contemplating her costly possessions. Why she is as she is, it is not our business to judge. It is enough that of her three daughters, Annabelle has freed herself by running away, Audrey has cut herself off and taken refuge in her husband and child, and Ariane, though failing to gain complete independence, has made a tolerable adjustment.

Dependent Parent

Another mother of three daughters is Mrs. S, at almost the other extreme of the social and economic scale. She was a widow of sixty-seven, living alone in a small walk-up flat where she was supported by her daughters. Before she first came to me she had been going to a clinic for her heart.

"I can't expect you to do much for me at my age—all I ask is some relief for the few months I still may have to live," she said appealingly.

She complained of palpitations, dizziness, pressure and occasional pain around the heart. She was restless and did not sleep well. Examination revealed high-blood pressure, some enlargement of the heart, and occasional missed heart beats. Medically one might well agree with her that she probably had not many years to live.

All three daughters became my patients, and eventually the family picture became clear. The eldest daughter had quickly freed herself of financial responsibility for the mother, claiming economic difficulties and her obligations to her own daughter. The widow's other two daughters were living in anxiety and guilt. When they visited their mother they were distressed by her loneliness. When they left her they were anxious about her health. I discovered that whenever one of them failed to visit her for a few days, my elderly patient's palpitations and shortness of breath increased and her pains returned.

Mrs. S had been my patient for several years when her daughters decided that it was not safe for her to live alone, and the eldest daughter took the mother to live with her. After a few months Mrs. S was carried to the hospital in a serious condition with uremic poisoning, followed by lobar pneumonia. She recovered and went to live with her youngest daughter.

After not very long, the old lady found it increasingly difficult to get along with her third daughter's husband. The situation became intolerable, and Mrs. S went to live in her middle daughter's home. But after a few months there, the friction with her second son-in-law became so acute that she returned to her youngest daughter.

This sort of thing has been going on for fourteen years. Mrs. S is now past eighty, and still talks of having "maybe another month to live." Her second and third daughters, for whose sake, as she continually reminds me, she never remarried, are losing years of personal happiness. Both are childless; both live in constant tension with their husbands. Both suffer the repetitious, nagging illnesses of a life lived in unrelieved emotional conflict.

Unconsciously this mother seems to be driven by her destructive instinct into injuring her children. Whether it is the children who are unwholesomely dependent on parents, as in the case of Mrs. T and her daughters, or the parent who leans on the children as does Mrs. S, the powerful emotions involved make the situation of parent-child dependence one of serious stress. A breakdown into illness of one kind or another is almost inevitable.

Illness involves, of course, more complex processes than a mere desire to flee from a difficult situation, like the daughters of Mrs. T. Also it is more than a purposeful punishment of others, in the way that Mrs. S seems to be punishing her daughters.

Illness comes as a result of continued stress with no prospect of relief. These people who seem to flee into illness become ill because they live in continued stress, and they live in stress because they are unable to resolve a situation fraught with emotion. The illness takes a form characteristic of the individual's emotional pattern; with Annabelle and her sisters, the dependency pattern, and in Mrs. S's case one of unaware hostility. This is why Mrs. S appears to be using her illness as a weapon against her daughters.

Illness may be acute, a way of getting out of a temporary difficult situation. Or it may become chronic, if the situation continues to be unresolved. The illness into which these individuals escape is costly, and it may be tragic.

PART **III** THE ROAD BACK TO HEALTH

—To take arms against a
sea of troubles,
And by opposing, end them.

10. ALLIES AGAINST ILLNESS

ONE of my professors used to tell his students: "I may have
erred many a time in diagnosis, but never in my therapy."

He was not merely making a joke. Medical therapy, or treatment, has of necessity been mainly directed at symptoms. We
have given digitalis for the heart, quinine for malaria, sali-
cylic acid (aspirin) for rheumatic fever. Of the thousand
drugs in the pharmacopoeia, these and a few more have been
considered helpful for certain diseases. The rest are for symptoms: something to bring down fever, something to alleviate
pain.

With vaccines we first began to stir up the body to build
its own immunity against a specific infection. With a few
earlier drugs, and now more successfully with antibiotics, we
come closer to the cause of disease: we kill germs. Still we
have not attacked the condition which made the patient susceptible to the germ in the first place.

With hormones we come still closer. We try to restore
a weak link in the body's defense system against stress. In
other words, with the endocrinologist's findings, we are able
to treat an earlier stage in the chain reaction of illness.

But have we attacked illness at its source?

Biological medicine exerts its strongest medicinal efforts.
Yet, with what we know today, there is still something more
to therapy than even the most subtle medication.

159

The fight against illness cannot be made by the doctor alone. The fight must be a collaboration of both doctor and patient, a working together in the fullest sense of the word. The sufferer who has roused himself to go to the doctor at last has only begun his job. He cannot passively hand himself over to the doctor and say, "Here I am. Cure me." He must actively try to understand what is making him ill. He must actively work to retrace the path which has led to illness.

He cannot be expected to do this all at once, nor to do it alone. Distressed, in pain, suffering not only from his sick body but from the fears and resentments which illness itself sets up, he must first have all the help which medical science can give him. He must be comforted in body and mind before he can be asked to take up arms in his own defense against illness.

The fight against illness is an alliance. But the doctor, the strong ally, equipped with his arsenal of scientific weapons, fights the first battle.

The Vicious Circle of Illness

Mrs. M, a woman approaching forty, came to me with complaints of colitis, fatigue, and migraine.

She was trim, chic, looking perhaps thirty. Competence gave a bright finish to her appearance and all her gestures, and an alert intelligence shone in her face. She seemed a model of that unique product of our culture, the American woman, eternally young, quick, and vital, capable both at home and in the business or professional world.

It is hard to believe that such women ever need the services of a doctor except to deliver their children. They seem equal to any situation, and it is difficult to imagine them ill.

But perhaps for the very reason that they are so capable on so many fronts, that they must meet so many kinds of demands both intellectual and emotional, intelligent modern women lead lives of considerable conflict and struggle, and they form a large part of the population in the doctors' offices. They do fall ill, and they do need help. This one did.

She had suffered first from a hyperthyroid condition for which she underwent an operation. Her first marriage ended subsequently in divorce, and she embarked on a career. Then she married again.

Now her pattern of illness took a different turn. From the overstimulated thyroid, a symptom related to the aggressive pattern, she reverted this time to the regressive side with colitis and fatigue, signs that she craved love and protection, and relief from responsibility. But she also suffered from migraine, a symptom of suppressed rage, on the aggressive side of the scale.

It is characteristic of the woman of our time that she undertakes, whether by choice or of necessity, rather more responsibility than one person should carry. A not infrequent consequence is that she rebels against the burden while conscientiously she continues to discharge her obligations. All of Mrs. M's ailments are symptomatic of this conflict.

Also, like many such women, she resented her illness. She had no time to be sick, she said. She had too many important things to do. Illness was for her no escape from responsibility, but an unwarranted disruption of her busy schedule. Moreover it was the cause of still more guilt piled on top of the burden she already carried.

This is the vicious circle of illness, from conflict to illness and back again to a sharpening of conflict because of the new problems set up by illness itself.

It is the doctor's first task to break through this vicious circle both by word and by deed. Only when anxiety is quieted, resentment allayed, and the pain of illness abated, can the patient take up his share of the real work of combating illness.

The first step is, of course, the obvious one of thorough physical investigation, both of the specific symptoms and of the patient's general condition. In this case, as in many others, the patient could honestly be assured that, according to the precise techniques which modern medicine has for examination, there was no organic illness.

Like most patients when they are relieved of their primary anxiety, she relaxed and began to talk. If there was nothing wrong, why was she sick?

"Don't tell me," she said, "that it's just nerves. I've heard that one too often."

She really wanted to know why she was sick. When a patient honestly wants to know, the first obstacle, that of resistance, is already hurdled. She wanted to know and she had a right to know. We talked about functional disturbances, and their origin in the emotions. We set up a diet to relieve her colitis, which was an independent medical problem no matter what its origin. We worked out medication to restore functional balance, and enable the patient to meet her difficulties with greater physical stability. This is the second step in the doctor's effort to free the patient from the vicious circle of illness.

In every relationship between doctor and patient there comes a moment when the doctor sits with all his charts, tests, and diagnostic findings before him, and the patient waits for the verdict. The patient is mute, thinking, "Now he knows more about me than I know about myself."

But the doctor can say truthfully, "Now I know everything about the illness of your body which modern medicine can discover. But about the cause of your illness, you alone know, and you alone can reveal it. Medicine can help you in your search, but yours is the task of seeking, and yours the gratification of its discovery—and the conquest of your illness."

In pursuit of the cause, I asked the patient for one more thing: a record of her symptoms, when they recurred, with what intensity, and what was the background of events or of her emotional reactions to events.

The question arises, if the origin of illness is emotional, that is, "mental," why do we not go to a psychiatrist? The answer is, we do. A medical man does not undertake to diagnose or to treat psychiatrically a patient suffering from severe personality disorder, and the psychiatrist is one of the specialists upon whom he calls, just as he calls upon the cardiologist, the neurologist, the gynecologist. In some cases we need a whole constellation of specialists.

At one end of the scale there are the acute cases of organic illness which require the quick action of the surgeon. At the other end of the scale are patients whose emotional conflict is such that it may best be helped by the psychiatrist. But between the two is the large mass of men and women, those who properly come within the province of the medical doctor, all the people who are struggling with the ordinary problems of living and who have reached a point where the weaknesses in their emotional constitution and the weaknesses in their physical constitution have together brought them to the point of illness.

In my experience, these people can be helped to understand the cause of illness within themselves, and when they understand it they can deal with it. It may be true, as Dunbar has declared, that eighty per cent of people walking around this country are in a neurotic condition and need psychiatric help. This does not mean that they cannot help themselves, nor that a medical doctor cannot help them. He does not need to throw half-understood psychiatric terms and explanations at their heads. With most sick people, he needs only to take the same interest in the patient's personality as in his illness. He needs only to listen as a human being to another human being in trouble.

Most patients can deal with their difficulties enough to get back on the right track. The cure may not be perfect. In a crisis they may again fall into the old emotional pattern and feel again the familiar symptoms of the suffering organ. But neither has psychoanalysis or psychotherapy a high score of permanent cures. In times of stress the patient comes back again to his psychiatrist for help over the rough spot.

Mrs. M was typical of this great mass of people who, once they know why they suffer, are able and eager to work toward the emotional health which will mean their physical health. At first the medication showed only moderate results. Her symptoms abated but did not disappear, and with every new situation which produced emotional stress, she suffered intense recurrences.

As she faithfully kept her record, however, she began to see a relationship between the events in her life and her sieges of colitis or headache or spells of fatigue. With each visit she wanted to know more about the way emotional disturbance affects the body, about the pathways from the emotional to the physical, about the effects on the organs of chronic emotional stress.

When she learned of the two groups of diseases and their relationship to the two basic emotional patterns, the aggressive and the regressive, her reaction was like that of Balboa discovering the Pacific. She went away very thoughtful.

It is difficult for each of us to face his inner self. We need time and patience to trace the path from emotion to illness. To understand with the mind is comparatively easy. To understand with the emotions—that is, to recognize and accept the necessity for changing one's emotional patterns—is more difficult. Inertia is a law of nature. The mind, like the body, like the physical world around us, resists change. We must apply power to move a stationary mass. In the same way, we must apply power to move ourselves out of old pathways of emotional response and physical reaction.

We have the power: that positive force within us, the will to live. This is the powerful ally of those whose profound wish it is to be well. In response to their rational, conscious effort, the will to live rises to their aid in a thousand big and little ways.

It is hard for a woman like Mrs. M, for all the Mrs. M's, so competent, so self-reliant, to realize that she needs love and is sick for the lack of it. It is hard for her to face her hostility toward her work—which interests her—and toward her husband, even toward her children. It is hard for her to accept the fact that all of us show two sides to those we love best, that we are both loving and hostile in some degree.

But women, I have found, are inclined to be more realistic

about themselves than men. They are not dogged by the "sissy" complex which demands of men that they be manly at all costs. There is nothing shameful to a woman, even to a very modern woman, about wanting to be loved.

After Mrs. M had been my patient for some time, her husband telephoned. He was outspokenly dissatisfied with his wife's treatments. "If she is sick she should go to a hospital and be operated on, like everybody else," he said.

Mrs. M submitted to her husband's demand and went to a physician who gave her mild sedation. But she would not submit to an operation. Instead she took a trip to Europe.

A year later she was back in my office. All in one week, her daughter had gone away to college; her stepson, of whom she was very fond, had gone into the army, and her sister had moved to another city. Her colitis had come back, and she felt her old state of fatigue. But she had no headache. She had observed that her husband was also shaken by this series of separations, and she felt only sympathy for him, no hostility. All she wanted was a little help over this spell of trouble.

"Now I know why I'm sick," she said.

Her next appointment was unnecessary. When she called to say that she felt fine and did not need to come to my office, she added: "I'd like a chart of those two groups of diseases. I want to hang it over my bed, to remind me."

Patient on the Defensive

The doctor's first task, that of breaking through the vicious circle of illness, is not often as easy as it was with Mrs. M. The doctor's personality and the authority of his knowledge, what used to be called his "medical art" or, less respectfully, his "bedside manner," was formerly his principal weapon against the hostility, resentment, and fear which patients bring with them into his office.

Now the doctor also has scientific weapons, with which to breach the patient's defenses and get at the real trouble.

Equipped with better understanding of the emotional origins of illness, and a knowledge of the physiological channels by which emotional disturbance acts upon the body, the physician can use medicine as well as what we inaccurately call "psychology."

An ulcer patient who has been to many doctors comes in with resistance bristling under his good manners. He waits for the doctor to say, "Barium test." He has made up his mind he is not going through that again, for the sixth or tenth time. He waits for the doctor to say, "It's all in the mind." But his pain is in his stomach, and the pain is real.

He has been through all the tests and submitted to all the traditional treatments. He has gone to a reputable psychiatrist, and has rejected the deep probing into his personality; it made his pain worse. He has come to still another doctor now because he is suffering and unable to function at his work. But he has begun to look upon doctors, all kinds, as strangers who make tyrannical disposition of his mind, his body, and his bank account.

But the wise doctor does none of the things the patient is waiting for him to do. He does not scoff at the pain as being "all in the mind." He does not dismiss tension and anxiety with the useless advice, "Stop worrying—take it easy," since these are precisely the things such a patient is unable to do, or he would not have an ulcer in the first place. Nor does he ship the man, in pain, off to a round of tests and X-rays.

He gives the patient a pill. Precisely what the pill is does not matter. Some doctors use one, some another; it is designed to relax the stomach spasm which causes the pain. With the pill goes an explanation.

This pill, says the doctor, will not cure your ulcer. Your ulcer is the end result of a great number of things, both emotional and physical. You cannot tackle all that now. First we must give you a breathing spell, a release from pain. Then we'll see.

The doctor, aware of all the physical and possibly dangerous connotations of the patient's condition, badly wants his tests done. He wants to eliminate any organic disease. But he must weigh the risk of waiting. Such a patient has an ulcer for the very reason that he is fighting his own need for dependence, for someone in authority to take care of him. He does not want to be pushed. He wants to make up his own mind. He is disarmed when the doctor does not even offer to make an appointment for the next visit. The patient goes away knowing that the decision to tackle the larger problem of his illness is still in his own hands.

Usually this patient calls for his next appointment in a very different frame of mind. The pill has relieved his pain and the explanation has relieved his hostility. "For the first time, I can think," he says. "What do we do now?" From then on—not always easily, not without setbacks—this patient is able to be a cooperative, intelligent partner in the larger task of changing the physical and emotional patterns which brought about his illness.

The Hostile Patient

A more pervasive hostility is found in the kind of patient who is suffering, for example, from high blood-pressure. His wife telephones for an appointment for him.

"Frighten him a little, doctor," she says. "Get him worried about his heart, so he won't smoke so much." It is obvious she has bullied her husband into going to the doctor, and expects to bully him back to health with the doctor as her accomplice. She does not realize that by such an approach she is reducing a grown man to the stature of a child. She is the wife-mother, dominating him "for his own good."

It is not surprising that he rebels, and, suppressing the rebellion, he suffers one of the chronic effects of hostility, an elevated blood pressure. We may assume that this pattern of suppressed rebellion and hostility was laid down long before, probably in childhood, and probably in relation to a similarly dominating parent. Now the continued emotional stress has had its effect at last on his arteries, and this is a medical problem.

But with such an introduction from his wife, the doctor may expect his patient to be hostile not only to the wife who badgered him into coming for an examination, and to others in his life situation. The man is bound to be hostile to the doctor as well, and to any diagnosis or treatment he may suggest.

You cannot get very far with a man who is figuratively pointing a gun at your head. You must first get him to lay the gun on the table. Then you can talk things over.

But he is not likely to lay the gun down if you ask him politely, or even if you command him with your authority as a physician. He may listen, but he will not hear. His hostility is unconscious; unconsciously it has dominated his behavior for years. Persuasion must be of a more subtle variety.

So we offer him a choice. We can give him temporary, superficial relief with conventional medication. Or we can take the next step, and determine what functional disturbances have developed in response to the stress of living. We tell him that we have ways of restoring balance, regardless of the origin of his hypertension. Then, when he is freed of his physical discomfort, he will be better able to deal with whatever is at the source of his illness.

He is a business man, and he knows that a business cannot run at a deficit. He understands that we must first balance the books.

The mind governs the body, but the condition of the body also affects the mind. There is no need to prove this out of the multitude of studies of people suffering from starvation or other physical conditions. We see it in our everyday life. A clever wife does not ask her husband for a new hat until after he has enjoyed a good dinner.

So with the bristling patient in the doctor's office. We do not cure his hostility. But by restoring functional balance we check the effects of stress on his system. By relieving some of his physical tensions, we soften the inner climate in which he must do his thinking. We persuade him, for the moment, to lay the gun on the table. Then we can proceed to enlist his conscious aid in the attack on his illness.

The Fearful Patient

Fear is another obstacle which the doctor must remove before the patient can become his ally. In medical practice, an acute illness is recognized as an emergency which demands prompt action. Fear can also be an emergency.

We have mentioned earlier that fear is often ignored in the practice of biological medicine, as are other subjective feelings of the patient to a greater or less degree. Out of sheer humanity a doctor may give an obviously frightened patient a reassuring word. But the patient who by great effort masks his fear behind a controlled exterior does not ask for such patronizing kindness, and generally he does not get it.

Yet fear is an emergency. Fear turns discomfort into pain, and turns severe pain into unbearable pain. Fear, built up over days, weeks, even months, has become acute by the time the patient has nerved himself to go to the doctor, and it must be dealt with promptly.

The fear that we are harboring a fatal disease is very common. Many people delay going to the doctor, unable to face the moment when their fear will be confirmed. This in itself is a self-destructive act. If there is a disease, the delay has wasted time during which the disease may be arrested or perhaps cured. If there is no disease, the continued fear is a needless torture; we know that a chronic state of fear can harm the body.

Terror can hide behind a calm, composed face. The doctor, assembling his diagnostic findings, must stop to deal with it, because the sooner he can dispel fear with knowledge, the sooner he has the patient as his ally against illness. The man with his inner eye fixed on the specter he fears is a demoralized soldier who has lost all hope of victory. Most of his energies are diverted to controlling his terror and displaying a calm exterior to the world.

Take for example one of my patients, a man in his fifties, a successful business executive with a high reputation and no financial worries. The exaggerated calm of his manner, his pallor, and a certain tense look revealed that he was in the grip of fear. For a month he had felt a soreness in his throat, not like a cold but like something stuck there which he could not swallow but which caused a constant tickling sensation. During the past week he had been increasingly tired and low in energy. He should have come before, he said apologetically. Now, he murmured almost inaudibly, it was "probably too late."

There was no need to mention what he feared. Naturally his mind dwelt on cancer of the throat. Mechanistic science demands that a thorough objective investigation should come first, no matter how long it might take, and that the patient's fear is of no importance. Since he had taken his time to come for examination, a few more days could scarcely matter.

But in such a situation, a delay of a few days, even a few hours is too much. Such a patient should not be sent home to suffer additional nights of self-torture before the diagnostic round of tests and X-rays can be completed.

So within the next twenty minutes this patient was in the radiologist's office being X-rayed. The films showed that there was no growth. The more detailed tests took longer, but at this first reassurance his fear receded, and he could talk.

He was smoking some sixty cigarettes a day. In addition, we discovered that an overconscientious housekeeper was spraying the closets at home with DDT, and one such closet was beside the head of his bed so that he was probably breathing the irritating fumes at night.

The spraying was stopped. Then after we discussed smoking, especially to such excess, as a self-destructive act, the patient gave up his cigarettes. In a few days all his symptoms disappeared.

This patient returns every so often, but not with his throat symptoms or his fear. He is smoking again, though not so heavily, and he engages in bouts of intensive work which result in fatigue. He understands that his way of life is in some respects self-destructive but like most of us, he likes his way of life and sees no pressing need to change it. He is active and creative enough, apparently, to counterbalance his mildly destructive habits. According to his medical record to date, he is maintaining himself in very good health.

11. INCURABLE?

"INCURABLE" is a fateful word. It has the finality of a slammed door. Yet doctors are driven to use it in many cases of chronic illness. When, on the record, every method known to scientific medicine for a specific ailment has been tried without success, it often seems to a doctor more wholesome to tell the patient that he must learn to live with his trouble, than to send him out again on the costly disheartening search for a cure which apparently does not exist.

But how many incurables are really incurable?

A woman of fifty visited my office with an "incurable" arthritis. Almost before she sat down she announced that she had determined never to go to another doctor, and had come only because a friend had nagged her into it.

She had had rheumatism since childhood. For the past four months she had had a sharp pain in her back and down her leg. She was full of bitterness against an osteopath, whose treatment she blamed for a new pain in her neck. It became clear that she was willing to submit to examination mostly in the hope of discovering some damage the osteopath had done so that she could sue him.

Her manner was witty and charming, but the camouflage was thin and an observant listener could hear hostility in every word she uttered. Her face, which showed remnants of youthful prettiness, also revealed hostility. Her features were sharpened and her mouth was compressed into a straight hard line.

Five years before, she had been in an automobile accident
172

with her husband, who had never before had an accident while driving. She dated the onset of her arthritis from this event. Of course she was not conscious of it, but she plainly nursed a grudge against her husband.

The patient slept poorly and was depressed. On this day, for example, she told me she had had no sleep at all the night before, was in pain from her shoulders to her toes, and felt "like jumping off the bridge." A doctor friend had told her it was all nerves and she must snap out of it.

As a starter, we used high doses of vitamins and other medication which had shown good results in arthritis. The patient submitted to treatment physically but resisted in other ways. As the weeks went by and her pains disappeared from her neck, her back, her legs, she concentrated on the shoulder pain which she still felt, complaining that it was excruciating, and she complained too of splitting headaches.

Although her improvement was obvious, her recently developed pattern of resistance did not allow her to admit it. Menopause, to many a time of stress, often brings out hostility.

As it happened, I knew of a party she had gone to, not long before, at which she had sung and danced like a young girl.

The following winter, some nine months after the patient had first begun her visits, we instituted cortisone treatments. Her improvement then became very marked. Even her face changed, softening noticeably.

After four treatments the patient interrupted this course for a trip out of town. Several months later she returned, with a mild recurrence of her old symptoms, some new symptoms, and an outspoken resistance to cortisone although it had helped her. This patient's vacillating response to treatment is one example of many who show permanent improvement only when they can change their basic emotional pattern.

A patient's determined persistence along a self-destructive course may explain many unsuccessful cases of medical treatment, as well as failures of psychotherapy. As Doctor Karen Horney says, "If there is no sufficient will to live, a person will go to pieces anyhow, analysis or no analysis."

Illness of Dependency

The hostile patient, one who is suffering from a disease developed out of aggression, is an individual who has tried to make an adjustment to difficulty, though an unsuccessful one. The regressive personality has not tried to make an adjustment at all. He has withdrawn from the difficulty, seeking refuge in parental protection and care.

The regressive personality is likely to be more cooperative on the surface, since his tendency is to seek help and the doctor is a person who will try to help him. Underneath, however, this type of individual has resigned from the struggle of life to a greater or less degree. He wants the doctor to do everything for him. He is unwilling to become an active ally against his illness.

The man with the thirty-year-old ulcer, mentioned in an earlier chapter, was an example of this. When his son, and then his grandson, appeared in my office with symptoms of the dependency pattern, one could see the long shadow cast by chronic illness over an entire family. As the Bible puts it, the fathers have eaten sour grapes, and the children's teeth are set on edge.

Fortunately most people are neither entirely aggressive nor entirely regressive. A purely dependent personality is rare, at least in a doctor's office. Most of us, though we may seek protection and love, still make some effort in our own behalf. Pride, the "sissy" complex which makes so many dependent individuals overaggressive in compensation, are evidences that we are trying to adapt ourselves to our environment although the adaptation is a poor one.

The elderly ulcer patient's son, a man of thirty-nine, was suffering attacks of heartburn. He revealed that he had had asthma since childhood, except between the ages of thirteen and twenty-one. He appeared happy at home and successful in business.

But behind him there was always the figure of his father, about whom he and the entire family were constantly concerned. Throughout most of his childhood, the family life had revolved around the father's "condition."

Now we have already said that asthma, like gastric ulcer, is considered one of the diseases of dependency. The son of the ulcer patient had been told that his asthma was incurable, and he had also been told that he was allergic to some variety of dust which so far had not been discovered in a long series of scratch tests.

In the course of medical treatment, the patient began to understand that the close relationship with his father was at the bottom of his illness. His excessive concern for his father's health was an expression of his need for dependence on his father. His father, also a dependent personality, was unable to give him the strong support which he had craved in childhood, and the need persisted unsatisfied into maturity.

The fact that the son had been free from asthma during his adolescent years was interesting. It suggested that during those years of growing strength and self-assertion he had achieved a temporary independence, but that with the struggle to face adult life and responsibility in his twenties he had slipped back into the childhood pattern of dependence.

This patient responded very quickly. His heartburn was the first of his symptoms to disappear. During a chest cold which he contracted, he had no asthma. His visits continued from November to March, a total of fourteen. But his recovery really began on the day he started to understand the connection between his asthma and his relationship to his father.

Fortunately other circumstances were favorable. A happy marriage, a successful business, and a strong wish to be well and enjoy his good fortune—perhaps also the example of his father's life of chronic illness—helped him to achieve a conquest of his asthma in a comparatively short time.

When his cure was well on the way, he brought me his twelve-year-old son. The lad had been suffering from summer allergies; significantly, the allergies first made their appearance at the time a younger brother was born, always a period of stress for the older child. Lately the boy had been having violent spells of sneezing, morning and night. He had been told he had a chronic sinus condition.

The boy admitted that he did not like school. He felt "gloomy." A catarrh of the sinuses was present.

A single visit and a small amount of medication was enough to clear up the boy's sinus condition. One can hardly claim credit for medicine alone in this cure. At home, the overcast of chronic illness in which the boy lived was lifting. As the father felt better, the boy was less disturbed. The father was turning from his painful concentration on his own father, the elderly ulcer patient. The younger man was freed to enjoy his own family. This, he now understood, was his proper responsibility as well as the source of his natural satisfactions. He was also able to perceive his young son's emotional insecurity before the competition of the little brother, and to help the boy make an adjustment to the necessity of sharing his parents' love.

Another patient, a small business man, is living comfortably with a gallstone the size of a cherry.

This is a man in his fifties, who for nearly ten years had been suffering from continuous stomach trouble. He had good cause for his anxiety. Most of his family were caught in Germany during the Hitler regime, and his efforts to rescue them were repeatedly unsuccessful.

On his first visit, suffering from acute anxiety, he was given medication to relax the digestive paroxysm which was causing nausea and vomiting. He swung back and forth during the next few years between stomach disorders on the one hand, and neuritis and skin eruptions on the other. These alternating illnesses seemed a classic reflection of his emotional distress: on the one side his longing to be relieved of the responsibility for his family which cruel circumstances prevented him from carrying out; on the other, his resentment against the Nazi persecution about which he could do nothing.

When he received news at last that his family were all lost, his ailments returned with double force. One day in 1947 he developed acute pain, and the unusually large gallstone was discovered.

This man surely had ample external cause for his illness. He was an indirect victim of one of the most barbarous episodes in the world's history. The question remained, could the damage which his body had suffered be repaired?

Gallstones are usually dealt with by surgery, and for such a large one an operation would seem the only recourse. When he understood the connection between his years of anxiety and his illness, however, the patient was willing to try getting along with his gallstone.

He realized that he must accept the tragedy of the past philosophically, and it is true that mass tragedy, in which our suffering is shared by many, is somewhat easier to bear than personal tragedy which must be endured alone. The patient also realized that he must not allow himself to become involved in emotional disturbances. He would have to live rationally, as a mature human being.

This he has been able to do with enough success to live and work in comfort. He has not had a gall-bladder attack for four years. He can eat almost everything. An occasional mild indigestion does not alarm him. He knows that stress brings it on, and that he can overcome it.

History of a Headache

With young people the word "incurable" must be used with the utmost care. To saddle a child with a conviction that he or she is permanently handicapped may cause incalculable damage to the personality, far more serious, indeed, than the physical handicap.

In some cases, of course, it cannot be avoided. There are conditions of actual destruction of nerve and muscle tissue, as in paralysis resulting from polio, which we may ameliorate but may not be able to eliminate altogether. It is better for both the child and his parents to concentrate their efforts on developing the capacities which remain, rather than in the hopeless attempt to restore the damaged limbs.

But where tissue damage is not apparent, we have no right to condemn a young person to an incurable disease. We have youth on our side, with its resilience of both body and mind, its willingness to learn, to change, to grow. In youth the patterns are not likely to be rigidly set, either emotionally or physically. When we close the door to hope with the word "incurable," we may be making a costly mistake.

With youth we have still one more valuable advantage in our attack on illness: the emotional pattern behind a young person's suffering is often dramatically clear. We also often have the parents still alive and very much on the parental job. The sharp edges of an unsatisfactory parent-child relationship usually show up in some way, and it is usually this relationship which is at the bottom of the child's illness.

One day a father brought in his son, a university student, who had been suffering from nausea and stomach pains for the past eight months. He had a history of frequent disabling headaches dating back to the age of seven, when he was struck with a golf club and received a severe skull fracture and concussion. A skull operation was performed at the time to remove blood clots; the extensive scar was a visible reminder.

The boy had had regular check-ups for his headache, and had been told repeatedly by various doctors that they were a consequence of his accident, that there was no remedy for them, and that he must learn to accept this permanent handicap which would limit his capacity throughout his life. The youth admitted that he was depressed, and well he might be.

These were the complaints which he voiced. Also pertinent was the observation that he had a bad acne, and that although he was almost six feet tall, his hundred and sixty pounds was twenty pounds too much for his age. He had the fatty thighs and lower abdomen which signify incomplete masculine development. His build suggested the type which in childhood has an overfunctioning pituitary causing early rapid growth—

the quick, alert lad who runs instead of walking. Under the stress of adolescence the overfunction in these boys may drop below normal, with the consequence of rather effeminate physique in young manhood.

After a reassurance that the headaches would probably respond to treatment, the father took over the interview, mainly to talk about himself. He told with a complacent smile of how he had worked his way through college, had acquired three academic degrees, and had built a successful business. Every boastful word was a gloved blow at his son's inadequacy. .

I remarked that something ought to be done to relieve the boy's feeling of inferiority, so greatly intensified by the medical verdict that he was permanently handicapped.

The father corrected me. "You don't understand—he is quite the opposite, difficult and demanding." To the suggestion that there was such a thing as overcompensating to cover one's real feelings, the father did not respond. But behind his parent's back the boy winked at me.

Silent and hostile until that moment, from then on the young man relaxed, and when we were alone he confessed that he felt himself different from the other fellows, that he was belligerent and did not get along well with his fraternity brothers.

At my request the boy kept a record of his headaches, their frequency and intensity. He brought in an admirably worked-out chart, with symbols devised by himself in a scientific manner. The chart revealed that his headaches were periodic, in a cycle suggesting the female menstrual cycle. This and other evidence indicated a decreased functioning of the sex glands.

We began treatments, using among other medications the anterior pituitary hormone stimulating the sex glands. We timed them to precede the intense phase of his headaches.

At an early visit he confided that he was secretly engaged and was certain his father would interfere with the engagement if he knew of it. After this confidence he confessed to

feeling much relieved, and his stomach upsets quickly subsided, finally disappearing entirely.

After three months the young man reported that he had
enjoyed forty-two consecutive days without headaches. Later
he had two separate attacks, one following the death of a friend
and the other when the family was moving. Four months after
treatments were discontinued he had had only one headache,
when he stayed up through the night "cramming" for an
exam. It was, he reported happily, "different from *those* headaches—it was the kind of headache the other fellows get."

Five months later, his acne had vanished, and he felt more
energetic. His thighs had thinned and assumed a more masculine contour.

Shortly following graduation he married the girl to whom
he had been engaged. He has since had a child and has made
a happy adjustment to adult life. His headaches are definitely
a thing of the past.

In the college student's case, endocrine treatment combined
with understanding had excellent results. Another young person, a girl whom I have watched at intervals for thirteen years,
is still struggling to overcome a bad start.

She was first brought to me by her parents at the age of
seven and a half with a chronic sinus infection. She was markedly below the average height for her age and twenty pounds
overweight, with a pot belly, heavy thighs and legs, short
arms, small hands and feet and a bloated face—all signs of a
glandular dwarfism called the Lorraine Levy type. She ate
excessively and drank large quantities of water. She had teeth
typical of rickets in infancy.

She had been treated for colds continuously since baby-
hood, but apparently the fact that she was a glandular type had
never been recognized. She was mentally slow and was considered a retarded child.

During examination, with her parents out of the room,
she confided that she hated school, that she knew she was very
ugly, and that the other children made fun of her. "They
think I'm dumb but I can't see the blackboard so I can never

answer." I referred her to an opthalmologist, who found that she was nearsighted and needed glasses; this also had escaped notice. I advised the mother to explain this to the child's teacher, and to enlist the teacher's help in restoring the child's self-confidence.

With pituitary injections the girl grew one and one-half inches and lost a little weight, a moderate improvement but it demonstrated at least that she could grow.

At eleven and a half she returned, suffering from intense headaches and drinking ever-increasing quantities of water. With pituitary and thyroid injections she grew two and one-half inches and lost seven pounds during this course of treatments.

At seventeen I saw her again. She was now five feet, one and one-quarter inches tall, but weighed 144 pounds. She was moody and depressed, and now her hostility toward her mother was openly evident. Withdrawn, unsocial, she was trying desperately to break the dependent relationship with her mother. She wanted psychoanalysis but the parents rejected it as too expensive.

From the beginning it was obvious that the mother was this girl's chief problem. The mother was plainly a disturbed personality; she herself was also obese. In her behavior toward the child she was overindulgent and critical by turns, dominating and completely without understanding. The father, mild, unaggressive, tried but was unable to help his daughter.

On one occasion, when I administered a sharp scolding to the mother for her behavior to the child, the father said, "That's just how she treats the kid—you could have been listening in our living room!" Although he knew intuitively that his wife was wrong, for the sake of peace in the family he did not oppose her.

But although she has been deprived of the psychiatric help which she needs, this girl has tried to help herself by reading and discussion. When cortisone became available we began treatments, and the improvement has been marked. She lost ten pounds in a few weeks. There are also noticeable personality changes. She is less aggressive, less hostile. She shows a desire to carry on friendly conversation. The intelligence which lay dull and inhibited through the years has begun to awaken. She is preparing herself for a business job.

Mental Antibodies

How far can we go with medical methods toward curing a so-called "nervous" disease?

The classification of some diseases as "nervous" may seem artificial, if we consider that all diseases may have an emotional origin and all proceed by way of the nervous and glandular systems. But there are unquestionably some purely functional symptoms which arise from an immediate emotional problem.

Such a symptom is nervous vomiting. Food and the act of eating are here used symbolically as they are in so many digestive disturbances. Psychoanalysts explain the spasm as an effort to reject or make restitution of something which one has taken. Guilt may be one of the reasons.

An intelligent woman of thirty-nine, a divorcee, had been suffering from this distressing symptom for five years. She experienced it usually at the end of the day, often during the day, but almost never in the early morning. The vomiting was accompanied by considerable pain in the upper abdomen and a burning sensation in the throat. After the attack she felt better. She had been told the cause was a chronic appendicitis. Her appetite was poor and she was losing weight. Examination revealed no organic explanation of the symptoms.

We tried to discover whether it was in relation to her work that she was suffering the disturbance. She was the director of a private school, and according to her own belief she was happy and effective in her work with the children. She was, however, often upset by her interviews with difficult and disturbed mothers. Furthermore she was constantly coping with financial problems.

From the fact that hers was a digestive disorder, we could infer that this woman was in need of love and a release from her responsibilities, that she wanted someone to care for her. The reason for the failure of her first marriage, as well as the origin of the guilt feelings by which the psychiatrist would probably explain her vomiting, could not be discovered except by a psychiatric approach. She claimed, however, that she was not ready for psychoanalysis, and that in any case she could not afford it.

After her fourth visit her vomiting stopped, and she felt only occasional pain. At the end of five more visits all her discomfort was gone. There has been no recurrence.

This therapy of a condition which had gone on for five years was completed in seven weeks. What accomplished the cure?

First we reassured the patient that she was in normal condition generally and there was no damage to any organ. This reassurance was based on thorough examination and testing. The assembly of specialists and technical experts with whose help we nowadays approach the physical side of illness cannot help but reassure a patient at the very start. Thus we exorcise fear.

Second, we attacked the symptoms themselves with medical weapons.

Third—and most important if a real cure is to be achieved instead of merely an alleviation of symptoms—came an understanding of what makes illness.

It is my experience that if a patient can understand what makes illness—if he can follow the causal pathway leading from emotional stress to physical tensions, and from physical tensions to physical illness—then improvement begins in earnest.

When the physical system is exposed to germs it forms antibodies. What happens in the patient who understands that his emotional disturbance is making him ill seems to be a mental process very like the physical one. I have come to call the process the development of mental antibodies.

When we inject diphtheria bacilli into the body, the body

forms specific antigenes against the bacilli, thus building a state of immunization. In the same way a patient, who comes to realize that a specific emotional reaction to a situation in his life is at the basis of his illness, seems to develop specific antigenes to that emotional reaction.

This wholesome mental reaction can be looked upon as part of the individual's natural process of adaptation of both body and mind to a situation. I have seen a man *refuse* to get upset by his mother-in-law or landlord or business partner. He does it by recognizing first of all that to get upset emotionally means bringing on his physical suffering. He then builds his defenses—develops his mental antibodies—against that situation and his emotional response to it.

Two conditions must be met before he is able to do this for himself, and in both he may need help.

First he must be assured that he is not born with a weakness which dooms him to illness, or that he is physically damaged so that illness must be accepted. In some patients this is a fear; in some it is a comforting delusion into which they escape.

Second, he must accept the truth that illness is not a visitation of evil fate, but that he himself brings about illness and he himself can avoid it. He must come to understand and to accept the connection between his emotional responses and his illness. He must see that by the way he responds to his problems he is inviting illness. He must be willing and able to make the effort to overcome this drive toward illness by changing the pattern of his emotional response toward his life situation.

Most people are aware of their living problems, on the one hand, and of their physical symptoms on the other. They are likely also to be aware, in many instances, that the problem and the symptoms are related.

We say, "He makes me sick!" of a boss or a colleague, and often we mean it quite literally. We are conscious of the rising nausea or the stab of gas pain, or of the throbbing which forecasts a headache. What comes as a surprise to most patients is that not the boss or the coworker, but our own emotional response to him is the cause of the indigestion or migraine, and that *we can learn to change this response.* The physical pain is the body's response to the emotional stimulus, as real as laughter when we are amused or tears when we are sad. If we can adjust ourselves to a situation so that the emotional stimulus does not arise, then the physical reaction will not follow.

Usually we sit and wait for the outside situation to change. But in order to get well, we ourselves must change.

It is not easy, nor is it an overnight cure. The patient must work hard, first to understand, and then to revise his emotional pattern.

There are some, of course, who cannot accomplish this re-education of the emotions without intensive help. There are the sufferers who must have psychiatric treatment, just as at the other end of the scale there are those who require the surgeon's prompt intervention.

Illness of the body can be looked upon as a sign of the struggle to make an adjustment to living. Psychotics, as Menninger and others have observed, are likely to be physically healthy specimens, and psychotics are those who have withdrawn from reality and thus escaped the need to adjust themselves to it. Therefore we have reason to say that the sick man or woman is one who is struggling to make an adjustment.

Most human beings are struggling with the common problems of living. While in our times the great majority show neurotic reactions to *some* of these problems at *some* time during their lives, they are not therefore incapable of dealing with them. For most people it is not necessary, and often it is not desirable, that the entire personality be revised, or that the original emotional foundations laid down in childhood be explored. With understanding and a knowledge of how mind and body function together, most people can themselves deal with the problems which are making them ill.

12. IN DEEP WATERS

ILLNESS is a kind of adaptation to the difficulties of living, though a costly one. We have seen how illness can have the effect of a temporary retreat from a difficulty, an opportunity to consider and regroup one's forces. It is an old observation of physicians that a man may come out of an illness wiser than he went in.

One may come out wiser, that is, if illness is understood, if the opportunity is used for considering our difficulty and setting a rational course toward resolving it. That it often is so, perhaps unconsciously, we have many examples to prove. "The whole experience has been tremendously maturing," one patient wrote me, looking back gratefully at his illness.

Acute illnesses in particular often have this salutary effect. I saw a sample of this in a refreshing incident, the case of a little girl of fourteen.

I had examined the child a few months before, when she had come home from camp. An alert, attractive, very popular and successful little girl, she stood high in her studies and got along well with her friends, both girls and boys. After the summer in question, however, her mother thought she seemed languid and apathetic. I found a strong bile reaction in one of the tests, and wondered what situation could call forth in this friendly, outgoing child the little sign of disturbance. She was in normal condition, and I so assured her mother.

During the winter she had an attack of flu, and afterward I was called with great urgency. The child was well, but she

186

refused to get up and resume her normal activities. She lay in bed, staring at the ceiling, rejecting any attempt by her mother to find out what was the matter. A member of the family who was a physician insisted that the child was in need of immediate psychiatric attention.

The anxiety in the household was acute, and the girl could not help being aware of it, but she was coldly unresponsive to her mother's hovering concern. When the mother left the room, the girl burst out bitterly, "Why don't they leave me alone?"

Examination showed that she was physically well and able to get up. But it was apparent that she needed to remain withdrawn from her active pursuits. She was evidently going through some effort at adjustment in which she must not be interrupted. My advice to her worried parents was to let her alone for a few days; the mother especially was to restrain her impulse to hover anxiously about the sickroom, and she was not to ask questions. A trusted maid, who had been in the household almost since the child was born, could look after the girl's needs.

Two weeks later the girl was back at school and behaving perfectly like her old self. Once or twice that spring her mother telephoned in anxiety to say that the child wanted to stay home from school again; I advised the mother to let her stay home and make no fuss about it. The litle girl made up her school work without difficulty, passed with her usual high grades, and went abroad that summer with an adult friend.

I afterward learned that the child had in fact suffered a setback of a social nature during her summer at camp, a trivial defeat but her first one in a short and successful life. As is often true with acute illness, her attack of flu was the opportunity for meditation and resolution.

She had to resolve the discrepancy between her sovereign position as a beloved child at home, and her lot as one of many, subject to rules and regulations like everyone else, outside the home. She had not quite figured things out to her satisfaction when the doctor pronounced her recovered from the flu and well enough to go back to school. A strong little personality, she insisted on taking all the time she needed to adjust herself to her first experience of defeat, and to prepare for whatever new experiences must come as part of the intense growing-up years of adolescence.

Encounter with the Death Wish

Acute illness, though it can be a maturing experience, usually begins as an outspoken wish to escape, sometimes to escape even into death.

What a person may feel, on the brink of death during an acute illness, was once described to me as a conscious experience, by a young woman of an adventurous temperament, an amateur aviatrix. Actually she was not ill when she had this curious experience, but perfectly well. She was alone in the cockpit of her plane, flying over the ocean at night.

What she experienced was a species of reverie, in which a friend and fellow flier, who had been shot down during the war, stood beside her and took her hand. "Come with me," he said. He—or her own thoughts—pictured the beautiful infinite world of space which went on and on forever, without cares, without fears, where all is quiet and soft as clouds.

"I must go now—are you coming with me?" he urged. She sat transfixed, while her plane roared on and out over the sea, away from land and away from reality.

Suddenly she came to herself. "If I hadn't turned back quickly," she said, "it would have been one of those flying accidents, a plane lost, down in the ocean. What's the difference whether you run out of gas or die of a fever?" she asked.

The analogy is apt. What this calm, poised young woman experienced during a moment of despair in the cockpit of her plane is not unlike what a patient experiences during the high fever of an acute and dangerous illness. When we hover in that unreal world between earth and sky, when everything that binds us to life, the faces of those we love, even our own limbs, waver and become unreal through the glaze of fever, then the mind confronts the death wish unmasked.

Returning from such an experience, a patient often says, "I was almost gone, wasn't I?" not in fear, but rather in wonder. And often, in that unguarded first moment of returning consciousness, comes the admission, "I wanted to die."

A young wife, just twenty, was having her first baby. Pregnant, she was radiantly beautiful. Her glowing skin, her lovely young features held such happiness that people stopped to look at her for sheer pleasure, and to watch her proud walk. She was an answer to the question of why the classic painters chose for their models young women in the early months of pregnancy.

When she came to the hospital for delivery, her pains developed normally at first from mild to medium strong, and then they diminished. The obstetrician became concerned and mentioned that he might have to use high forceps. Present at the husband's request, I observed the patient's face rigid with fear, and I begged for time to bring her out of her state of anxiety. The obstetrician feared the umbilical cord was strangling the infant, and decided to go ahead with the instrument delivery.

The delivery was difficult. Even under anesthesia the young mother's muscles were rigidly contracted. She was delivered of a normal baby boy, but she suffered a dangerous hemorrhage from a broken blood vessel. By the next day her temperature was soaring. She had developed bronchial pneumonia. The day after, the bronchial pneumonia seemed to be checked.

But very early the following morning I was desperately summoned by her husband. The hospital had informed him that his wife was dying.

The young mother had sunk into a coma and was in fact next door to death. She had developed an embolism in the lung. Her temperature was 105.5, her pulse was scarcely perceptible, and her breathing was shallow even in the oxygen tent.

The whole arsenal of medicine was now thrown into the

battle to save her life. She had penicillin, streptomycin and aureomycin around the clock, intravenous heart stimulants, and another blood transfusion.

Toward evening she became semiconscious. "You have a boy!" I shouted into her ear.

"I don't care," she murmured, and fell back into unconsciousness. The fight went on.

Two days later the first trace of color came back to her bloodless lips. By that time we knew we would probably save her. She wanted to talk.

She had heard the supervisor saying, "Call the priest," and a nurse answering, "She won't last until you come back on duty tonight." She had heard the wings of great birds beating above her, higher and higher, and had come back to hear the nurse say cheerily, "Well, dear, I thought by now you'd be pushing up the daisies!"

She could not remember the delivery, but she remembered her terror of the high forceps, and of anesthesia. She remembered one thing more: during the nervous last days of waiting for labor pains to begin, her husband had become very jittery, and she had insisted that he go off for a day in the country.

"He needed to go," she said, justifying her urging and his going—but she had wanted him to stay. "How could I know he loved me?"

She had gone into labor not sure she was loved, not sure she wanted to live. Fear added its deadly measure to the balance. Her pains, which had begun normally, stopped, and the rest followed almost inevitably, the death wish growing steadily more irresistible as the body succumbed to one dangerous development after another and the will to live grew weaker with the body's weakness.

Something of this girl's history may explain the extreme measure she was driven to, because she was not sure of being loved and because she was in fear. She was still a child, barely twenty. She had never known the security of love. She had been brought up by nurses and governesses, had been sent to a convent for her schooling, and had seen her mother once a month.

Her marriage brought with it the first home she had ever known, and the first relationship of love with another human being. How permanent, how dependable that love might be, she could not be sure. In her immaturity, and without knowing that she was testing that love, she had urged her husband to go away for a day. The fact that he had innocently taken her at her word and left her, though only for a day, was enough to shake her confidence in his love.

This she admitted with great difficulty, and in far fewer words than I have put down here. But even if she had not been so young, even if she had not had such a loveless childhood, she might have swum out into dangerous waters in that delivery, because of fear.

Childbearing is a normal, healthy experience. But we have surrounded it with terror, with all the stage setting of a major operation. A woman must indeed be strong in her self-confidence and her will to live, to carry out this creative act without fear in the setting we have provided for it.

Once she had talked a little about her encounter with the death wish, this young mother gained strength. She had two more embolisms, and was not out of danger for some days, but she recovered. She was, after all, young, and youth is a great ally. Her unconscious wish to destroy herself had not had time to damage her youthful resistance. She swam out almost too far, almost into the deep waters, but we were able, with her own young strength and the mighty weapons of modern medicine, to bring her back.

After the Storm

And after we bring them back, what then? If you jump into the water to save a drowning child, do you leave him shivering alone on the shore? No, you see that he gets safely home.

In order to develop its present scientific weapons against illness, medicine had to free itself from such imponderables as the patient's personality and the doctor's personality, from the inexact, elastic approach to healing as an art. But surely it is time to remember once more that the patient is a human being, and that after we have cured the illness, the human being still remains. It is still our responsibility to see that he gets safely home after his dangerous bout with the destructive instinct.

It is not enough to cure the ulcer or the asthma, not enough to save the patient from death by pneumonia or a heart attack. If the inner drive which has led to illness is not understood, it will break out again in the same or in another, possibly more perilous, form. Physician and patient must together attack the inner force which has driven the sufferer toward disaster once and may conceivably do so again. Only then can we grasp the full possibilities of therapy, a word which means "to care for, to nurse, to serve."

The reader will remember the very first patient with whom this book began, the woman who sat on the edge of her chair and said, "Maybe there's no help for me." Now, with our new knowledge of what makes illness and what must be done to conquer it, we can bring that case to a close.

Her medical treatment, we now understand, was designed to break the vicious circle of illness which made an endless round of fatigue and indigestion and headache back to indigestion and fatigue. Next it was designed to relieve the tensions which were driving the physical system around this endless circle. And third, it was aimed at restoring homeostasis, that glandular balance which emotional conflict had shattered.

As we retraced the pathways of illness by medical means, we were retracing them also in our discussions. With each visit the patient was able to illuminate more of her deeper difficulty, and from each visit she took home new questions about herself and her life to which she wanted to find the answers.

The simple device of asking a patient to keep track of the occurrence of symptoms, their intensity, and the events—either external or within the patient's own private emotional world—which form the background of the attack, automatically makes the patient an ally in the doctor's work. It does more. It gives the patient a specific, though simple, technique for self-observation and for self-evaluation.

You cannot note the times and degrees of your pain and the events which went before, without seeing a connection. You cannot watch your own suffering after a quarrel with a member of your family or your business firm, without becoming aware of the emotional climate within yourself during and after the quarrel.

In time you will come to be aware of your emotional state before the quarrel, and perhaps of the way in which that preliminary pattern precipitated the quarrel. It does not take more introspection than most of us are capable of, to develop this wisdom about ourselves. If we have a technique for it, and if we use the technique, we soon learn to see our illness, our relationships, and finally our own emotional patterns with some objectivity. This is the road back to health.

So with our patient of Chapter 1. After three months she was still occasionally depressed, but her depressions were neither so deep nor so dark. Six months later she was feeling really well. Once in a while she had a bad day, but she was not distressed and she rose again quickly. "I don't let trouble get me," she said. She was still taking hormone treatments about five times a month. She was not depressed any more, nor moody.

In fact she felt so much better that she became pregnant. Pregnancy had twice before been an escape from chronic illness for her, but this time she did not seek it as an escape. She had a positive desire for another child, a sturdy wish to give creative expression to her growing contentment with life.

How had she achieved this contentment? What actually had changed?

"My husband says he is the happiest man in the world," she said, characteristically giving her answer first through another's reaction. She was still, and will probably always be, a shy and modest woman.

But how was she really working out her problem?

"I think I try—well, to be a better person. I think of ways to please him, to be more loving. I find he tries to please me in return. I realized that I had everything to gain that way. I was selfish before, but I only hurt myself by my selfishness."

When she became pregnant she called for an appointment, but the day of the appointment she called again to cancel it because her younger child was sick. Her pregnancy was going wonderfully well. It was quite different from the other two. During those earlier pregnancies she had been free from her usual symptoms, but she had had severe morning sickness. In this one, which she had entered upon with quite different emotions, she did not even have a moment of nausea.

Still, a pattern of anxiety is not easy to overcome. A sudden though unimportant telephone call during the night frightened her; her knees buckled and she almost fainted. She began to have pains, and shortly afterward she suffered a miscarriage.

She came to the office when she had recovered. She was not downcast about the failure of her pregnancy. On the contrary, she was eager to get into good condition for another. She sat in the office in a glow of healthy activity, talking animatedly, looking at her watch now and then. She wanted to be sure to leave on time. She likes to be home when her children, now ten and seven, come in from school. She wants plenty of time to prepare a good dinner for her family.

She still, she said, has to overcome a certain monotony in her life. Her husband still goes out four nights a week to his club and his card games.

She stood up briskly. Then as she buttoned her neat coat, she said with a confident smile, "But I'm sure I can work that out, too."

13. A REGIME FOR STRESS

In the foregoing chapters we have talked of what makes illness. We have shown how the alliance of doctor and patient can cope with illness.

For most of us, illness for which we need a doctor is not a continuous experience, although when it comes it may be a crisis in our lives. Someone has said that people devote the first half of their lives to making money, so they can spend it in the second half of their lives getting back their health. The gibe has the sharp but partial truth of most gibes. It would be more accurate to say that we spend a good part of our lives trying to work things out for ourselves, alternating between success and defeat, between greater and less happiness, between better and poorer health.

It is to the many people who are not sick, and who would like not to be sick, that this chapter is addressed. It is also addressed to those who have illness in the family, and who would like to guard themselves from breaking down under the stress which illness brings to all those whose lives it touches.

Most of us try to carry our responsibilities, but rarely do we achieve the best of which we are capable. In some way, conscious or unconscious, we acknowledge this. We may strive toward a goal or we may be content just to "get by." Whichever way we choose, we are generally traveling blind. We function, but at a price, because we lack understanding.

Even while we are well we pay a price for ignorance; we work harder for what we want and have less happiness than we might have. And there is always the threat that one day the struggle may become too much for us, and we will be sick. Since life is a struggle, and none can escape times of stress, this possibility is always present.

How then can we manage better? How shall we live to achieve the best in us, the most in accomplishment and the most in happiness?

Most people would like to manage better. Those who profess perfect contentment, who seem self-satisfied, perhaps smug, are likely to be deceiving the world, or themselves, or both. Behind the most complacent exterior there may seethe the greatest discontent.

The answer is that we must learn to cultivate the will to live.

The will to live is so powerful a force that we may think it can very well take care of itself. Yet we have noted throughout this book—and we can see in our own lives and those around us—how we ourselves lay hidden traps for this valuable life force. We have seen that in everyone's life there are periods of danger, situations of danger, and directions which lead to danger.

The will to live can be weakened; it can be destroyed. Otherwise we would not have the spectacle of people falling ill and dying before their time, or of living at half capacity, or of killing themselves outright.

The will to live is not a will, in the sense of that conscious or "free will" by which we like to distinguish man from the animal kingdom. It is a biological and psychological force. It is the product of many factors. Like an iceberg which is seven-eighths under water, the will to live is largely submerged below the surface of our consciousness. We can unconsciously weaken and destroy it.

But though the will to live is mostly unconscious, it can be strengthened, nourished, cultivated—and *this we can do consciously.*

Each of us is the sum of what he was born with and everything that has happened to him up to this moment. He is the product of his inheritance, environment, cultural background, the personality of his parents, school influences, religious influences, the customs and morals of the society in which he lives. On the other hand some psychologists are telling us today that we can throw all these big words out of the window—if our mother loved us.

Most of what has made us what we are, including our mother's love or the lack of it, was beyond our control. We realize this, not to weep over it, but also not to let it pursue us throughout our life. We cannot rewrite the past. But we can modify the present. And we can reshape the future.

We can do this in two ways. First we must know how to support the will to live in times of stress, so that we may come through the inevitable crises in life with the least damage, and with the most momentum for proceeding on our route. Second is the long-range program, the cultivation of the will to live in all possible ways in order to make our lives as rich and happy as they can be made.

Emergency Measures

First let us frame an emergency program for the stressful situations through which we must all find our way.

What is stress and what does it do? The word seems self-explanatory, but biological scientists are now using it with a specific meaning. It is the effect on the body of disturbance, either external or internal or both.

A conflict with a business partner or a marriage partner, sexual dissatisfaction, illness or injury to somebody close to us, the threat of unemployment or the reality of it, a death in the family, a disaster that threatens or befalls a child, all these and many more produce stress.

Stress may be produced by our inner reaction to an external situation. We fear a challenge or an obstacle, or doubt our ability to meet it. Or we cannot make up our minds on the best way to meet it. Or we suffer a setback in dealing with it and cannot accept the defeat. As we have seen in earlier chapters, stress may also be produced entirely within ourselves, as a result not of any specific external situation, but by our own anxieties, resentments, and conflicts.

If the stress is temporary—if we can fight the battle or run away from it—then the body relaxes and no harm is done. This is what the body is built for.

But prolonged stress, either external or internal, gives the body no chance to regenerate, refuel, regroup its forces—what we mean when we say "relax." In prolonged stress the body is maintained in a constant state of mobilization. Reserves of energy are constantly being poured out, tensions are mercilessly sustained, and organs like the heart and those involved in complex chemical processes are driven to their utmost capacity without pause.

In prolonged stress we are racing a high-powered motor at top speed—in neutral. We are burning up fuel. We are wearing out parts. But we are not going anywhere. This is the destructive effect of prolonged stress.

We might say, let's avoid stress. We can certainly say, avoid unnecessary stress. But it takes the wisdom of experience and maturity, and also some courage, to decide in advance what stress is unnecessary. We can learn to distinguish. But not all stress can or should be avoided. We cannot live under glass. To avoid stress means to avoid living, because stress is an inescapable part of living. So we must find a way of meeting stress.

What Stress Does

Stress mainly does two things: it sustains tension, and it spends energy. We must therefore answer it with two kinds of measures. We must find ways to break tension. We must learn how to conserve and replenish energy.

Intuitively we seek ways of breaking tension. You call up your older brother or have lunch with a trusted friend. Some of us flee to the movies; others take a hot bath. Some people take a walk and some take a nap. Some actresses and ballet dancers lie down with the feet higher than the head. People who can keep going for long stretches at a time generally have a talent for the short nap, in a train or plane or car. Napoleon is said to have napped sitting on his horse.

Breaking tension is an art at which many men who bear weighty responsibility learn to become most skillful. During the terrible tensions of the war Churchill would undress completely and go to bed for ten minutes, if ten minutes was all the time he had. Roosevelt joked with his circle of experts, or withdrew for a quiet time with his stamp collection.

These men were coping with the most desperate problems on a world scale. They were daily called upon to make decisions on which the fate of nations and of continents might hang. But their problems were external. The art which they mastered was the art of putting aside the problem for a few minutes, to take a deep breath, to stretch the muscles, and then to return refreshed to the task in hand.

This is not to say that the leaders of nations do not suffer illness under stress. Quite otherwise. The foreign correspondent Burnet Hershey, in an article in *The Nation,* quoted General Marshall at an Overseas Press Club dinner, describing some of his difficulties while he was Secretary of State.

"Ulcers have had a strange effect upon the history of our times," General Marshall said. "In Washington I had to contend with, among other things, the ulcers of Bedell Smith in Moscow and the ulcers of Bob Lovett and Dean Acheson in Washington."

The general himself underwent a serious operation. Senator Austin and Herschel Johnson, American delegates to the United Nations; Hull, Stettinius, Byrnes, Sumner Wells; General Eisenhower, General Clay, and a long line of American statesmen and military leaders past and present have been on the serious sick list during the stressful times of their public service.

Nor are the European leaders immune. Atlee's ulcer and eczema, Bevin's tired heart which finally gave out, significantly, after he had retired on his seventieth birthday; the French statesmen Queuille and Schuman with their stomach ailments; the Italian de Gasperi's arthritis and siege of gastric trouble; Vishinsky's ulcer, Molotov's insomnia, and Gromyko's visible aging all testify that the human body's reaction to stress is no respecter of national or ideological differences.

At the French government's banquet to the Paris conferees in the fall of 1948, says the same article, the Big Four delegates scarcely touched their plates. "This one was 'off' coffee; that one couldn't smoke; pills were taken in place of cocktails; and always the chorus, 'nothing fried.'"

Because our problems are on a less heroic scale, limited to one person, one family, one business or professional crisis, this does not make them less important to each of us, nor does it lessen the stress which they impose on us. We struggle as hard with our problems as leaders of nations do with theirs. The winning of a first case may be as important to a young lawyer as the winning of a war to a president or a prime minister. And perhaps the young lawyer suffers more in his struggle. Few of us are given the superb talents and the integrated personality possessed by some of history's great men.

A leader of peoples is moreover carried by the trust and faith of millions. Their confidence strengthens him. They share his anxieties and buoy him with their hopes. But the individual making his lonely struggle must carry his burden almost alone. Sometimes those closest to him do not help but only increase his difficulty.

We also add our inner conflicts to our external problems. The more personal the problem, the more self-doubts we suffer in our dealing with it. This is why most of the ways of breaking tension which the average person chooses are not good ones. Most of them are not so much relaxation as *evasion*.

A man may run to a bar, or the races, or sit up all night in a card game. A woman may go shopping, or redecorate her bedroom, or flee to an afternoon visit. There is nothing wrong with these occupations, or any occupations which may suit a particular individual's taste. The question is, do they refresh the body and mind? Can the man who sat up at an all-night poker game, or the woman who returns from an exhausting shopping expedition, truthfully claim that he or she returns to the stressful situation refreshed and better able to deal with it? Haven't such devices served as an escape from facing the problem, rather than a genuine breaking of tension in order to cope with it?

This does not mean that we must grimly stare the problem in the face every waking minute. There are times when it is better to put the problem aside and engage in some other activity. But it must be an activity which truly refreshes, not one —like shopping or gambling—which is accompanied by more tension.

Sexual activity serves many people as a means of relieving tension, except in those situations where, perhaps because of guilt or underlying hostility, the sexual relationship is in itself stress-producing.

We may put our problems out of mind for a romp with our young child or a game of ball with an older one. We may undertake a pleasant gardening task or a limited household chore. When the Norwegian mother in *I Remember Mama* was troubled, she got out her brush and pail and scrubbed the floor. The modern housewife has many lighter tasks to choose from.

We may go out to bask in the sun for a while, or take a solitary walk. If it is inadvisable to go outdoors, try looking out of the window. It will remind you of the world beyond the four walls which hem you in with your difficulty, and thus help you to gain a little perspective.

Lunch hour can be a real break in the day's tensions, but not the way most of us take our lunch. We say, "I run down to a counter and grab a sandwich, and when I run back I don't feel so well." The pattern is so familiar that even the words scarcely differ from patient to patient.

One man who complained of indigestion after lunch protested that he did take a walk before he went back to his desk, but his troubles walked right with him. The man was habitually stooped as though he carried the world on his shoulders, and his troubled face was bent always toward the ground.

"You take a walk," I told him, "and report to me how many pigeons you see flying along Fifth Avenue."

He looked blank at first, and then he saw the point. "I'll try it," he agreed.

I did not see him again for six years, and then he came in with a minor ailment. "I'm still counting pigeons," he reported cheerfully.

A woman may walk two miles from store to store and counter to counter, but this is no relaxer of tensions. A walk should be undertaken for exercise and relaxation, not simply to get somewhere.

A "change of wallpaper" is the prescription an old-fashioned doctor used to give his patients. A trip or a visit away from the physical setting of your problem does not solve the problem, but it may give perspective, time to think, time to consider.

These are ways of breaking tension. They are also ways of conserving energy during a period when energy is being used up at a rapid rate under stress. Any devices which suit your situation and your inclination are good, provided they fill these twin requirements: they must break the tension of stress, and they must conserve the energy which is being used up under stress. Any device is good to include in your stress regime if it does either, and better still if it does both.

To ignore these needs of body and mind for refreshment under stress is to be a traitor to your will to live. If under stress you go without sleep, eat carelessly or irregularly, ignore the symptoms of strain and fatigue, then you are courting disaster. You are aiding and abetting the destructive instinct.

To let yourself get run down because you are under stress is no excuse. What you are indulging in is a self-destructive act.

This is the most baffling facet of self-destruction. As you seek relief from its oppression, it creates new harmful appetites—another drink, another cigarette, another box of chocolates, another sleeping pill. The curse of evil is that it creates more evil.

But once you know that the drink or the cigarette or the sleeping pill is not a solution, but only a temporary crutch, then you can safeguard yourself. Once you glimpse what is going on inside you, you can take rational steps to answer these destructive appetites in good ways. This is what is meant by supporting and strengthening the will to live under stress.

A Stress Diet

We know from laboratory experiment a good deal about what happens in the digestive organs under stress. We can thus work out ways of eating which will replenish the energy being squandered in the stressful situation, and at the same time put the least extra strain on organs already being strained to function under difficult conditions.

Some people stop eating altogether under stress. Others eat too much. Still others choose the wrong things to eat. All three are destructive reactions, and all can lead to trouble.

The self-starver is likely to suffer from depletion, since he is spending energy and not replenishing it. Fatigue, irritability, and loss of efficiency are obvious prices which he must pay almost at once, and serious illnesses may result. Certainly, not to eat is a self-destructive act.

The nervous appetite of which many of us are conscious under stress is a more logical expression of the body's need, since there is a demand for more and more fuel when so much of it is being used up. We must eat. But how shall we eat?

Stress makes heavy demands on our metabolism. We are asked to keep a war machine constantly supplied. Our fuel storage depots in the liver and other parts of the body are being emptied into the blood stream to feed the heart, muscles and brain. At the same time our digestive organs are likely to be either inhibited or overstimulated. We must make it easy for them to deliver what is required. We must give them food which they can digest under these difficult conditions.

For example, a group of laboratory dogs were shown a cat. Immediately the constant flow of bile from the liver through the biliary duct into the gall bladder either slowed or stopped entirely for twenty minutes. Then the dripping of bile began again, slowly, and in one and one-half hours the normal flow was restored. Of all the dogs observed during several experiments, only one dog remained unperturbed by the cat, as revealed in the uninterrupted flow of bile.

One individual, like one laboratory animal, may retain the privilege of reacting differently. But for most of us the average reaction is the one which we may expect. Bile is ejected from the gall bladder into the upper part of the small intestines in the digestion of fats. Without bile, fats cannot be digested. If, under stress, bile is in short supply, then the logical conclusion is that under stress we should not eat fatty foods.

The fact that we do eat fatty foods and that we should not is given ample and uncomfortable testimony by the millions of sufferers from gall-bladder disturbances throughout the country. Twenty per cent of all male patients and twenty-five per cent of all female patients in the United States have gall-bladder disorders, and this does not include the many who do not go to the doctor.

The disturbance of the biliary tract is only one aspect of what happens in the digestive system under stress. The entire system is similarly disturbed. The factory is working short handed, with diminished power, with machinery at half efficiency or less.

The man or woman who gets acid indigestion under stress, or who reacts with diarrhea or constipation, is now understood to be showing an unconscious need for protection and appreciation. We have seen how in the infant the need for love becomes associated with food. This association persists in the unconscious. When in a stressful situation we long for someone to protect us from our difficulty, or to solve for us a problem which we feel unable to solve for ourselves, this longing is expressed by a stimulation of the digestive organs as though we were about to receive food.

Thus we have the oversecretion of digestive juices in the stomach under stress, causing indigestion and setting up conditions for possible peptic ulcer. We have the overactivity of the intestines causing diarrhea, or the reverse, a rigid spasm causing constipation, or an alternation between the two.

The stress diet must therefore be designed to counteract this overactivity of the digestive system, and to avoid causing further stimulation. This is what we mean by the familiar "bland diet" with which almost any stomach sufferer who has ever been to a doctor is acquainted.

We choose protective and nonstimulating foods according to three principles: chemical, mechanical, and thermal. Chemically, the foods must tend to the alkaline side so as to counteract the hyperacidity, and they must not be rich, heavy, or spicy dishes which stimulate the stomach to still more digestive effort. Mechanically the foods must have a minimum of roughage, to avoid further irritation and further stimulation. Finally they must not be excessively hot or excessively cold.

Meat protein is one of the complex foods which demand extra digestive effort, and so are fats, not only meat fats but cream and butter as well. (Small amounts of uncooked butter are well tolerated.) Spices, as any cook knows, are used with the specific purpose of stimulating the digestive juices. Sugar in large quantities, especially cooked sugar, can cause fermentation. A large amount of food at one time puts an extra strain on the already overstrained stomach.

Besides this, the stomach which is secreting gastric juices at an excessive rate needs to have those juices used at frequent intervals. The sheer accumulation of them causes distress.

Under stress, therefore, we should eat little, but often. Instead of three substantial meals, we should divide the day's requirements into five or six small meals. An individual whose stomach reacts to stress with oversecretion of the gastric juices should eat something every two hours: a few crackers or zwieback, a small glass of milk, a piece of fruit if the accompanying irritation is not severe—and it is better to peel the apple or pear. Citrus fruits are effective in neutralizing acid.

People who cannot leave their work every two hours to eat might try keeping a jar of honey in the desk. A spoonful of this simple natural sugar is soothing to the overactive stomach, and to some of us its quick energy is as stimulating as a shot of whisky is to others.

Where diarrhea is the tendency, the same regime of frequent light meals is good, with particular avoidance of roughage, sugar, milk and fatty foods. Scraped raw apple, which we give to infants, is a specific for diarrhea. Apples have a high content of pectin, the natural jelly-forming substance in fruit. If you haven't time to fuss with a knife, gnaw on the apple; your teeth are a good scraper.

For constipation, the remedies are legion, but prevention is better. The continued use of cathartics actually encourages the continuation of constipation. A patient of mine embarked on a trip to Europe and after the ship had left the dock discovered to his dismay that he had forgotten the little pills without which, as he thought, he could not survive. After a few days on shipboard he forgot he had ever needed them, and he never used a cathartic again.

Part of the reason for his liberation was, of course, the relaxed atmosphere of an ocean voyage. He was free of the situations which caused his tensions. We can achieve the same liberation, even under stress. Precaution can be as good as a pill. When the tensions mount, take a breather. Get a drink of water. Go out for a walk even if you have to invent a small errand.

The important thing is not to let tension pile up. A tense day may bring a tense night. You know this, but under stress you tend to forget it; perhaps this forgetfulness is another instance of the destructive instinct at work. Lean back at your desk and consider whether the problem which is making you tense is really worth all the discomfort you are likely to suffer later. If you will remember the connection between this moment's stress and tonight's or tomorrow's physical distress, you will find ways to break the tension before it gets hold of you.

People who unconsciously overeat, and gain weight under stress, would also do well to remember the connection. It helps them, too, if they will keep a record of what they actually eat, both at meals and in that off-the-record nibbling which they are so prone to forget. It is not enough, however, to curb the appetite by an effort of will. One must also remember the emotional tension which causes the appetite, and give earnest thought to understanding its cause.

A low-calorie diet is meant to yield less energy so that the body fat will be used to fill out the needed supply. Such a diet is therefore low in fat and carbohydrate and high in protein. To fill the stomach comfortably such a diet also contains salads and leafy vegetables, and fruits with low sugar content.

The patient suffering from high blood-pressure is put on a rice diet. We can explain this now: continually geared for a battle which is continually postponed, he is in constant need of quick energy. Rice is an ideal quick-energy food, high in easily digested carbohydrate, low in protein, and without fat. When his body is quickly supplied with the energy it needs, that part of his tension which results from the depletion of his energy supply is relieved. He is calmed; his blood pressure subsides.

Nietzsche remarked that rice makes for Buddhism, and beer —another source of quick energy—for German metaphysics. Certainly the peoples who live on rice are less combative and more meditative than the meat-and-fat eaters.

Alcohol is an even quicker energy source than rice. When after a tussle with unpleasantness a man says, "I need a drink," he is obeying a specific demand of his body at that moment. He can use a drink. Alcohol is a stimulant with quick food value besides. To take a drink for relaxation is healthy. But a dependence on alcohol to dull the senses and evade the problems of living is obviously self-destructive.

The elements of the stress diet now emerge: simple starch or sugar, no fat, a low amount of protein. The protein should not be eggs, which have a high fat content, nor meat. Milk and milk products such as the fresh cheeses, and vegetable proteins, are the proteins the body can handle best under stress. And no rich desserts, no creams, custards, or pastries which are full of fat. Coffee has a certain amount of fatty acids; tea is comforting and less irritating.

What's wrong with a good steak, you would like to know. Nothing at all, if you pick the right time to eat it. After a real battle or a siege of hard work, you can take on a steak—because the stress is over. The jungle animal first fights, and then eats. It is safe to assume that the tiger does not suffer indigestion on his regime. But no animal eats under stress, except man.

Still, you can have that steak even under stress, if you take your time about it, both before and after. It is mere common sense that you don't come straight from the tense business conference and sit down to your steak. You take a drink, perhaps, and wait half an hour or even an hour. Then you can enjoy your dinner.

And give yourself an hour or so afterward to digest it. Take a tip from the tiger, who goes to sleep after dinner.

Eating a good meal is like building a fire in the fireplace: first you must have the energy to build the fire. The digestive organs are the first to be robbed of energy by the alarm reaction of stress. You must give them something to work on before you can ask them to digest a heavy meal.

This is why we are sometimes so disturbed, or so tired, that we cannot eat. To force yourself to eat because you know you need energy is not the answer. I have found that a cup of some uncomplicated liquid (except a meat broth or consommé) works well. My own choice is strained, lightly salted oatmeal gruel such as we give to infants. A cup or two washes down old mucous and bile in the digestive system, and gives quick energy at the same time. Half an hour or an hour later you are hungry and can eat.

If you think that all the tempting things are left out of our stress diet, here is a surprise for you. The most perfect stress diet ever devised is: caviar and champagne. Caviar is very compact in food value, and champagne, besides its quickly useful alcohol content, is also a stimulant for the circulation. So order up the caviar and champagne—unless another stressful situation will arrive with the bill. In that case, you better have oatmeal gruel.

How to Get a Good Night's Sleep

A problem looks much less formidable in the light of morning than at night, as we all know. It dwindles still more if the night has been restful.

But when we are under stress a good night's sleep seems the most elusive of luxuries. The more troubled we are, the more cunningly sleep escapes us. Yet there are ways to invite sleep, both common-sense ways and scientific ones.

Sleep is good even if it is occasionally induced by a drink or a sleeping pill. We have liquor, we have sleeping pills, and they are for use in an emergency. Sleeping pills are habit-forming. Especially when we are under stress, we must guard against becoming dependent on them. Such dependence is, of course, an overt evidence of a dangerous self-destructive trend. But to take a sleeping pill for one night's needed sleep, or in order to break a pattern of insomnia, comes under the heading of protection of the body under stress, and is an aid to the will to live.

Our grandmothers, and their grandmothers before them, had many homely devices for inducing a good night's sleep, and some of them are sound. They were on the right track when in chilly weather they tucked the would-be sleeper into a warm bed with bed socks or a hot-water bottle for his feet.

Quiet, a comfortable room temperature, absence of light, and security from disturbance are the combination which invites sleep. Of course some of us prefer other combinations. The mother of a patient of mine always asked the hotel clerk which was his noisiest room. "Oh, but madame, I won't give you that room," he would protest, and her answer was, "But that's just the room I want!"

The amount of sleep we need varies enormously with the individual. Some of us get along well on four or five hours, others need eight or nine, and some feel worse the more sleep they get. It is the height of unwisdom to argue with anyone who insists that he has not slept a wink. A woman (or a man) says, "I tossed all night," and her husband (or his wife) retorts, "You were snoring all night!" and then the battle is on. Rest is a subjective matter. It makes no difference whether or not we slept. What is important is whether the sleep was refreshing.

There is a distinction between acute and chronic insomnia. Acute insomnia—a night or a few nights without sleep—is a common experience. Its cause may be a specific problem, or nothing more than a strange bed, different noises, or no noise at all, such as a city dweller's first night in the country. Chronic insomnia has its cause in anxiety, and this requires looking into. The sufferer from chronic insomnia also needs careful preparation for sleep.

A bear shuts himself in the depths of a quiet, dark cave to hibernate. The anxious seeker after sleep should go to bed with the same cozy confidence that he will not be disturbed. If he does not have to get up at a certain time, he should make sure beforehand that no one is going to awaken him. But if he is obliged to be up, someone else—or an alarm clock— should take over the responsibility of getting him up on time so that he can dismiss that worry from his sleep.

Sometimes the alarm clock itself becomes a source of worry. The sleeper wakes in anxiety that it will not go off on time, or that it has not been set, or contrarily he dreads the shattering sound which will wake him. In such a case another member of the family should, if possible, take over both the alarm clock and the waking-up job.

Sleeplessness is commonly intensified by anxiety about losing sleep. This is often instilled in us in childhood. A mother, trying to get a child to bed on time, urges, "You'd better go to bed or you'll be tired tomorrow." It is a fact that lack of sleep is not fatal. We would wake up fresh enough after a night of little sleep, if we were not convinced that we ought to feel tired.

One who has been fitful and tense during the day is likely to be the same at night. This is why it is important to "let go" during the day. It is a mistake to go to bed tense. Prepare for sleep by relaxing first.

To eat or drink before going to bed is a common-sense counsel. We observe that in nature animals sleep after eating; it follows pragmatically that we might do well to eat before sleeping. Physiologically, when the digestive system is engaged, the rest of the body tends to be dormant. The parasympathetic mechanism is in control. Brain and muscles, heart and circulatory activity are quieted by a diminished blood supply and a minimum of glandular stimulation.

This is why we get drowsy after a heavy meal. But this does not mean that to eat a heavy meal will bring on restful sleep. Quite the opposite; when the body is under stress, eating the wrong food or too much food is like taking a bomb to bed with you. All your careful plans for rest will fly up in splinters.

Yet against all good sense, men who have been wrestling with problems in a late evening conference will adjourn to a restaurant and put away heavy meat sandwiches or egg and meat dishes, and then top this off with rich pastry and a second cup of coffee with cream.

Those for whom the conference was successful may be able to sleep on such a midnight meal. But if the evening's problems were unsolved, or if some of the conferees suffered personal defeat or disappointment, there are miserable nights ahead for some of the group at the table.

The bedtime snack must follow the rules for a stress diet. It should be light, easily digested, carbohydrate, with low protein content, little meat, and no fat. If it is warm rather than cold it helps the warming of the body which encourages sleep. A milk or chocolate drink is generally a safe sleep-encourager.

Much of what we are suggesting here may sound naive and obvious. Yet these are the little snags on which people get caught. Whether your favorite relaxation is reading or soft music, a drink or a cup of milk or a dish of breakfast cereal, the important thing to remember is that the accumulation of tension is the cause of your sleeplessness. No real lesson is learned in a day, and no method of inviting sleep should be discarded after one unsuccessful try. You must practice your lesson in relaxation.

A suggestion which often shocks the weary seeker after sleep is that he should take a vigorous walk, a really long one of a couple of miles, before he goes to bed. Exhausted as he is, how can he go out and tramp through the dark? Surely he will drop in his tracks.

Not at all. We have heard and talked a good deal about the power of mind over body. Such a walk will reveal to him the power of body over mind. But he must perform the experiment correctly. He cannot let his depressed spirits do his walking for him, with reluctant lagging stride. He must step out strongly with a long and rhythmic pace, body swinging, head and chest up, lungs filling with deep breaths. It is obvious that he must be dressed properly for a good walk, with appropriate clothes, comfortable shoes (this for the ladies especially), and no encumbrances.

Such a walk has more than one useful purpose. First of all it draws blood away from the brain into the muscles, thus quieting the spinning mind. The movement and the full regular breathing stir the circulation which has become sluggish in the limbs, and the body is warmed and nourished throughout. Nervous tensions are gradually relaxed with the rhythmic muscular movement and the relaxation of mental activity. Soldiers have been known to fall asleep on the march, while continuing to trudge along.

As the body begins to enjoy greater comfort, so does the

mind, since the two are one. The inner climate changes. Even the very problem which has been whirling unresolved may emerge with greater clarity as the smoke of inner battle clears. The sleeping pill simply puts the problem away until morning. But the long walk may bring the problem closer to solution, if only because it has been seen more clearly, or been placed in better perspective by a sky full of stars.

Back home, after a hot bath and a drink of something warming, you climb into bed in a quiet and well-ventilated room. Your body is tired, but your mind is quiet. You have left the problem outside your door, like a pair of shoes to be shined and picked up again in the morning. You have every reason to count on a good night's sleep.

14. AMATEURS IN THE ART OF LIVING

THE BOOKSHOP counters are laden with books that tell us how we can live longer, eat better, be happier, richer, and more beautiful, and find inner peace. Many of these books appear for months at a time on the best-seller lists. According to their sales figures, we ought all to be young, beautiful, healthy, happy, long-lived and rich.

That we all yearn for these good things is no surprise, nor is it surprising that many of us wishfully believe we can buy long life, inner peace, etc., for $2.95, more or less.

Generally these books offer very good advice. Time and again someone will say to you that he has just finished reading such and such a book and "it made sense." Yet you will observe no perceptible difference in his life, and a week or a month or six months later he can scarcely tell you what the book said that made such good sense.

The fault is often not the book's but the reader's. We buy books as we take pills, or trips, or go to the doctor or psychoanalyst, looking for an easy answer to our discontent. We seek endlessly for some magic which will banish trouble and make life fall into a more comfortable pattern, like the woman who asked me once, "Can't you give me a hormone which will sweeten my disposition?"

The doctor, like the book, gives us very good advice. He says, "Relax," and surely that makes sense.

The hitch is that making sense is not enough. We must go deeper than the *make-sense* level. The reassurance which you can get from a book, even this book, is momentary. You feel

214

for the moment that someone understands, that someone has answered your questions and solved at least some of your problems. But no one else can do this for you. When you close the book the reassurance vanishes before reality. Your problems still haunt you. Your dissatisfactions still gnaw at you. Nothing is changed unless you change it yourself, unless you embark on a program of change.

This does not propose any heroic transformation. A long-range program is exactly what the words mean: a slow, patient, brick-by-brick building of a new and sounder structure for living. Life is made up, not of great decisions and noble moments, but of small acts and choices day by day, a word here, a deed there. "There are no big moments you can reach unless you've a pile of smaller moments to stand on," says a character in Lillian Hellman's play, *Autumn Garden*.

A New Year's resolution which is too hard to keep is simply not kept. All we get out of such brave beginnings on too large a scale is one more defeat, to add to those under which we already smart. If we are modest in the demands we make on ourselves, but persistent, we have a better chance of making progress. It may be slow but it is progress. You won't move the mountain, but you may climb over it, if you set your goal within reach.

A long-range program has two phases. There is the distant eventual goal, the specific form which your idea of a better way to live may take for you, whether you call it inner peace, better health, a better relationship to your work, to your family. All are related, but one aspect may appear more vital to you than another. You want to know what you are aiming for.

The other phase is the daily lesson. A pianist practices every day. A singer vocalizes every day. A boxer, a runner, a baseball player trains every day. When a doctor is away from his practice for a month he returns to find his familiar routine strange.

If you think through your day you will discover that a great part of it is daily habit. To add one more habit to your routine of tooth brushing and bathing is not too large an order. The new habit, of taking daily account, can become as much a part of your day as any other. Many people find that keeping a diary is a help. The idea of a diary, whether or not you write it down, is a good one.

Postponing your stocktaking from day to day is another habit, the lost-day habit, which can become as hard to break as any habit bad or good.

This daily lesson is your step-by-step examination of yourself. You are your own stock; your assets and liabilities are all within yourself. In the business of living, no man can get by forever without re-evaluating himself.

The search for a better way to live begins with self-searching. Man has been granted this unique gift: he can stop and think things over. He can re-evaluate a situation in the light of new knowledge and new experience. He denies himself a precious human prerogative if he fails to make use of it.

Most people now and then spend some thought on trying to find a connection between events and their reactions to them. Doing this occasionally is like playing a musical instrument occasionally.

The man or woman who takes stock *occasionally* remains an amateur in the art of living.

Self-Appraisal

Whether you come up with the right answer in your stocktaking depends on how deep you dig for it.

A young business man said to me, "I ate shrimps for lunch and they didn't agree with me." What he left out was that whatever he eats at lunch with his boss disagrees with him. Should he therefore avoid shrimps? Or his boss?

Perhaps he is sensitive to shrimps, but he will not make much progress if he stops there; his body's reaction is only the top answer. He will have to examine his attitude toward his boss, toward his work. What fears, what resentments toward his work and the symbol of authority, his boss, does he swallow along with the food he takes at the weekly luncheon?

The closer he can come to the kernel of the difficulty within himself, the better will be his relationship to his work, his boss —and his lunch. The discovery of the something beyond shrimps which is giving him his indigestion is a long step. And incidentally he may get rid of his indigestion.

What makes self-examination a hard job is that we must penetrate behind the overt behavior, the *strategy* which each of us has adopted in our dealings with the outer world. One person wears a cloak of modesty to hide his driving ambition, and another carries an aggressive chip on his shoulder to cover up his self-doubt. One is all sweet compliance, with a heart full of rebellion, and another says "no" to everything like a child blindly striking out for an independence he knows no other way to achieve.

Some people beat their breasts with guilt for everything that happens, whether they are guilty or not. The more usual device—one with which all of us trick ourselves on occasion— is to blame everyone except ourself, like the young woman who burst into my office one day and exclaimed, "Today everyone is fighting with me—my husband, my mother, and just now my maid! What is the matter with *people?*"

If our self-examination is to be fruitful, we must get behind our own masks. The penalty for lying to the world is severe, but the price of lying to yourself is disaster. Sooner or later the lie catches up with you. However successfully you deceive the world, you never really deceive yourself. Deep within you, in some way, you acknowledge the fiction, and the deeper it is buried, the more power it has to do you harm. We can add one more truth to Abraham Lincoln's homely wisdom: you cannot fool all the people all the time, least of all yourself.

The next step after blaming everyone else for the things that happen to you is to blame the state of civilization we live in. Certainly there are aspects of our way of life which put severe pressures on the individual. Indeed the farther we travel from the primitive state, the more difficult our struggle for adjustment.

To complain about the state of the world and do nothing to improve it is futile. The healthy way to protest is to work for a better world. A constructive effort, in a way which seems right to you and which is within your capacity, will at once remove much of the sting of frustration and impotence before conditions which strike you as unjust.

How big a job you do seems less important than the doing of it. To work for one's neighborhood school may bring as much satisfaction on a personal level as a university president derives from stating his principles of education to a nation. The joy is in the creative effort, whatever the scope of the work.

Still, progress is slow, and a dramatic improvement in the world within the lifetime of one individual is unlikely. This is the world you were born into, and no matter how you may work to better it you must nevertheless learn to live in it.

Often people who feel that the world is bad, that everyone is against them, are expressing a discontent more with themselves than with the world. They may be suffering from a lack of recognition or appreciation. They have perhaps set unrealistic standards for themselves, and their complaint against the world is in the nature of an alibi for failing to achieve those standards. They are like the boy who won't play unless he can be captain.

The Stiff Upper Lip

Learning to live in the world does not mean that we must accept without question a way of life as it is handed to us. The most commonplace rules for living can be dangerous, if only because they take no account of individual differences. Slogans can act like a lid on dynamite.

Take for example the "stiff upper lip" of the English, or

the American version, "Be a good sport about it," and the scornful "You can't take it." On the surface this is good counsel. What cannot be cured must be endured, and one may as well put a good face on it.

The danger lies in what is behind the stiff upper lip, and what is under the sportsmanlike behavior. If the good sportsmanship is nothing more than a cap on top of rebellion, if the stiff upper lip is only a stopper on resentment, then you are setting up perfect conditions for a volcanic explosion. "I'm ready to burst!" we exclaim, and it is a precise definition. Few of us break out into the open rebellion of delinquency or crime. But the toll in self-destruction is universal.

To screw the cap of good sportsmanship on tighter is no solution. What is necessary is a genuine acceptance of this failure or this defeat, whatever it may be. Like a good boxer, one must roll with the punches. This time you lost. Why did you lose? What can you do better next time so that you can win? Or, you might ask, is it important or necessary to win? Being a good sport in terms of absorbing what happens to you, and turning it to your realistic use, is the productive, the creative, the healthy kind of sportsmanship.

Which Basic Reaction?

We learned in earlier chapters about the two types of basic emotional response to difficulty, the aggressive, and the dependent. In our self-examination, we will come upon now one and now the other response in ourselves. The average human being has a little of both, and swings back and forth between the aggressive effort to deal with life by fight or flight, and the regressive tendency to seek protection.

Our mixed responses may make it harder to understand ourselves. But they are one more evidence of the effort of the human being to achieve and maintain balance in what seems often like a precarious walk on the high wire. The fact that an individual swings from one response to the other is one of his best claims to being normal. It suggests that he is making a positive effort to cope with his problems and manage his own life. It indicates the inner restlessness of growth toward emotional maturity.

Suppose, like many men actively engaged in the competitive business world, you are a go-getter on the surface, but underneath you have longings to be taken care of, to be protected, to be dependent. So well have you covered up your dependent needs that you may never have been aware of these longings, perhaps until you read this book, and realized that your delicate digestion was a tip-off to the inner softness which you have so long denied.

Now that you begin to penetrate the aggressive outer crust of your personality, you may realize that the woman you married is a strong individual. You may observe how you have tended to attach yourself to a strong business associate, or that you turn to your lawyer for that protective relationship which you need, or to your doctor.

You may also discern within yourself a certain hostility toward these very people from whom you crave love and care. You are perhaps sharp and dominating with your wife, argumentative with your business associate, inclined to disparage the advice your lawyer gives you or complain about his fee.

What's wrong here is not that you have a need for dependence, although that is an immaturity and you must recognize it as such. What's wrong is that you deny your dependence, cover it up, suppress it, and feel guilty about it. This is why you are combative, hostile, resentful, and it is also why you have a delicate digestion.

Suppose you were to recognize the fact that you have a need for a certain amount of love, of "mothering." Suppose you could accept, for the moment, this immaturity in your personality. So you need love. Why don't you ask for it?

In your own way you are asking for it now, but the way is not a good one. Pride prevents you from asking in a mature way. You hide your need and expect those around you—your wife, for example—to guess what you want. When she disappoints your unexpressed demand you are resentful. Perhaps you provoke a quarrel, when you really want to be loved. Perhaps you try to dominate her, to prove that you are stronger than she and to earn her respect. But respect is a poor substitute for the love you seek, and in any case you are more likely earning her hostility by your tactics. If she is a strong personality she resents your effort to dominate her.

There are good ways of asking for love. One of them, and probably the best, is to give love. How much thought have you spent during the past month on your wife's happiness and contentment? How much interest do you show in her achievements? How much do you really care about her? How do you show her that you care?

When did you last take her out to enjoy a dinner she did not have to cook? A present of flowers can mean as much to a woman as a new bracelet. More, perhaps, because it is only when the relationship has reached a state of mutual hostility that she needs to be bribed or placated by a showy, expensive tribute.

(To put the shoe on the other foot for a moment, one might say without fear of contradiction that any woman worthy of the name knows a thousand small but effective ways to show love. If she declines to practice them it is probably not out of ignorance. We are told that we forget things for unconscious reasons. Perhaps forgetting small errands and comforts for a husband can be understood as a concealed gesture of hostility.)

If you—the go-getter with the dependent tendency—are true to type, you are ashamed, or too proud, to show your wife that you care for her. You are so busy keeping her from finding out that you need her, that you have no time to think about her side of the life you live together. What if you let down the bars and admitted that you need her? Not sloppily, not childishly, but as one adult to another. If at the same time you can show her that you are genuinely interested in her, that you value her for herself apart from what you can get out of her, that you cherish her rights and privileges as an independent human being—then you are likely to get a response from her which will support and strengthen you in your own effort to achieve independence.

One thing you can be sure of: from the moment you recognize and accept your need for love, you are on your way to independence. And you may never get that ulcer, after all.

He Who Fights and Runs Away . . .

Let us see what the aggressive side of your personality reveals in this self-examination. You are a man or woman who does not evade responsibility. You do not turn to someone else to take care of things for you. You are trying to deal with your problems in an adult way, that is, by your own efforts.

But often you are frustrated. It is one of the conditions of living that people do not always behave as we want them to, and situations do not resolve themselves as we have planned. When you have lunch with your boss—or dinner with your in-laws—or receive an unsatisfactory telephone call or letter or come out at the wrong end of an interview, you may not get indigestion, but by the end of the day you have a splitting headache.

What is wrong? You have tried to deal with a person or a situation in an adult manner, and all you have got out of it is a headache. But not quite all. Behind the headache lie rebellion and resentment against the way things have turned out, a feeling of helplessness, a suppressed rage. The headache is what you are aware of. The other feelings are buried because they are not acceptable. It is not *right* to be angry at your family. It is not *safe* to fight with your boss. Fear has kept you from fighting back. Fear of the consequences may even have kept you from fighting for what you wanted in the most effective way, with careful preparation, with a minimum left to chance. You yourself may thus be responsible for the frustration which now irks you.

A patient of mine came in one afternoon in a state of jubilation. "I feel marvelous—I feel as though I had had a workout in the gym—I feel the way I felt when I was twenty, after a hard game of tennis," he said.

What had happened was nothing unusual in the course of business. A colleague had offered unexpected opposition to his favorite project. But this time, unlike many previous times, he had first looked into himself before confronting the colleague. He had considered the consequences of opposing the other man. He had decided that he could afford to accept the consequences. Having first looked his own anxieties in the face and found them not realistic, he was freed to fight for his project.

Two discoveries astonished him. First he discovered that once he had consulted his own fears, he was able to tap reserves of courage and energy he did not know he possessed. He went into his conference with the confidence that he could win his point. There is no doubt that the strength and conviction with which he entered the fight were important factors in his victory.

His second discovery was his feeling of *physical* wellbeing after the fight was over. His body felt limber, young, resilient, as after healthy athletic exertion.

There is an important moral to be drawn from such an experience. We can say with positiveness that in most of the difficulties which we must face in life, it is not the external situation which trips us up, but those inner forces within ourselves *which we have not consulted*. It is because we have not consulted them that they hamper us. It is because we have ignored or suppressed them that they block our way.

Those inner voices rise up to torture us afterward. We turn a situation over and over, when it is too late. The French have a phrase: *esprit d'escalier,* the wit that comes to us on the stairs after the interview or conference is over, the answer we should have given, the way we should have acted. We have a bad night, or many bad nights, with our *esprit d'escalier.* We are annoyed with ourselves, and often with the world as well.

We say of someone, "He is his own worst enemy." The same is potentially true, to a greater or less degree, for every one of us. If we will take time to recognize those inner forces, if we will pay them the respect which is their due and confer with them before we confront the outer world, then we are in a fair way to achieve inner unity. We may in time turn to the world a united front, an integrated personality.

Sometimes, after consulting with ourselves, we do not come out fighting. A realistic evaluation of our position points to defeat if we fight. Flight is the better course.

Here is a common source of confusion. It is considered "sissy" to run away. It is considered weak and cowardly to decline the challenge of a stronger opponent. We applaud the little man who tackles the big bully, even though the little man takes a fearful beating.

It is true that the little man, for all his inadequacy of size, may be moved by such stong indignation that he wants to fight, he must fight, and even though he is beaten he is satisfied at having fought. But more often we fight because we are ashamed not to fight. We go into battle already defeated, and come out with only the small comfort that we were right in expecting defeat.

The animal in the jungle feels no obligation to be that kind of hero. Confronted with a known enemy, he acts according to whether he is likely to win or lose a battle. A stag will fight another stag for a doe, but he will probably not attack a leopard if he has a chance to flee. He is not ashamed to run from a natural enemy stronger than himself.

I was once briefly lost in the Burma jungle, and came suddenly face to face with a panther. He gathered himself to spring, but he did not spring. He waited, glaring at me, and I waited, not daring to breathe. Then he turned and glided away. I went away too, at a run, grateful that the powerful cat had more sense than to charge an enemy whose strength he could not estimate.

Flight from a situation is not cowardice. We ought to get as much satisfaction from successfully escaping a situation as from successfully fighting it, because either course is healthy depending on the circumstances. The reason most of us do not is that we have been brought up to identify flight with cowardice, and a reasonable fear of defeat with a want of manhood.

How shall we flee from a situation which we cannot fight? A woman patient, after considerable self-searching, realized that her visits to her mother-in-law's home were the occasions for her headaches and backaches. The older woman was fighting for possession of her only son, and behind a deceptively loving exterior she took every opportunity to undermine her son's attachment to his wife. Our patient was the innocent victim of this struggle between mother and son, the one for possession and the other for independence.

The young wife saw that she could neither fight her mother-in-law nor stay away without endangering her marriage. Either course might force her husband into making a choice between his mother and his wife.

Since she could not escape the situation in fact, she escaped its emotional effects. She carried a mild sedative in her hand-bag; when she felt the tension rising, she excused herself from the room and popped a pill into her mouth. With its help she was calmer during the visit, and able to be more objective.

She became more confident of her husband's love, now that she did not put upon it the added strain of competition with his mother. She began to understand the older woman, in time to pity her, especially when she saw her mother-in-law suffering from chronic attacks of an irritating skin rash, evidence that the older woman too was under the stress of emotional conflict. It followed that with her growing inner strength the wife became a source of strength to her husband, and the bond between them deepened into one which no immature relationship with his mother could disturb.

15. THE CHILD WITHIN THE MAN

WEISS and English speak of man as having four ages: chronological, physical, intellectual, and emotional. It is not unusual to encounter a man who is forty years old according to his birthday, but may have the physical vigor of thirty, the intellectual development of fifty, and the emotional age of ten.

Our chronological age is automatically decided for us, but our three other ages are more or less subject to ourselves. We can make rational efforts to maintain the body in a state of youthful vigor. We can reach out for intellectual growth through study, reading, and the companionship of well-developed intellects.

Of the three ages beyond the chronological, the hardest to develop is the emotional. The groundwork for our emotional growth is laid down in early childhood, when we have nothing to say about it. Whether we know it or not, we are the people our childhood made us.

So it should not surprise us that, in the course of our self-examination, we may find clinging to us traces of the child we once were. Growth is by nature an uneven process. We leap suddenly ahead, and then for a time we seem to stand still or even to slip backward. Educators are aware of "plateaus of learning." A child learns in spurts, alternating with level periods in which no progress or very little is apparent.

Since growth is so uneven, and may take place on different levels of the personality at different periods, we must be prepared to find that some aspects of our growth are slower, and some may be definitely held back. Freud was the first to point out that an emotional shock in childhood may arrest an individual's emotional growth at that point. *Fixation* was his explanation of many nervous illnesses which had puzzled medicine, for which there was no apparent organic cause, such as paralysis, blindness, deafness, vomiting, tremors, compulsions and phobias. Behind them, Freud found arrested emotional development.

All of us are familiar with certain kinds of childishness in adults. Sometimes it shows through plainly. The individual who habitually reacts with screaming, desk-pounding, uncontrollable rage is the child given to temper tantrums, only in a man's body and very often in a man's position of responsibility. He may even be your boss.

The man who is "just like a baby when he has a little pain" is in fact a baby asking for a mother's care, though he is a grown man. The woman who spends forty dollars for a new hat and then finds she cannot pay her butcher is the same little girl who ate all her party candy at once and then cried because the other children still had some to enjoy later on.

More often we cover up our childishnesses, as much from ourselves as from others. Our devices for hiding our immaturities are cunning, and it is hard for us to discover them.

Yet we must not be discouraged in our search for them. An emotional immaturity is a weakness in structure, and under stress it is likely to crack. Even without extraordinary stress, our immaturities may exact a constant price from us in happiness and achievement.

On the other hand, we are rewarded almost at once for our effort to achieve maturity. In proportion to the effort we make, we feel ourselves freed of the dragging burden of our childishness. It is as though we can put down at last the heavy baby we have carried, as though the childish hand which has clung to ours has loosed its grip, and the childish footsteps which have slowed our pace have ceased at last to follow us.

Some Common Immaturities: The Eager-to-Please

The more the students of childhood tell us about children, the better able we are to penetrate the immaturities which persist into adulthood. Some childish patterns are so commonly found in adult behavior that we can label them immediately— in other people. We are naturally slower to recognize them in ourselves, and some of us refuse to recognize them at all.

A powerful motive in children is the need for approval, especially the approval of adults. In a child this is readily understandable. He is dependent on the good will of grownups for his continued care and protection. He is constantly confronted with the necessity of meeting adult standards. His behavior is good if it pleases his parents. His school work is good if it satisfies his teachers.

As he grows to maturity, this need for outside approval should diminish in proportion as he develops his own standards. The desire for approval cannot disappear entirely, since we are human and therefore gregarious. Each of us needs to be accepted in some community, whether it be the family, the office or factory, the congregation or neighborhood.

The mature adult achieves a balance between his own standards and those of his community. The immature adult, however, continues to live for the approval of others, even at the sacrifice of his own needs and wishes. He is thus thrown into conflict with himself. The needs which he buries are in conflict with his outer behavior, which is designed to satisfy others, not himself.

We know about people who "grow away from each other." At the end of the war many young wives and husbands who had been separated came together to discover that they were not the same as they had been. Sometimes a separation has the effect of freeing one or the other partner from having to live up to the other's expectations of him. A separation plus a profound experience such as war service—or, equally, the wife's experience of carrying on alone at home—may be genuinely maturing.

If the two young people can accept each other's new status as more mature individuals, then their marriage will flower in ways which were unlikely before. If one or the other cannot make the adjustment to the new relationship, then the partnership founders, and indeed many such marriages did.

The question you must ask yourself is not whether you need to be liked and approved by one person or many in your life, because you have a right to this need. The question is, how much do you depend on this approval? How much of yourself will you sacrifice to win it? How much are your decisions and your behavior governed by the desire to please others, not yourself?

Child psychologists tell us that the child who is too obedient is often in greater difficulties than the one who expresses his rebellion by antisocial behavior. In adults this can be equally true. The adult who conforms too docilely to the standards of his class or group or parents, who never dares to express his individuality, is also likely to be in difficulties. His way to maturity is to learn to understand and respect his own needs as an individual, and to overcome his fear of expressing them.

If this seems difficult—and for the cautious conformist, the Mr. Milquetoast, it really is difficult—then he should remember that he can begin in little ways. The smallest assertion of himself will give him courage to attempt the next one. If he makes his small self-assertions pleasantly, not as an attack on the other person involved but genuinely for his own positive reasons, then he is likely to find himself not less popular, but more respected in consequence.

Sometimes an individual will go through his whole adult life unconsciously trying to earn the approval of a parent, or to prove that parent wrong. I know a woman who is beautiful and very successful in her social aspirations. She has been courted by men of world importance, has become wealthy and is accepted in the most exclusive circles of international society. She has made one socially acceptable marriage after another, but has been unable to find happiness in any.

This woman was born in an obscure middle-class family in a small American town. She has achieved the success she sought solely by her own efforts. Her tragedy is that she does not believe in her achievement and cannot enjoy it. When as a girl she dreamed of such a life as she now leads, her mother warned her, "You will never make anything of yourself." It seems that she has spent her whole life trying to prove her mother wrong. The constant need to assert her self-importance above any man with whom she begins a relationship soon defeats the relationship.

Unhappily it is true that standards are often set for us in childhood which we can never meet. Must we let this poison our whole life? Can we not try, by self-searching, to exorcise this need to prove ourselves worthy to a father or mother whom we should long ago have outgrown?

Rebel for Rebellion's Sake

Peer Gynt sailed the seven seas, vainly searching for happiness, unable to accept the necessity for conforming to any society. He is the symbol of perpetual adolescent rebellion, as Peter Pan is the symbol of perpetual childish rebellion. A young patient of mine set out to find happiness by crossing the country on horseback. This was his second great idea. His first great idea was to write a new philosophy which would replace all previous philosophies.

There are slippery corners in all our lives, points at which a wholesome drive may be deflected into unproductive channels. The need to rebel against authority and find our own way is a good and healthy one, just as the need to work and earn our own living is a good and healthy one. But the boy who sets out to earn his living may turn into the man who wants money for money's sake, or for the power that money may bring. Just so, the child who rebels in order to reach his own full development may turn into a rebel for rebellion's sake, without cause and without direction.

The rebel who channels his efforts toward a goal may become a great reformer, a leader, a breaker of new trails in man's struggle to improve himself. Menninger's clinic reports that those who were rebellious children make good psychiatrists. But the rebel who is only running *away from something* and never *toward something* is wasting himself. His sturdy spirit is arrested at an immature stage, with the result that his potentiality for effective achievement in the world is thrown away.

Most of us do not run away. Most of us remain in the home, the job, or the marriage to which we are committed, and nourish our rebellion in secret. This is a real danger point. Unacknowledged rebellion is, as we have seen, the beginning of many an illness. It is a free grant of power to the destructive instinct to turn against the self. It is a constant whittling away at the very sources of the will to live.

Attention-Getters

One of the French poets, it is said, dyed his hair green, in the latter part of the nineteenth century when green hair was only one of the milder efforts to shock the complacency of a Victorian world.

Some individuals will go to any length to attract attention. I read a story from the London *Times* of a century ago, describing the performance of a criminal at his own execution.

He had dressed with great care for the occasion. His proud, graceful walk to the gallows was made to the accompaniment of vociferous admiration from the crowd. At the foot of the gallows he bowed with great dignity, received a torrent of applause and cheers, and climbed grandly to his death as the fitting climax of the greatest moment of his life.

Hangings are no longer public, but opportunities for attention-getting are far from lacking. Recently a dowager was pictured on front pages across the country when she put her feet on a table at a Metropolitan Opera premiere. A jealous rival for attention stood on his head for the photographers outside the opera house. In another city a woman was photographed carrying a basket of ripe tomatoes with which she planned to assault a concert artist who had declined her invitation to dinner.

Fortunately for the dignity of mankind, not many of us take such extreme measures in the effort to achieve distinction. But some of the subtler ways we take are far more damaging to ourselves. There are people, both men and women, who devote most of their adult lives to being seen with celebrities and claiming to know famous persons by their first names. I know at least one woman who will drive her husband and herself to exhaustion and perhaps bankruptcy in order to live like her wealthy friends, with a large expensive home staffed with cook, butler, and maid. She does no useful work herself, because the women by whom she craves to be accepted do not work.

The need to be noticed by association with the rich or famous betrays a sad lack of faith in our own worth. The need to attract attention by being different is a confession of profound self-doubt, just as taking refuge in perfect conventionality betrays a lack of self-confidence.

I can think of one example of an attention-getter who was nevertheless true to himself. When I was a boy in school a new youngster joined our class. Tall for his fourteen years and thin as a lath, he wore a pince-nez with a little chain, and English knickers though they were not yet in fashion. The fact that his father was a well-known novelist did not impress his classmates. But this boy found a way to impress us.

An ordinary boy would toss a nickel or a dime in the air. Left severely alone during recess in the school yard, this boy tossed a twenty-dollar gold piece. When it fell and rolled away he did not leap for it, but nonchalantly walked to the spot, kicked the dirt away, and stooped with languid indifference to recover the coin. It did not take long for him to be accepted as one of the leaders in our group. But once accepted, he proved himself a worthy member, no sissy but as able to take the rough-and-tumble as any of us. He has since become a successful film producer.

The Poor in Love

Love is said to be a cure for everything, but many adults are not capable of love. They confuse love with possessiveness, clutching at the loved one and giving little in return. They treat love like securities, to be kept in a vault but never used.

Some are afraid to give love, as though it were money and if you gave it away you would have no more. Or they are afraid of rejection, of ridicule, of hurt, or of a foreign invasion. Or they express a contempt for love as a weakness, like the woman patient who described her suitor as a weakling because he had not been able to resist falling in love with her. Is she really contemptuous of love? Or is she rather afraid, seeing in his expression of love a demand for her to give love in return?

People rarely die of love like the woman in our second chapter, but many dry up for lack of it. I have been watching a patient, a young widow, for several years. She is drying up physically. Her skin is dry, her hair is dry and thinning, her fingernails are dry and brittle. Her whole personality is drying up. Even her income is drying up, because she mistrusts the people who could help her with her investments.

She says, "I haven't had my share of happiness. Someone will come along." But she has not gone out to find that someone. Instead she withdraws still further. When a man shows interest in her, she at once begins to destroy the relationship by arguing, trying to prove herself his superior. She offends men by her aggressive prudery even before they make any approach to her. Her friends have warned her, but she is superior to her friends too, and gradually she is losing them. She wondered why, one day, she found in her young son's

pocket a piece of stale bread. She could not understand that
the boy too was suffering from her inability to give love, and
had taken the bread with the plan of running away from home.

This woman is a deeply unhappy person who defeats herself completely, even to rejecting the medical help which
might save her. Many people defeat themselves in love, though
not to such a degree. They are people who did not learn in
childhood how to give love.

We learn in childhood to give love if we are first loved by
our parents or by those who stand in the relationship of
parents to us. Well, then, perhaps you were not loved enough
as a child. Unconsciously you resent your parents' lack of
love for you, but unconsciously you are visiting that same
lack of love on others now. If you have children, you may be
failing to love them as your parents failed to love you. Must
the chain of lovelessness go on unbroken from generation to
generation? And must you live out your life without love,
because you never had enough of it to begin with?

A little child is born selfish. He is the center of his own small
universe. Others, like his parents, are important only as they
give to him, as they satisfy his needs. As he matures, he learns
to share his parents' care with his brothers and sisters, his toys
with other children, his pleasures with other young people.
He can do this if he is secure in his parents' love. If he is not
sure of their love, he clings to the symbols of love: food,
attention, toys. He clutches these to himself. He remains a
selfish little animal. As a grown man he may make generous
gifts to charity, but possibly this is only a cloak for his selfishness, for he has learned that to be obviously selfish is not socially acceptable. To those closest to him, and in that coin
which is least material and most valuable, he is still miserly.

How can such a person learn to give love? He can make
a beginning by taking a different kind of interest in those
around him. He can begin to look upon them, not for what
he can get out of them, but for what will best help them to be
themselves. He can turn his center of interest outward, and
try to understand others—not merely some unidentified peo-

ple whom he does not know and for whom it is easy to write out a check, but those whose love will really warm him if he can win it.

Until now this book has urged us to turn our eyes inward, on ourselves. But sometimes the first effort we must make in self-discovery is to turn our eyes outward, on those around us. In learning to give love, we must first learn the needs of those around us.

Johnny Appleseed strode through the country, planting the seeds of trees of which others would enjoy the fruit. He is a homely symbol of love freely and lavishly given, and he lives in the legend as not only a good man, but a happy man.

And I remember a story in a school book about a man who had the finest apple tree in his county. All year he nursed and tended his tree, but when the apples were ripe and the boys climbed the wall and stole them, he did not stop them. He wanted the boys to have not only the apples but also the fun of stealing them.

Learning to give love is like learning to use a new skill. At first we feel awkward, perhaps frightened. It is necessary to go slowly, to work in small, familiar, even trivial ways, and not to be discouraged if the response is slow in coming. We cannot change a pattern of years with a single gesture, an occasional word. But love freely given, without strings attached, without even a demand for thanks or gratitude, will sooner or later win love in return.

THE LIST of common immaturities in adults could go on and on; by now the reader may be adding his own observations of childishness in grownups he knows.

We meet immature adults in the office, store, and factory: the executive who surrounds himself with yes-men, like the willful child who must have his own way; the floater who keeps changing jobs, like the child who is always beginning projects and never finishing them; the slave to routine, like the child who is upset if things are not always done the same way.

We meet them in the home: the husband who is always reminding his family how hard he works for them, the wife who makes her housework a martyrdom. I know a woman whose husband provides her with a maid all week, but who cannot join the family outings on Sunday because that is the day she does the laundry.

We all know men who work nights as well as days. Such a man might ask himself whether his long hours of work are really necessary. Any business or profession may require occasional periods of intense work. But to drive yourself to work grimly day and night, month after month, is one more kind of self-destruction.

We know people who cannot make up their own minds, like the man who asks his wife which suit he should wear, or the woman who goes shopping for a dress, looks at suits, actually buys a coat—and returns it the next day because a woman friend was critical of it.

Why we are as we are is less important than whether we

236

recognize ourselves. It is no shame to be immature in one way or another. The human being is a complex creature in a complex world, and it takes him a long time to grow up.

From time to time we may be aware of a childish trait, but it is easier to suffer an hour or so of remorse and self-criticism, and to bury the weakness out of sight again, than it is to make the effort to revise it. With the effort we waste covering up our weaknesses we could make quite a lot of progress toward working them out constructively.

What is lacking, generally, is the incentive to make the effort. We do not realize the price we pay in happiness. We do not estimate the loss we suffer in productivity. We do not face the danger we run, of illness.

A buried dissatisfaction with life leads to fatigue, to irritability, to inefficiency. A failure or rejection leads to worry, fear, and tensions which in turn lead to more failure and more rejection. We pay the price in happiness and achievement first; the body's illness is likely to follow more slowly.

Boredom and Health

Boredom can be a serious illness. Boredom is that invisible disease caused neither by germs nor toxins, nor by organic change. It is the mental counterpart of that physical state which we call fatigue. Boredom can be chronic or acute.

Acute boredom can arise from discontent with a given situation. The company or the occupation does not suit you, or there is somewhere else you would rather be, someone else you would rather be with. It may be a stage in creative work, the time before the birth of an idea, the fallow period when we are regenerating. Acute boredom is temporary boredom and not necessarily a sign of trouble.

Chronic boredom is serious. It is an evidence that the creative instinct has surrendered and the will to live has handed in its resignation. Boredom is a total absence of the incentive to go on living. But whether or not we accept the fate of dying of boredom, either metaphorically or in fact, is eventually up to ourselves.

We can reverse the decision and cure ourselves of the disease of boredom, but only if we will take rational action against the symptoms and make an earnest examination for the cause.

Wellbeing has its symptoms too, of joy, kindness, and interest in life and people. A healthy adult, like a healthy child, has energy left over for play. A healthy adult, like a healthy child, is interested and curious and wants to learn things and do things. It is normal to enjoy your work and the rewards it brings, both the material rewards and the satisfaction of achievement and recognition. The enjoyment of both work and play are symptoms of a flourishing will to live.

It is true that our complex industrial civilization offers less and less scope for the majority to find individual creative expression. Many of us must work at routine occupations and many of us do work which we do not enjoy.

The solution to the problem is still the same: fight, or flight. Either we deal with the situation aggressively and find a rational solution within it. Or we get out. We do not resign ourselves to it, if resignation means, as it usually does, that we remain in the situation while secretly rebelling against it. That way is suicidal.

A young dentist complained that he was unhappy in his profession, and particularly in his work as an assistant in a large fashionable office catering to wealthy patients. His gall bladder was giving him trouble, he was subject to dizziness and spells of faintness, and it was obvious that he could not continue in work against which he was in such protest that it was making him ill. He wanted to be a writer. But he had a wife and young child to support. He received treatment for his symptoms, and in the course of his visits I suggested that he might try to find a workable solution, one which would not jeopardize his integrity.

He found his solution. He moved his family to a small town where the cost of living is considerably less than in the metropolis. His house is tiny and almost bare. He keeps limited office hours for patients, just enough to pay his living expenses, and devotes the rest of the time to writing. His first novel had a fine reception, and his second, still in work, is already sold to a good publisher. The austerity of his life troubles him not at all. He is a happy young man, and a healthy one.

His solution combined both fight and flight. He escaped from the particular conditions of work which were unacceptable to him. At the same time he found a way of combining the professional earning of a living with the work he wanted to do.

Not many of us are so fortunate as to have another kind of work which we are longing and able to do. But if we must remain in work which gives us no joy, then we must make a *positive adjustment* in our lives. We must make the unsatisfactory work a part of a more satisfactory whole. We must seek ways of spending our leisure time which will give expression to those creative impulses to which our work does not give scope. To ignore this need, to refuse the choice of fight or flight, is self-destructive.

The same is true in our attitudes toward home and family, toward parents and children, toward marriage and our marriage partner and our parents-in-law. *Resignation is not adjustment.* The only true adjustment, the one for which the human mind and body are equipped, lies in the choice between fight, which is an effort at adjustment, and flight, which is the act of getting out of an unwholesome situation.

Resignation does not end our dissatisfaction. We do not "forget it." We only stifle the open protest. We bury the conflict—and thus give our dissatisfaction the greater power to do us harm.

When we say we resent our work or our marriage because we have no success or happiness in it, we may be stating the case the wrong way 'round. We may first resent it, and therefore fail to make a success of it. We tend to wait passively for someone or something outside ourselves to change. We try to reform a husband or revise the personality of a wife. But we cannot change other people. We can only change ourselves.

Some people extricate themselves from one unsatisfactory

relationship only to enter another and divorce one wrong partner only to turn to a similar one. But most of us make the effort, with more or less success, to learn from our mistakes. Critical events can change us. A serious accident or illness, sudden wealth or the loss of it, a birth or a death among those close to us—such experiences may push us with the shock of strong emotion either farther along on the path of maturity, or backward toward less capacity to deal with life. It is obvious that the better an individual understands himself, the more capably he can deal with the big and little events of living.

Each human being has his specific way of reacting to situations. The difference between the normal and the neurotic is only one of degree. The normal itself offers quite a spread. The medical normal in blood pressure, blood sugar, metabolism, height and weight, is never a single point like 98.6 on the thermometer, but a spread between two figures. To find oneself somewhat outside the normal spread occasionally is not necessarily serious. An occasional limp is not an illness.

Everyone becomes confused now and then, stuck in a dead-end road, not knowing which next step to take. To run away from ourselves at such times is to court confusion as a permanent state. Precisely in time of stress is when our personality weaknesses show. Precisely then is when we have most to gain from examining ourselves.

The difficulties we encounter in life are not insoluble. If we cannot find a solution through either fight or flight, then our thinking about the situation is faulty. A situation with no possible solution is rare in real life. Usually, we fail to discover the solution because it is one which we are unwilling to accept: that of making a positive adjustment.

Our refusal to face a solution is nourished by our own destructive instinct. To resist solution is to destroy oneself.

Preparing for Later Years

As our birthdays mark the passing of youth, the will to live is apparently challenged by a failing body.

We can seriously question whether it is really the body which fails. We can ask whether we have not unconsciously crippled the will to live in our earlier years, even before we reach our prime.

A significant observation was made by the physiologist Rubner about twenty years ago, in a study of the physical symptoms of aging. Rubner found that the average man does not begin to age merely in his later years. The first signs of physical aging actually come *at the beginning of his adult life,* at the time when he has finished his schooling and settles down to the practice of his chosen occupation.

This early aging of the body, Rubner explains, is the result of "narrowing the mental horizon, sinking into . . . purely occupational tasks, neglecting any further development of the self."

This self-limitation reveals its full destructiveness when a man retires from his business or profession. He finds that without his work he has nothing to do. He has no interests, no direction, actually no reason to continue living. It is, therefore, not surprising that so many men, vigorous until they retire, fail rapidly afterward.

"Knowledge and timber," said Oliver Wendell Holmes, "should not be used until they are seasoned." But Dr. Holmes did not intend that we should never use them at all. By the time knowledge should have seasoned into the wisdom of maturity, most people have given up both the acquisition of knowledge and the use of it. Most adults tend to live, not by knowledge, but by the set patterns of habit.

Childhood and youth are periods of many interests and activities. A characteristic of the normal child is his eagerness to learn and explore. Youth has the privilege of rushing forth to make its own discoveries, without thought and without plan. But there is no natural law which prevents the mature man from continuing to explore and discover. Only, because he is mature, it is characteristic that he should first stop to consult with himself on where he is going and how best to get there.

Most of us, however, shed not only the rashness of youth, but also youth's eagerness to discover. When we reach what is hopefully called the age of reason, when we finish our youthful preparation for the way in which we will earn our living, then we discard most of the activities and interests of our youth, even though they could continue to give us both pleasure and profit. We put them aside, we say, until we have more time. This is the moment at which we begin to grow fatty tissues in our muscles.

How many musical instruments, how many collections and handicraft tools, how many skis and skates, bats and balls, books, records, albums are gathering dust in your attic? How many arts and skills are withering in you, not from aging, but from neglect?

Often we throw these things aside in a gesture of rebellion. We are thumbing our noses at authority. Many a graduate hurls his books into the farthest corner. I know I did.

We feel we must make good. We are afraid to take time out to play. Life, we are warned, is not meant to be easy.

A young person puts on the trimmings of maturity. He smokes and drinks like his elders. He represses his young hopes under cynical talk. He plays bridge instead of baseball. He carries a brief case as though this will magically make him a man of affairs. His old interests seem childish; they threaten his new dignity. He makes a clean sweep, not stopping to question which things are really childish.

Resting or Rusting?

Mountain climbing is a strenuous, perilous sport, a young man's sport. But a man who continues climbing can climb still, and enjoy the exhilarating sport far into his late years. Rubner mentions the number of men who are good mountain-climbers at sixty and sixty-five. As a young man traveling in the glacial heights of Switzerland, I was myself amazed at the aged Englishmen who gathered at the mountain resorts for the season's climbing. If these men had stopped climbing in their twenties or thirties, postponing this pleasure until they had more time, they would never have climbed again.

Making up for lost time solely on vacations and weekends is not, however, the way to keep muscles young. We don't need to prove that we are still young by playing three sets of tennis in an afternoon after not playing for a year. Exertion in spurts is a dangerous risk for people in their middle years. We keep our bodies young, not by putting intermittent violent strain on them, but by using them habitually in enjoyable physical activity.

While muscles which are used do not age until late in life, a mind which is used need never age at all. The idea that learning stops with the end of the school years denies us knowledge and pleasure. It is also self-destructive. It invites old age.

The belief that only young people can learn has been thoroughly disproved by the current flowering of adult education in this country. People in their middle and late years who want to learn, and who are not ashamed to learn, have no trouble in learning. Adults who never touched a musical instrument, or who were forcibly exposed to one in childhood, are learning to play music for pleasure now that they turn to it of their own free will.

I know a man in his sixties who recently began to study philosophy. He took private tutoring and graduate courses, and has collected a library which is a pride and pleasure to him. The sharpness of George Bernard Shaw's wit was not dulled even at ninety.

When we stop learning, we begin to grow old. When we stop being interested, we begin to grow old. When we stop using our bodies, we begin to grow old. There is no physiological age at which we must stop all activity. Hence there is no age at which we *must* grow old. Like Shaw, we can be fully alive until we die. We need never be old.

The interests, arts and skills which we recklessly toss away on entering adulthood may be the very tonics which could lift us over the darkest moments of our life. If we put them aside until we have leisure to pursue them, then we are inviting old age before our time. When at last we come to the advanced years, when the sharpest struggles are over and we are freed to enjoy the fruits of our life's labor, there may no longer be any fruits to enjoy. We have let them wither, long before. All our efforts to prolong life may mean that we do not live longer, but only die more slowly.

With science each year adding new length to the average life span, a new branch of medicine has been developing to preserve our health and enrich our lives during these added years. Geriatrics specializes in the diseases of old age. Gerontology is the branch of research devoted to old age. A mass of data from research and practical work with old people has already accumulated. All our knowledge points inescapably to the need for preparation during our young and middle years of interests and attitudes which will maintain us in health during these added years. Dr. Harry Benjamin in the magazine *American Medicine* pointed out that the problem is not to add years to our life, but to add life to our years.

Second Childhood

There is another aspect of aging, which is not merely emptiness or dullness but actual deterioration. It has occurred to me that those old people who have reached the second childhood of senility may have been just as childish all their lives as they reveal themselves to be in old age.

When a man must deal with the world as an adult, he is obliged to hide his immaturity behind a front of seemingly adult behavior. If he has position and prestige, if he becomes rich, the childishness he may show is tolerantly called eccentricity; he is a "character." In old age there is no longer the necessity nor the energy to maintain the front, and such a man may revert to his true childish self. He could not grow old with dignity, because he never grew up.

Otherwise how shall we explain the fact that some old people do not become senile, but maintain to their last day the dignity and wisdom which properly belong to advanced years? Oddly, we often find that these beautiful old people also retain their physical faculties. They see and hear, and their minds are not only tolerant and kind but also alert. They are rare people, and they are memorable.

Many of us cherish the image of such a grandparent or wise old family friend. We remember with gratitude having known such a person, although we may be mystified to explain the basis of his or her unique quality.

I will make bold to say that the reason is not mysterious. I believe that a man or woman who grows old beautifully is one who has achieved maturity. Such a person may have been gifted with a fortunate constitution at birth, or may have had a nurturing environment. It is just as possible that he or she overcame by great effort a disadvantage of birth or environment, or a critical experience in youth. If we were to know everything about the lives of such people, we would find, I am certain, clues to the maturity which illuminates their old age.

I believe that to grow old in dignity and wisdom we must first grow up. We must deal with those immaturities left in us from childhood. We cannot merely hide them, or trust passively that years of living will do away with them. We must consciously seek maturity by making that positive adjustment to living which is maturity.

To live long, not only in years but in the enjoyment of them, we must understand and control the forces which shorten life. Both early and late, we must take time to cultivate the will to live.

He that wrestles with us
strengthens our nerves and
sharpens our skill. Our
antagonist is our helper.

EDMUND BURKE

17. DOCTOR AND PATIENT

THE IDEA of medicine in people's minds is a ragoût of what
they hear and what they read, seasoned with childhood im-
pressions, left-over superstition and old wives' tales. But the
solid content of what they know about medicine is learned
from their doctors. Therefore we would do well to turn our
attention to the doctor, whose attitude affects not only our
health or illness but also our understanding of it.

The doctor holds a unique position. Among the motives
which lead him to choose his exacting profession is the ideal-
istic wish to serve. For the layman the word "doctor" has
emotional overtones. It is touched with the mystery of childhood's belief in magic and its accompanying awe. When we
were children the doctor was an almighty personage called
in times of anxious need and capable of performing miracles.

He was more powerful than other adults, more powerful
even than parents. A mother or father could be struck down,
sick and helpless in bed, but the doctor always appeared
robust and hearty, with the fresh cheeks of outdoors. He went
confidently about his ritual, dispelling anxiety, spreading an
air of comfort. He made us feel that all would be well now
that he was there.

We remember fear and anger, too, when he pressed down
our tongue and stuck a needle into our flesh. To some he was

247

a threat: "If you don't take your cod liver oil I'll call the
doctor!" In other people's minds the doctor has inherited the
mantle of the high priest, and some physicians are not averse
to trying it on now and then.

Yet the physician is not made of different material from
other human beings. He is subject to the same natural laws,
the same feelings and reactions as any other man.

In his own life the physician is not spared stress. He has the
same anxieties and conflicts, the same alternating hope and
depression as other men. Finally a doctor seems more disposed
than the average man to die of an illness which we consider
"unnatural"—that is, premature—such as a heart attack.

We know that he carries the burden of anxiety for his
patients in addition to the problems all other people have.
We may suppose that his profession sharpens for him the
conflict experienced by conscientious men in many fields,
the conflict between ideals and the practical demands of living.
His economic struggle is made acute by the frequent inability
of his patients to pay. Many a doctor is confronted almost
daily with a choice between the need for his services, regardless
of fee, and the needs of his own family. When Talleyrand said
that a married man will do anything for money, he was only
exaggerating a bitter truth.

Physicians fall into the same classifications as other men.
We find among them too the regressive or dependent type, and
also the aggressive, hostile one. One is so shy that he cannot
talk to patients. Another assumes a chilling remoteness, but
he cannot control his nervous tic. Still another is dictatorial,
covering his self-doubt with bluster or intellectual superiority.
The walls of some doctors' offices are papered with diplomas,
to the patient an effective reminder to keep him in his place.
Others set receptionists and nurses to guard their inaccessibil-
ity.

Doctors too must struggle to make their adjustments to
life. They hide anxiety and insecurity. They mask rebellion
and resentment. We have doctors who are emotionally mature
and doctors who are as immature as the most retarded of their
patients. We must point out that their immaturity does not

necessarily make them bad doctors. It does, however, put them under greater stress in their work. It makes a good doctor-patient relationship more difficult to achieve.

A doctor who is emotionally immature is likely to be upset by immature behavior in his patients; perhaps he sees in them a reminder of his own difficulties. A doctor's skill and intellect may be developed to the highest power, while emotionally he may remain a child who meets another child's antagonism with his own antagonism. Many a patient limps away from the doctor's office, his ego bruised, forgetting that he himself threw the first snowball, remembering only that the answering snowball felt twice as big, with a rock inside it.

The doctor has voluntarily chosen a life of dedication. Yet not all doctors can be expected to have the strength of a Kant, who lived up to what he wrote at twenty-two, "I have already fixed upon the line which I am resolved to keep. I will enter on my course and nothing shall prevent me from pursuing it."

Patients are not inclined to see the doctor as a human being, fallible and subject to weakness. They do not want to see him in any disappointing human form. For many patients the doctor is the last substitute they can find for a father. They cling to their belief that he will look after them, will see that nothing bad happens to them. Each one likes to think that *his* doctor will take care of everything with his little pills and his magic injections.

Though they cannot expect the doctor to be superhuman, they have every right to expect him to be superior, not only in his skill and knowledge, but in his humanity. Unlike most other professions, the doctor deals almost exclusively with people in trouble. The patient and his family are frightened, confused, full of anxiety and tension. They must put their trust in the doctor; they have no other recourse. The patient's family are often more difficult for the doctor to treat than the patient himself. Nevertheless, can the doctor afford to vent on them an outburst of temper, a dictatorial unreason, or a cold indifference?

Illness brings out the best in some people, and in others the worst. Doctors speak of good patients and bad patients. The good patient is quiet, docile, grateful, and moreover he responds well to treatment. The bad patient demands explanations, comes up continually with new complaints, takes the doctor's time, and worst of all, his symptoms are as stubborn as himself.

The doctor must be prepared to deal equally wisely with both types. The question has been raised whether purely biological training prepares young doctors adequately for this aspect of their practice. But there are signs that the doctor-patient relationship is now being regarded in a new light, in accordance with our modern understanding of the psychological aspects of illness.

The Impersonal Routine

The word "doctor" comes from the Latin word meaning "to teach, to instruct." For many years now, since the great development of medicine as a natural science, doctors have seen no actual need to teach their patients how to be well. The doctor felt he could depend entirely on his highly developed methods of testing and prescribing.

Ours is an age of experts, each trained in a particular part of a most complicated whole. We gratefully acknowledge the necessity and the value of detailed research in modern medicine. But we must face the danger of getting lost in the details. We must understand the error of seeing the whole as merely the sum of its parts. A human being is something more than the sum of our medical specialties. The physician who does not go beyond being an expert at mending a bone or treating a fever does not know how to treat a human being. He is not likely even to see the need of dealing with the human being as someone whose emotional troubles may be a cause of the broken bone or the fever, someone whose life situation may delay or prevent his recovery despite all the doctor's scientific skill.

We have talked of the family physician who knew his patient as a person. He could give sound advice, and he did.

He warned and scolded. Sometimes he went outside his medical domain to find positive ways of helping a patient in difficulties. He got a man a loan if he needed money, reconciled differences between husband and wife, persuaded a parent of a better way to deal with a child. The authority of a doctor in those days was based on his personality scarcely less than on his professional knowledge.

In the modern big-city doctor's office, two strangers meet, and when they part again they are still likely to be strangers. The atmosphere is businesslike and to the point. Of the two, the patient is too intimidated to make any advance toward a more human relationship, and the doctor is too busy. A patient who had been to many doctors confessed to me that she had come to my office once before her first official visit. On that occasion she had stood for a long time before the office door, and then she had gone home. She felt unable to face again the chilling routine she had learned to expect in a doctor's office.

Partly in self-defense, partly as a result of his training, the modern doctor keeps his personality under wraps. He does not expose himself to questioning or criticism. Caught in the routine of modern medical practice, many a doctor becomes estranged from the deeper meaning of his title.

There are times when the doctor himself experiences the shortcomings of that method. Young physicians in war service began to see the necessity for a change in their approach to illness. What we broadly call psychosomatic medicine existed long before World War II, but the recognition of psychological factors in illness took a tremendous leap into public consciousness during the war and after it, in response to a felt need.

The doctor is in a difficult position. He is justifiably afraid to step off from the safe shore of what he knows—his physiological science of medicine—into unknown waters. He may wonder whether he is even needed any more. Will the medical man become extinct while the psychoanalyst takes over? And what about his bread and butter? In the end he lances the abscess and lets it go at that.

Insecurity sometimes makes a man more dogmatic and unapproachable than he might otherwise be. Occasionally a patient, with more self-confidence than the average, tries in a small way to make friends with the doctor. One such patient, having his blood pressure taken, asked, "Doctor, how do you read that machine?"

"That, my dear fellow, will take you four or five years to learn," the doctor replied, without troubling to discover that he was talking to a man who had earned his Ph.D. in science.

More and more physicians are seeking a way for doctor and patient to meet as two human beings, not pitted against each other, but allied with each other against illness. The change is coming. Weiss and English write:

"The day is here when the general physician should be able and willing to administer minor psychotherapy [as he always performed minor surgery] and recognize the criteria for major psychotherapy. Now and then there may be a patient whose inability to understand or whose reluctance to look within himself may cause him to go elsewhere in search of the more traditional therapies. But sincere patients will not do this. If we believe that personality problems are an important cause of psychosomatic disorders, then it is useless to compromise, to be indirect in approach, or to try to hold the patient by giving him what he thinks he wants."

Medicine as Service

A physician who does not feel a sympathy for individual human beings should not feel obliged to practice. There is a need for pure scientists in medicine, for research men whose intellectual gifts can make enormous contributions to the cause of health. A man who is not emotionally dedicated to medicine can achieve the rewards of his intellect in those fields. He should not subject himself to the tensions of dealing with people.

Why must the physician be dedicated above most other

professions? Not so much because of the long years of training, nor even because, both waking and sleeping, he is at the mercy of his patients' needs. He must be dedicated principally because the material of his work is not drugs nor mechanical appliances, not chemistry nor physiology, although he must use all these. The material of his work is human beings.

He cannot afford to indulge in impatience or intolerance. He cannot make moral judgments on his patients' behavior. He cannot preach. He may not approve nor disapprove. He must only help.

He must consistently put his patients' interest above his own. This is a first principle in his ethics, and when he set out on his long and arduous training this was undoubtedly a principle to which he subscribed with all his heart. But ideals often become tarnished in the rough world of reality, and aspirations which seemed within reach in the cloistered halls of learning recede farther and farther under worldly pressures. The doctor, like any man, must make practical decisions. His skill and his time must pay him a living.

Yet it is a mistake from every point of view, even the practical, to regard a medical practice as a business in which patients come to buy so many pounds of health at so much per pound. A few patients may approach the doctor in this trading spirit, and a few doctors may make a good living out of selling their skill as a commodity.

But medicine is essentially not a business. It is a service. Most doctors accept it as such. My professor of anatomy started his first lecture in this wise: "Gentlemen, before we begin, I want you to take serious thought. Any one of you who is guided by other motives than devotion can still withdraw from medicine. Banking is a better profession in which to make money."

Most doctors are not rich men. Most doctors enter upon their profession without any expectation of wealth. They hope to be able to make a living. In this reasonable expectation, the doctor who is truly dedicated to his work is not likely to be disappointed.

The patient is not necessarily impressed by a fine office and showy evidence of a prosperous practice. On many patients this atmosphere has a chilling effect. They are repelled by the suggestion of mass production.

I had a young patient, the heiress of one of the country's great enterprises. When she was approaching the final months of her pregnancy she declined the services of a city obstetrician and went to a small New England village.

"I want a country doctor," she said. "I don't want a big production. I want a normal delivery, and a normal baby."

The patient cannot judge the doctor's skill and knowledge. These he must take on faith. But he can judge the doctor's attitude toward him. He can feel the doctor's interest in him as an individual.

To this interest the average patient responds. When he knows that the doctor is laboring unreservedly in his behalf, the patient will generally give his cooperation, his gratitude, and his loyalty. Even a very rebellious patient, hostile and unmanageable, is likely to return again and again to the doctor who does not answer hostility with hostility, but who continues to work in the patient's own interest.

How the patient responds to this attitude in a doctor, even during a first interview, is described by Binger in *The Doctor's Job:*

"In the course of such an interview something transpires. The patient reacts to being listened to with a certain half-perceived feeling, which he may indicate with look, gesture, or word. What does this mean? It means, I think, this: 'I am in trouble. I need help. I have found someone who cares and who wants to help me.' *That is the beginning of the therapeutic situation.*" (Italics mine.)

"What I am talking about now," Dr. Binger says further, "is a simple human experience so common that it often goes unnoticed. It does not belong exclusively to the realm of medicine. It exists between lawyer and client, as it does between teacher and pupil, pastor and parishioner, or in any situation in which one person seeks and receives help from another. In medicine, and more particularly in psychiatry, we see the situation in 'pure culture' because the seeking and receiving of help are, after all, the basis and intent of the relationship."

The doctor's reward is first a security in his practice. Since, for all his ideals, he must still pay his bills, this is a matter of no small importance.

But he has a deeper reward than the economic, deeper even than the satisfaction of work well done. It is in what he gets back from his patients in depth of fellowship and breadth of human understanding. The doctor can learn medicine out of books, but the practice of medicine he learns from his patients.

The Doctor's New Job

Where must you go to find such doctors?

Most doctors are like that. The big-city specialist, separated from his patients by his very specialty, is not typical. In rural areas, in small towns and cities, in the neighborhoods and suburbs of the metropolis itself, doctors give themselves thus freely and devotedly as a matter of course. A patient who is concerned with impressing his own superiority on the doctor may never see this.

It would not occur to us to question the devotion to service of the average doctor, except for one thing. The doctor now stands at a turning point in his profession. He faces a change like the change of a century ago from the art of healing to the science of medicine. He needs reorientation, and he needs reassurance.

Hegel said that we arrive at truth by thesis, antithesis, and synthesis. Virchow's great achievement was that he set illness of the body apart from all other considerations, and focused the sharp eye of science upon it. By fixing the point of attack on disease in the diseased cell, he set in motion a great wave of scientific research upon the physical aspects of illness. Thus was developed the thesis.

Ever since, man has suffered from this dichotomy, this division between mind and body. Against the most stubborn opposition, the psychologists and psychiatrists have persisted in presenting the importance of their science of the mind. Psychoanalytic psychology represents the antithesis.

Now we are approaching the synthesis. The truth is not a monopoly of either branch. Virchow's position in the scientific firmament is rather like Darwin's. Darwin pointed the way to understanding the development of man from the simplest form of life, but he could not tell us how life began. In the same way, Virchow uncovered a rich vein of knowledge of the physical progress of disease in the body, but he could not tell us how disease began. We must move in an opposite direction to find the force which brings on the structural change in Virchow's cell, just as we must seek in new directions to discover the first spark which ignited life.

Like the golden mean of Aristotle, the truth in medicine will be found somewhere between the clinician and the psychiatrist. Until now, the physical and mental sciences of medicine have seemed to be in opposition. Now they meet and fuse, and their fusion will be felt most profoundly in the general practitioner.

To the doctor in general practice today, the prospect is alarming. He is confronted with an entire new field of study, one surrounded by mystery. How shall he satisfy this new demand, added to his already complex medical science? Must he go back to school and learn to be a psychoanalyst?

An impressive practical demonstration of how the general practitioner can prepare himself to meet this new demand is reported from Cincinnati, where the Department of Medicine and Psychiatry of the University's College of Medicine, and the Cincinnati General Hospital, have been conducting a psychosomatic clinic for medical residents and fellows.

The report, in the *Journal of the American Medical Association* for June, 1950, covers the treatment of 170 patients. The success of the clinic from the patients' point of view was clear from the minimum number of sign-outs; that is, of patients who voluntarily gave up coming to the clinic although they were not well enough to be discharged.

Seventy-five per cent of the patients had physical disorders such as hypertension, various types of organic heart disease, asthma, peptic ulcer, diabetes, skin diseases, migraine, epilepsy, hyperthyroidism, obesity. The remaining twenty-five per cent had primarily neurotic disorders; that is, the symptoms of which they complained showed no physical evidence.

The majority of the patients showed a symptomatic improvement. For example, the man with high blood-pressure felt better although his blood pressure might have subsided only a little or perhaps not at all according to the machine. About half the patients showed real improvement in their capacity to function; they were able to return to almost normal life at home and at work.

What is most significant, however, is the reported effect on the doctors: "For the first time, the medical residents began to develop feelings of stability and security in dealing with patients who have emotional disorders." They were not upset by the provocative behavior of patients, once they understood the cause of it. They observed how even a most difficult, belligerent patient calmed down before tolerant kindliness in the doctor.

The resident physicians found that most patients are willing to talk about many vital personal matters "if the physician not only listens but by his accepting attitude conveys the impression that such material is important and meaningful in the general medical illness from which they suffer."

In every way the relationship between doctor and patient was humanized. The patient always came to his own doctor, instead of to just any doctor who happened to be on duty and available. The interview was personal, not conducted before a group of students with the patient as a guinea pig for the purpose of instruction. Compare this with the practice in psychiatric clinics in many hospitals, where the whole spirit of psychiatry is defeated by the use of the patient for demonstration.

The necessity for "maintaining the patient's dignity, self-respect, self-esteem" was stressed. The doctor was expected, and was given the opportunity, to develop a real interest in the patient as a human being. The "basic reassurance stems from the patient's conscious and unconscious awareness of the strength, integrity, and *sincerity of purpose* of the physician," the report points out. (Italics mine.)

The goal of the clinic toward the patient was threefold: to relieve his symptoms, to improve his total functional capacity, and to prevent a recurrence of his illness. Social agencies were called upon to help solve the patient's realistic problems, finding a dwelling or a job, providing legal aid.

To the general practitioner who has not had psychiatric training, the report makes these suggestions:

First, the doctor must be persuaded to accept the new approach to his patients. In the case of students, lectures and case demonstrations were presented to introduce them to the psychosomatic point of view. Seminars for senior students were offered, and enthusiastically received. Weekly psychosomatic case conferences were held.

Second, the practicing physician is asked to recognize the importance of the *individual* doctor-patient relationship, and to allow his interest in the patient as a human being to take its full development.

Third, the physician is asked to understand the value of hospitalization for a patient during periods of emotional stress, even though his actual physical condition would not ordinarily require his going to a hospital.

Fourth, the physician is asked to realize that psychotherapy is positive therapy. To the medical man, positive therapy means a prescription, a pill, an injection. The report points out that psychotherapy was as effective a part of the clinical treatment as the prescription, and in many cases it was the only therapy which proved helpful. With psychotherapy the doctor will find, says the report, that he can help patients whom many previous doctors could not help. He will also be likely to find a basis for hope in patients whom he once would have dismissed as incurable.

Out of such promising experiments the future of the general practitioner emerges as far more satisfying than it has ever been. He will find that he is doing a better medical job. His insight into the patient's personality and the background of the case will guide him in his purely medical therapy. He will attach his patients more securely to him. He may win back to medicine the lost sheep who have wandered to "healers" for understanding.

He will work better at less emotional cost to himself. He will be spared most of the irritation, frustration, even anger which a patient's bad behavior formerly aroused in him and which he forced himself to suppress. Understanding the causes of such behavior, he will become more objective. In the end the pursuit of such a humanized approach will also give the doctor greater economic security, for a practice grows and flowers on trust.

In the new relationship between doctor and patient, not only the patient but the doctor as well will have everything to gain.

A Hospital for Health

The doctor's areas of activity are three: the office, the patient's home, and the hospital.

The doctor, concerned with the emotional as well as the physical side of illness, knows that there are times when a patient needs to be removed from the home setting, even though his physical illness does not seem to require hospital care. The patient needs to be lifted physically out of an emotional situation. He needs a protected seclusion, where his wants are impersonally tended and his need for rest and quiet can be guarded. This may make the difference between a long, wasting illness and a speedy recovery.

In such cases, the doctor comes to see the hospital with new eyes. He begins to see it, rather, through the patient's eyes.

The beautiful, efficient institution is the dream of modern biological medicine. It is a vision realized in stone and steel, in gleaming apparatus and laboratory test tube, in immaculate corridor and starched nurse and precise records in triplicate. But to the patient made sensitive by illness and emotional suffering, it is a prison house of intimidating routine. In his state of emotional disturbance, he has only a narrow margin of tolerance. It is exactly this routine, which rationally he should accept, to which in his condition he cannot accommodate himself.

What such a patient needs is a substitute for the care he had as a child. He wants, not institutionalizing, but mothering. He wants the preferential treatment of a sick child. He wants the reassurance of love while he works out the problem behind his illness.

Small wonder that the conflict between treating disease and treating human beings should be intensified in the hospital, the one place that is dedicated to the sick. The marvel of the modern hospital is nearly new-born in the progress of medicine. Much less than a century ago, in the latter half of the 1800's, the famous hospitals of Paris had wards with three to four hundred patients, seven or eight in a bed. Death reaped a splendid harvest there. Indeed only the poor went to hospitals, and then but to die. The hospital retained for a long time its sad reputation as the last stopping place before the grave. It was far safer, as well as more comfortable, to be sick in your own bed, if you had a bed. In terms of medical history, the modern hospital is an overnight miracle.

Yet the doctor who knows the emotional condition of his patient may look at the hospital askance. For the emergency or the surgical case in a state of semiconsciousness the hospital's efficiency is no hindrance but a help. Its instant access to the scientific tools for saving life is priceless. But to the patient who needs not an oxygen tent but an atmosphere of friendliness, not a blood transfusion but a transfusion of confidence, the hospital is no refuge.

The more we know about the emotional origins of disease, the more we can anticipate the onslaught of serious illness. We can work in advance, gauging the emotional pressures, seeing the first signs of trouble in glandular and nervous disturbance, listening for the complaints which do not yet show in the physical tests but which forewarn of organic illness to come.

We can say, such a patient is slated for a bad time, unless we can break the chain reaction of which we can already see the first steps being enacted. But sometimes we cannot break the chain reaction without taking the patient bodily out of the situation which is bringing on illness. In such cases the modern hospital is not the proper place.

To a patient close to a breakdown but not "sick" enough for the hospital, the doctor often urges that he must go away. At this point the weary patient groans hopelessly. Where shall he go? He cannot face the noisy social whirl of the ordinary resort. But even supposing that he can find a quiet place, he cannot cope with the many questions to be answered, the many details of making arrangements. The writing or telephoning for accommodations, the journey, the arrival, the choice of a room—all these trivia loom enormous to a person already worn down by stress. And if he needs medical care or watching over, he will not find it in his quiet resort.

Or we may have a patient in convalescence after a serious illness or operation. Remembering the possible maturing effects of grave illness, we hope the patient will use this time to see himself and his situation in perspective and that he will arrive at a resolution of his difficulty. We want to make it possible for him to avoid another grave illness, another operation. We want to give him the perfect conditions for true convalescence, a convalescence in which he will recover not only from the illness but from the cause of it. The hospital does not provide these conditions.

Then there are the walking sick. There are the weary and

confused. There are the chronic sufferers whom even medication and good management cannot cure while they remain
surrounded by the pressures and conflicts of living. Inescapably the doctor who is concerned for these aspects of illness and
the possibilities for prevention of illness will see the need for a
new and different kind of hospital.

He will want a hospital for his patients who are sick but
not bedridden, who need care but not emergency care, who
above all need to be removed from the setting of their difficulties and given time to regain balance and clarity. He will
want, for such patients, a sanctuary where they will feel protected and cared for, but not reduced to a case-number.

The modern hospital is not the place to care for such patients as these. Very sick people are likely to be docile under
routinized care. Those who are not very sick but only in danger of illness, or those who have been sick and are recovering,
are not easy patients. They are often bristly, demanding, un-
cooperative. Or they endure the impersonal invasions of their
privacy quietly on the surface, but seething within, and this
is no help to their recovery.

The hospital has other disadvantages. Often it is located in
a big city, and the pace and tensions of urban life seep in, to
say nothing of the noise. It is too accessible; friends and rela-
tives bring with them into the patient's room the very anxieties and pressures from which he needs to be temporarily
extricated.

The new approach to illness needs to be translated into a
new kind of hospital, with the same thinking about the patient, the same individual approach, the same doctor-patient
relationship.

There were in Europe many famous sanatoriums, often
staffed and equipped like first-rate hospitals, but with the setting and atmosphere of a more or less luxurious country estate.
The medical care was personal and individual. It dated, not
from the new humanized science of medicine which is emerging today, but from the earlier art of healing. The head and
guiding spirit of each of these establishments was generally a

physician of very high standing and reputation. City doctors referred their patients to the care of this physician in his sanatorium, as to another type of specialist.

There are some, but comparatively few, institutions in this country which fit this description. There are nowhere near enough to meet the need. Most country homes are either mental institutions, or for invalids, the aged, or other special disabilities. We are at a loss to recommend a place to a patient in need of general care.

What is needed is a small hospital, in a country setting where the climate is wholesome and the natural surroundings peaceful and beautiful. A mild regimentation, a minimum but necessary routine would establish an atmosphere of order and care, giving the patient security in the same way that a young child derives a sense of security from the fact that the essential activities of his day, his eating, sleeping, and play, are organized for him.

But that tyranny of the clock, which seems inescapable in a big institution if only to get the work done, need not dominate a small hospital. No patient has to be awakened from needed sleep as the clock strikes seven, by a nurse whose professional cheeriness is to the irritable patient only an added offense.

More important is the attitude of doctors, nurses, and therapists. In a small hospital of which the individuality of each patient is a guiding principle, those who care for the patient will be concerned for him as a whole human being, not merely as a sick body.

He will find himself treated with unvarying friendliness whether he behaves well or ill. His uncooperativeness will be met, not by a punishing attitude of reprisal, but by an understanding which focuses on the causes of his resistance rather than the resistance itself. This is not to say that the staff need to permit undisciplined behavior. They are serious scientists. The basis of their science is an insight into the whole human being, his emotional as well as his physical disturbance.

The value of such a small country sanctuary both for the

cure and the prevention of disease can be incalculable. I know because I have experimented with it. This was the place where the patient in Chapter 2 made her strong bid to overcome her destructive trend, and almost succeeded.

Surrounded by a restful setting, with a staff to care for their medical needs and to provide the dietary and other regime prescribed for them, the patients there felt cared for and protected. At the same time the permissive attitude of the staff left them free to seek their own outlets for a returning vigor of mind and body. Some worked and some played. A gynecologist, one of the patients, organized a labor battalion of women who had never before worked with their hands. They pruned shrubs and made paths where those who were less well could take their walks. A retired professor of medicine organized evening entertainment. A European diplomat gave lectures in history.

A wholesome spirit of belonging grew up spontaneously. Security encouraged in each member of the community a tolerance and generosity toward the others. The most withdrawn patient could find a place for himself in the relaxed relationships. Some who came for a weekend visit to a patient remained for weeks. Husbands who saw their wives markedly improving stayed to refresh themselves in the happy atmosphere.

One vital purpose, among all the others, can be accomplished in such a place as nowhere else. That is the program of physical and emotional re-education for a healthier life.

The man or woman who has been ill needs to learn how to keep from becoming ill again. More particularly, the obese and the underweight, the insomniac, and others under stress need to learn how to manage their emotional lives better.

The obese person is a case in point. We can reduce overweight by medical means, but we often see one of two consequences. Either the patient begins gaining weight again as soon as the radical regime is ended, or else he slips into another, possibly more serious, form of self-destruction. We cannot remove the outlet of an emotional disturbance and leave the emotional disturbance unchecked, without incurring these risks. The abnormal dependence on food which brings about obesity is widely recognized as stemming from emotional disturbance. If we really want to cure the obesity, we must work at its source. This is a process of emotional re-education, the depth of which can be determined only by the depth of the individual's disturbance.

Psychotherapy of this kind can be many times more effective if the patient is removed temporarily from the real-life situation, relieved of responsibility for his eating habits, and placed in a protected situation until he has gained enough self-understanding and emotional balance to undertake responsibility for his own future program.

I envisage for the future three institutions of equal rank: the general hospital for acute physical illness, the hospital for serious mental illness, and the hospital for health.

Obviously we need the great modern hospital in the fight against acute and infectious disease. We need it for surgery, for emergency. We need it to save lives which are in desperate danger. Its sister institution, the hospital for health, must develop in answer to just as real a need. It should be a natural outgrowth of the more human approach to illness.

Of course there will be difficulties. There is resistance to any reference to emotional disturbance, which is still a stigma. In the hospital for health, as in the other aspects of the new approach to illness, this must be eradicated.

Then there are economic considerations. When such institutions are privately run they must make a profit, and the profit motive is not always compatible with the care of the sick. We may find through the great foundations for medical and hygienic progress the funds to establish such hospitals for health on a non-profit basis. Or we may find a way to establish them as branches of the great hospitals, when the hospitals begin to absorb the humanized medicine of the future.

It is conceivable that just as the hospitals are beginning to establish psychosomatic departments and psychosomatic clinics, they will discover how to fill the need for psychosomatic branches away from the mother institution, physically as well as philosophically distinguished from the efficient machine for saving life which is the modern hospital.

The hospital for health is an aspiration toward which laymen and doctors might work together.

18. IT IS EASIER TO HATE, BUT HEALTHIER TO LOVE

Laplace is reputed to have said on his deathbed that science was mere trifling, and nothing was real but love.

The historians who coin titles for the successive eras in man's history may argue how to name our time. It has been called the machine age. More recently it became the atomic age. Man's advances until now have been materialistic for the most part. In his quality of humanity he has made little progress. He lives differently, dresses differently, travels differently, fights differently. Tools and methods have changed but man himself has remained basically the same.

Now we stand at the threshold of a new era, perhaps a crucial one. It should be named the Age of Ambivalence.

Ambivalence is a psychological term meaning the simultaneous existence within us of opposite emotions toward the same object or person. We may be outwardly, consciously friendly, and inwardly, unconsciously hostile at the same time.

Ours is the age which has discovered, by way of science, that a man may speak with conviction of friendship and brotherhood, while inwardly he is moved by active antagonism. To establish as scientific theory this two-sided oneness of man's strongest emotions, love and hate, was Freud's contribution.

Freud was not content with calling the convulsive emotions of enmity, bias, bigotry, and intolerance merely "human nature." In the same way, he had not been content merely to observe the wilderness of paralysis, spasms, and tremors, the nervous disorders for which no name and no understanding existed; psychoanalysis was his answer to these human ills. With his explanation of the Janus-like character of the emotions of love and hate he gave us the clue to man's contradictory behavior.

Ambivalence explains man's darkest eras, those of persecution, of sadistic tribunals, the burning of witches, the extraction of confessions by torture, the killing of people en masse like vermin, and last, the burning of books, all in the name of progress.

In *Man Against Himself* Menninger writes, "To relate this destructiveness, this evidence of spiritual malignancy within us, to an instinct, and to correlate this instinct with the beneficial and fruitful instinct associated with love, this was one of the late flowers of the genius of Freud."

In many eras before ours, men may have thought that this or that discovery placed them at last on the doorstep of the final truth. Perhaps there is no final truth. Perhaps William James was right when he wrote: "There is no conclusion. What has concluded that we might conclude in regard to it? There are no fortunes to be told and there is no advice to be given. Farewell."

But man's seeking mind cannot remain long in a state of negative resignation. William James died in 1910, before the concept of ambivalence had come into existence in his own science. Today, whatever doubts we may have, one truth seems reasonably certain. With the new, hitherto unimaginable depths of insight given us through our understanding of the unconscious, man for the first time can examine his acts. He has now both the opportunity and the obligation to achieve real maturity. Before the judgment of history, man must henceforth willy-nilly assume responsibility for his deeds.

In the thousands of years of his childhood man could be irresponsible. He could follow his drive toward cruelty and destruction unpunished, not even understood except by a future century. Because he was a child, and knew not what he did, he could be forgiven.

Today he has no excuse. He cannot continue to be a man with the mind of a child. Emotional immaturity speaks with the voice of the beast, whatever the alleged noble cause it may put on as a garb.

It is a clear issue on which each one of us must take a stand. It is a question which none can evade. There is no way to withdraw from membership in the human race. There is no way not to participate in the common fate of man.

The sixteen-year-old who shot three in a family we recognize as a sick adolescent. The nineteen-year-old who stabbed seven and killed four is no longer dismissed as merely mad, a freak to be put in an asylum for the insane and forgotten.

Today we see these in desperate youths a reflection of all mankind. We understand at last that if either of them had had the intellect, the opportunity, the education, but no basic change of character, he could have achieved a position of power and wreaked his destruction on a world scale. We have seen the expression of hate and destruction on a world scale in our time. It cannot be brushed off as national insanity or national suicide.

It can happen again, as it has already happened. The destructive instinct cannot be dealt with in terms of discipline or punishment, of prisons and insane asylums. It cannot be isolated like leprosy or manacled like a criminal, because it exists to some extent in every human being. We must open our eyes to destructiveness everywhere. We must deal with it at its roots in human nature.

Those who declare that men are either good or evil are at best naive, or else they themselves are the disciples of destruction. Those who say that wars will always be because wars have always been do not believe in the progress of mankind since they do not love mankind. To assert that human nature cannot be changed is an expression of the destructive instinct.

Human nature can be changed. It is being changed. It has always been capable of change. Leaders have arisen in age after age, who have changed human beings into beasts, or into men. False propaganda can change friendly human nature to hatred, and truth can change enemies into friends.

Science shows us how the "human nature" of a child—self-centered, greedy, fearful, destructive, but also needing to be loved and to love, needing to be taught and to learn—is changed into a thoughtful, considerate, self-contained, mature man or woman. Science shows us also how that child can be arrested in his growth, and can carry with him into the recognized outer form of maturity the unsocialized instincts of the child. The child in a man's body, with a man's power, is the enemy which men of good will must seek out everywhere.

Overstreet, in *The Mature Mind,* quotes Diderot's assertion that all children are essentially criminals, and adds his own comment that all childish minds are dangerous, but particularly when those minds are housed in adult bodies, for then "they have the power to put their immaturities fully and disastrously into effect."

This realization, that man may be mature in body but in mind childish, that he may speak of creation but do destruction, gives us new measurements by which we may guide our judgment of men and deeds, of beliefs, prejudices, and causes.

Human Nature Can Be Changed

Nietzsche called upon men to live dangerously, to erect their cities beside Vesuvius, to send their ships to unexplored seas, to live in a state of perpetual war. He might have been extoling the wholesome impulse of man to deal aggressively with the physical world in which he must live. He might have been summoning man out of ignorance and sloth. He might have been spurring the creative instinct. He spoke these words after a serious illness had inspired him with an ardent yearning for health. They might have been interpreted as a call to the will to live.

But his words were seized upon by men who felt joy in

building with the anticipation of destruction. They were another expression of ambivalence. The immature drive in man to create so that he may have something to destroy is like children on a beach first building a sand castle and then destroying it. Nietzsche's own life was such an expression. He wrote in *Thus Spake Zarathustra*, "I love him who willeth the creation beyond himself, and then perisheth." He left powerful works to the world, but he himself retreated into insanity.

Words like Nietzsche's appeal to people who find action better than inaction and war better than boredom. In the end all these roads lead to destruction. Freud's words are more sober, and more mature. It is as a scientist that Freud says, "There is nothing to be learned from destruction."

There are signs that man is growing up to the realization of his responsibilities. His ideals are no longer only the dreams of a few good men. They are the results of new and solid psychological gains.

What our new self-knowledge may do for mankind on a global scale is suggested in the report of the Unesco Conference on World Tensions and the International Congress on Mental Health, held in London in August, 1948. The conclusions of the joint conference, as reported in the *Journal of the American Medical Association,* are based "on the premise that human emotions ('human nature') can now be scientifically studied, understood, and even changed, both for the individual and the group.

"Wars are unnecessary," continues the report, "and are not considered an inevitable consequence of human nature. Some needs are vital to all men. These include freedom from disease, insecurity, and fear. Men everywhere desire at the same time fellowship, respect of their fellow men, and a chance for personal growth and development.

"One group may be wrongfully led to see another group as a menace through acceptance of false images and oversimplified solutions. Myths, traditions, and symbols of national pride, handed down from generation to generation, plus social and nationalistic symbols, are believed to hinder free movement of thought across artificial political boundaries of an interdependent world.

"This newly clarified concept of the modifiability of human nature through insight into otherwise unconscious obstructions suggests ways of removing obstacles to personal and social development. . . . The primary factors leading to better mental health are the acquirement by the individual of self-knowledge and group social insight."

What this conference suggests as a way to better mental health may be broadened to include better physical health. Even the plagues which sweep men into death by the hundreds of thousands are now recognized as a concern not limited to the biologist and the sanitary engineer. There are causes behind the virulent germs, causes behind the unsanitary living conditions.

"Human history shows that [the] root [of epidemics] is not the epidemic disease but poor health," writes Dr. F. K. Meyer under the title, *Global Strategy in Preventive Medicine* in the Annals of Internal Medicine for 1950.

"An epidemic of malaria in Ceylon was recorded after an economic depression, with an enormous mortality rate in a disease the cause of which is known and for which specific treatments are available . . . Men fight," says Dr. Meyer, "not only because they are hungry, but because they want to extricate themselves from the cycle of sickness-hunger, hunger-sickness."

The influenza epidemic of 1918 followed upon four years of war and hunger in Europe. It is estimated that five hundred million people fell sick in that epidemic. Fifteen million of them died.

The World Health Organization's constitution, now in preparation, has a paragraph which reads: "The health of all people is fundamental to the attainment of peace and security and is dependent upon the fullest cooperation of individuals and states."

Which comes first, the mental or the physical health, the

elimination of economic misery or the prevention of war, scarcely matters. As we now understand that we must deal with physical illness simultaneously in the body and in the mind, so we now see that the sickness of peoples must be dealt with on all levels of science.

We curb the germs of epidemic disease, and the physical conditions in which such germs thrive and spread, on the same principle as we relieve the symptoms of illness in the individual, the fever and infection of the body. But simultaneously we recognize the deeper causes. These are the causes with which it is our new responsibility to deal, tirelessly and vigorously, because now we know about them. We know how they work.

For or Against Mankind

"When men are friends," said Aristotle, "justice is unnecessary. But when men are just, friendship is still a boon."

Justice on a world scale is a present aspiration of men of good will, but justice is not enough. We will still need friendship, and understanding is the first step toward friendship. The more we understand ourselves and our neighbors, the greater is our hope of health, both as individuals and as a world. This is the new and greater task of the doctor, to teach us to know ourselves and each other.

Doctors have never shirked their responsibility. Prevention has always been the physician's most hopeful principle. Preventive medicine has written a glorious chapter in man's history. Today the physician wants to do more than put together bodies shattered by shellfire and bombs.

In his introduction to *The Story of Philosophy* Will Durant says, "Science tells us how to heal and how to kill. It reduces the death rate in retail, and then kills us wholesale in war." The Surgeon-General of the United States Army reports that 98 per cent of the wounded now live, as against 95.5 per cent in World War II and 92 per cent in World War I. This is a bitter sort of progress. The physician of today would prefer to spend his skill on keeping men whole and well. This was his longing when he embarked on the profession of medicine.

But the doctor cannot succeed without the patient. The fight against illness, as we have seen, is an alliance of doctor and patient. On the larger scale, the long struggle for world health, physical and mental, cannot achieve its purpose against a laggard mankind clinging to ignorance.

This is the task which we in our time must begin together, doctors, educators, jurists, political leaders and all leaders of men. The issue is not of one political doctrine or another. The issue is for mankind or against it, for creation or destruction.

Voltaire's words, that we shall all leave this world as foolish and as wicked as we found it, need no longer be true. As the new knowledge of man's ambivalence enables us to understand and thus work for health, it will enable us to understand and work for peace.

Peace and friendship grow from the same roots as health and happiness. As we strive for the one, we win the other. All are the flowers of a sturdy and vigorous will to live, in every man and in all men everywhere. To hate is easier, but it is healthier to love.

INDEX

275